"The Doctrine Committee of the Scottish Episcopal Church is to be commended for this volume where a range of authors explore what it means to be a human being in the modern world. From within a spectrum of perspectives questions of how, over centuries, humans have considered themselves to be 'different', 'special', even 'unique' creatures are examined. The authors face up to change and evolution in western understandings of *Homo sapiens* viewing human beings from perspectives both traditional and contemporary, theological and secular. That each chapter is accompanied by further reading and questions makes it additionally rich both for individuals and reading groups alike."

— **The Most Revd Stephen Cottrell**, *Archbishop of York*

—

"Being made in the image of God means living and loving in creative relationship with God, neighbour, and creation itself. This volume offers an imaginative and faithful opportunity to challenge and re-shape theological conversation in and beyond 'church'. It includes provocative questions for reflection and/or discussion—many worthy of expansive, life-long wrestling."

— **The Rt Revd Dr Katharine Jefferts Schori**, *XXVI Presiding Bishop of the Episcopal Church*

"These essays are reminiscent of the three Wise Men in W. H. Auden's poem 'For the Time Being', in seeking to discover what it is to be human. They try to make sense of what that means in relationship to God, Jesus and the whole created order by drawing on many different disciplines and traditions, in insightful, profound, and original, if demanding ways."
— **The Rt Revd Dr Barry Morgan**, *former Archbishop of Wales*

—

"*Made in the Image of God* offers a multi-faceted and multi-disciplinary exploration of the opportunities of human living and dying in response to a world of divine resonance. I commend both the breadth and the depth of these essays. Together they make a kaleidoscope of analysis engaging, often more through probing questions than through ready answers, with a creation that in its totality needs to look at itself afresh in terms of mutuality, justice and compassion. Scientific and philosophical perspectives combine with biblical and theological approaches to provide a window of honesty on Christian doctrine today."
— **The Most Revd Dr Michael Jackson**, *Archbishop of Dublin*

Made in the Image of God

Essays on Religious Anthropology

EDITED BY

— MICHAEL FULLER & DAVID JASPER —

Sacristy
Press

Sacristy Press
PO Box 612, Durham, DH1 9HT

www.sacristy.co.uk

First published in 2021 by Sacristy Press, Durham

Sacristy Limited, registered in England & Wales, number 7565667

British Library Cataloguing-in-Publication Data
A catalogue record for the book is available from the British Library

ISBN 978-1-78959-170-5

Contents

Acknowledgements

Thanks are due to many people who gave of their time and expertise during the writing and editing of this book. In particular we would like to thank Miriam Weibye, the Church Relations Officer of the Scottish Episcopal Church and Secretary to the Doctrine Committee, and Natalie Watson and Richard Hilton at Sacristy Press. We are also very grateful to the Drummond Trust for its generous assistance with funding for the publication of this book.

Unless otherwise stated the New Revised Standard Version (NRSV) of the Bible is used throughout this book.

Contributors

Margaret B. Adam lives at St Stephen's House, Oxford, where she is Visiting Tutor for Contemporary Christian Ethics. She has previously taught theology and ethics at Loyola University Maryland, the University of Glasgow, the Scottish Episcopal Institute, and the University of Chester. Currently, she is the postdoctoral researcher for the three-year AHRC-funded project, the Christian Ethics of Farmed Animal Welfare, which has recently produced a free policy framework for Christian institutions: see <https://www1.chester.ac.uk/about-cefaw>.

John Davies is Research Fellow in the College of Arts, University of Glasgow and teaches in Theology and Religious Studies. His fields include the history of the medieval Church in Great Britain and Ireland and the history and practice of Christian worship. He is a member of the Liturgy Committee of the Scottish Episcopal Church and teaches liturgy and worship in the Scottish Episcopal Institute.

David Fergusson has recently taken up the post of Regius Professor of Divinity at the University of Cambridge. He was previously Professor of Divinity at the University of Edinburgh (2000–21). He is author of *The Providence of God* (Cambridge University Press, 2018).

Michael Fuller is Senior Teaching Fellow at New College, University of Edinburgh, where he works in the field of science and religion. He has written a book and more than thirty articles relating to this field and is Lead Editor of the "Issues in Science and Theology" series (Springer). He has also published papers exploring theological themes in literature and in music and is a regular contributor to the *Wagner Journal*. He is an Honorary Canon of St Mary's Cathedral, Edinburgh.

Robert Gillies was Bishop of Aberdeen and Orkney in the Scottish Episcopal Church until his retirement in 2016. He is an Honorary Research Fellow in the University of Glasgow. With Liz, his wife, he lives in north-east Fife. His recent publications include *Guilt and Forgiveness: A Study in the Thought and Personality of Paul Ricoeur* (Handsel Press, 2019), and *The Approaching Word: A Companion to Reading New Testament Epistles in Sequence* (Handsel Press, 2020).

Harriet Harris MBE is University Chaplain and Head of Chaplaincy Service at the University of Edinburgh. She is Honorary Fellow of the Divinity School at Edinburgh, the Co-Director of the Global Compassion Initiative, and Associate Fellow of the Clinical Educator Programme at Edinburgh. Her publications include *Fundamentalism and Evangelicals* (Oxford University Press, 1998, 2008) and *Faith and Philosophical Analysis* (Ashgate, 2005).

Trevor Hart is Rector of St Andrew's, St Andrews in the Diocese of St Andrews, Dunkeld and Dublane, and Honorary Professor of Divinity in the University of St Andrews. He was awarded his PhD by the University of Aberdeen. His recent publications include *Between the Image and the Word: Theological Engagements with Imagination, Language and Literature* (Ashgate, 2013). He is a member of the Doctrine Committee of the Scottish Episcopal Church.

Alison Jasper was Senior Lecturer in Religion and Feminist Studies at the University of Stirling. She was awarded her PhD by the University of Glasgow. Her recent publications include *Because of Beauvoir: Christianity and the Cultivation of Female Genius* (Baylor, 2013). She has served on the Liturgy Committee of the Scottish Episcopal Church.

David Jasper is Emeritus Professor at the University of Glasgow where he was formerly Professor of Literature and Theology. He was Changjiang Chair Professor at Renmin University of China, Beijing. He is Convenor of the Doctrine Committee of the Scottish Episcopal Church and Canon Theologian of St Mary's Cathedral, Glasgow. His recent publications include *Literature and Theology as a Grammar of Assent* (Ashgate, 2016) and *The Language of Liturgy* (SCM Press, 2018).

John McLuckie is Rector of Old St Paul's Church in Edinburgh and an Associate Tutor of the Scottish Episcopal Institute where he teaches Spirituality and Discipleship. He is also Convenor of the Scottish Episcopal Church's Inter-Church Relations Committee.

Delyth M. Reid was Staff Scientist at the Institute of Medical Sciences in the University of Aberdeen. She has over forty publications in photoreceptor research, autoimmunity and immunology. She is a member of the Doctrine Committee of the Scottish Episcopal Church.

Eric Stoddart teaches practical theology in the School of Divinity of the University of St Andrews in Scotland. He is a co-founder of the international Surveillance & Religion Network which promotes research into ways in which religious communities are subject to monitoring and how such communities use systems of data collection and analysis. Having taught on the Open University's first wholly online course about the internet, in the late 1990s, he has since developed Masters-level modules at St Andrews in theology and digital technology, most recently on surveillance.

Nicholas Taylor is Rector of St Aidan's, Clarkston, in the Diocese of Glasgow and Galloway of the Scottish Episcopal Church. He was awarded his PhD by the University of Durham and has published in the fields of New Testament and origins, and the interface between theology, liturgy and ministry. He has taught in universities and colleges in the United Kingdom and in central and southern Africa and is Canon Theologian of Mutare Cathedral.

Made in the image of God

The Most Revd Dr Mark Strange
Primus of the Scottish Episcopal Church

There has, perhaps, never been a more pressing time for Christians to reflect upon the nature of what it is to be human made by God in God's image, as we read in the book of Genesis. As I write these words, we are in the midst of a pandemic that has shaken human society to its very core, its threat to our wellbeing felt by all, but leaving cruelly exposed the weaknesses and inequalities in our way of life. For the divisions between wealth and poverty have grown even greater, the ensuing suffering made greater still by political events that have served only to divide us even further. I write in the depths of winter when days are short, the weather freezing and we remain locked in our homes, dreading the human contact that we also crave.

The essays in this book do not seek to offer answers or simple solutions to profound problems. But they are written in hope and with the purpose of, perhaps, making their readers a little better informed and thoughtful. Their authors are all practising Christians closely linked to the Scottish Episcopal Church, engaging here in a discussion between theologians and scientists, those engaged in the pastoral ministry of the Church or teaching in colleges and universities. No doubt they can be criticized for what they omit, but they do embrace a wide range of topics, from the question of artificial intelligence to the treatment of animals and the matter of transgender and much else besides.

At the very heart and centre of the book is an essay on the nature of compassion. The *Oxford English Dictionary* begins its entry on this word "compassion" with a reference to two early Christian writers,

Tertullian and Jerome, then indicating the root meaning as "suffering together with": "*com*—together with + *pati*—to suffer". Do we find our true humanity when we are drawn together in our sufferings and in our concerns and hopes?

Harriet Harris' reflection on compassion, human and divine is perhaps the pivot around which these essays turn, each in their own way. I am grateful to the members of the Doctrine Committee of the Scottish Episcopal Church for this book, together with guests who have contributed, and I hope that it will help to inspire further reflection on the question of what it is to be truly human, made in the image of God.

Introduction

Michael Fuller and David Jasper

We live in dark times: lives and economies threatened by a virus that has already killed millions globally and wrecked economies, the balance of nature threatened by human carelessness and greed, our Western democracies fragile and under threat from "populism" and perhaps worse. Now, therefore, it may be important to stop for a moment and reflect a little on what it actually means to be human, with all its privileges and responsibilities.

In the first account of the creation in the book of Genesis, we read, "So God created humankind in his image, in the image of God he created them; male and female he created them" (Genesis 1:27). The essays in this book explore what this statement might mean for us, drawing on many perspectives and disciplines. Although these essays are the result of a great deal of discussion between the authors, each has a particular voice and there has been no attempt to edit them into a single point of view, nor to eliminate technical language from different disciplines (although explanations of technical terms are given where necessary). Each remains independent, the only common thread being that all the authors are practising Christians. The book began in discussions within the Doctrine Committee of the Scottish Episcopal Church, and most of the authors are members of that Committee.

The first essay by Nicholas Taylor establishes the discussion of what it means to be human, made in the image of God, within a biblical context, drawing upon both the Hebrew scriptures and the New Testament. Here, from the outset, the themes of privilege and obligation are introduced. There is, furthermore, an eschatological dimension, for being human for the Christian is not merely a matter of this world but embraces also the mystery of death and resurrection. John Reuben Davies, in the second essay, continues the theme of going beyond ourselves, exploring the terms *homo religiosus* (the religious human), *homo orans* (the praying human) and finally *homo adorans* (the worshipping human), in whom the full identity of humanity is reached.

The third essay by Trevor Hart continues the theological discussion, addressing the theme of the ambiguity of our humanity—humans being the pinnacle of God's creation and at the same time "pathetic wastrels" bearing responsibility for the fall in Eden. This discussion is extended in Robert Gillies' essay, drawing upon his own pastoral experience as a priest and bishop, and seeking a "radical re-framing" of Christian eschatology. Gillies' essay expresses both lament for human failure and hope for the future in God.

John McLuckie explores perspectives on what it means to be a human from the Eastern Orthodox Christian tradition, drawing on the 2015 Buffalo Statement produced by the International Commission for Anglican-Orthodox Theological Dialogue. The first section of the book concludes with Harriet Harris' discussion of the concept of compassion, seen from social-scientific, psychological and theological perspectives. Harris distinguishes carefully between compassion and empathy, and indicates how the two may interrelate in therapeutic contexts; and she analyses how the idea of divine compassion may be compatible with the idea of divine impassibility. Harris also opens the theme of "human flourishing", and how far that condition demands human compassion in our relationships with one another.

The second part of the book is both more contemporary and more interdisciplinary. David Jasper begins by placing our understanding of what it is to be human in the context of the post-Enlightenment world, concluding with Charles Taylor's sense of the secular age in which we live. In this context we have the first of the scientific contributions from Michael Fuller, who indicates the parameters which scientific thinking places around our consideration of what it means to be human. He explores the idea of human uniqueness in the light of reflections on extraterrestrial life, our understandings of animal behaviours, and the drive towards a "posthuman" future. Delyth Reid offers an understanding of humanity based on physiological, genetic and biochemical criteria. She draws attention to the ways in which scientific understandings of the human organism can point towards those things which make us continuous with, yet also distinct from, other members of the animal kingdom, and also to correlations between such human experiences as moods and emotions with particular levels of hormones and other complex biochemicals. She also points out some of the ways in which our increased understanding of ourselves and our natural environment might be open to misuse.

The creation narrative in Genesis with which we began speaks also of God giving to humankind "dominion" over the creatures of the earth—the fish, the birds, the cattle and all wild animals (Genesis 1:26). Margaret Adam brings our focus to bear upon our relationship with animals, and especially at a time when we are increasingly conscious of the cost to created life of barbaric and intensive methods of farming to provide food for human consumption. Our concern should not merely be with human flourishing, but also with animal flourishing—and the two may be far more closely connected than we sometimes imagine.

Moving from the animal world to the human, Eric Stoddart explores the development of artificial intelligence, and the predictions of the role this will play in the lives of human individuals and societies in the not-too-distant future. Stoddart looks at the potentialities of both transhumanism and automation to radically change our future, not least regarding working practices. How important is work to self-identity, and to human dignity? Economic and ethical questions come to the fore in this analysis, which makes the point that there are no easy answers to the important questions which it raises. Finally, Alison Jasper addresses the matter of gender and transgender. How does the Christian tradition, with its biblical imagery of male and female, manage the contemporary challenges to the binary understanding of human gendering? Jasper gives a detailed exploration of the ways in which the opening chapters of the book of Genesis portray the creation of men and women, in order to challenge normative gendered readings of these texts. Analysing them in theopoetic terms, she suggests alternative approaches which challenge engrained assumptions, and which can be affirming of more radical and non-hierarchical approaches to sex and gender.

The book is brought to a conclusion in a summary Afterword by David Fergusson of the University of Edinburgh. We hope that these essays will provoke thought and discussion at a moment in time when humanity, it may be, is at greater risk from itself than ever before. Its questions are not trivial—indeed they may involve the very survival of our planet as we know it.

CHAPTER 1

In the image of God: Being human in the biblical tradition

Nicholas Taylor

The canon of Christian scripture opens with the creation narrative in Genesis and closes with the vision of the new creation in Revelation. Between these biblical bookends are to be found a diversity of texts which express human responses to the experience of God and the world, to collective and to a much lesser extent individual life on earth. It would not be possible within the parameters of this chapter to treat all relevant texts in any detail, or to reconstruct at all comprehensively the development and coalescence of diverse traditions through the Hebrew scriptures and their reinterpretation in the Christian New Testament. Rather, attention will focus on what is arguably the most significant theme found both in the literature of ancient Israel and in that of the apostolic Church, that of humanity as created in God's image, with some reflections offered on ways in which the traditions in Hebrew scripture have been reinterpreted in the light of Christian experience.

The human being will be viewed as an integral person, and not divided into corporeal and non-corporeal components. Any attempt to distinguish between supposedly physical and non-physical aspects of the person would be anachronistic.[1] The human being, rather, must be understood as an integral living organism, variously understood in different cultural contexts to be able to transcend the limitations of terrestrial life through a spiritual force of divine origin.

---

[1]   E. Hill, *Being Human* (London: Chapman, 1984), pp. 99–108.

Humanity in creation

It has, since the beginnings of critical study of the Old Testament, been recognized that the opening chapters of Genesis include two distinct creation narratives: that of the creation of the world out of primordial chaos in six days, traditionally ascribed to the post-exilic priestly source P, connected or in continuity with the reforming or reactionary movement associated with Ezra (Genesis 1:1–2:3); and the account of the creation of Adam and Eve, and the planting of the Garden of Eden, followed by the story commonly known as the "Fall", attributed to the Yahwist or J tradition associated with the Davidic court (2:4–3:24).[2] It is also recognized that both myths draw upon much more ancient traditions common to ancient Near Eastern polytheism, and in particular the Mesopotamian creation myths, attested in some diversity of surviving texts found over a broad geographical area and dating from a period of well over a millennium.[3] In both Genesis accounts, however, conflict and intrigue in the pantheon are replaced by the word and action of a single creator God, whose polytheistic antecedents are, in the P myth, reflected in the plural form *'elohim* (literally "gods", rendered "God" in English translations) and in the hortatory form, "Let us . . ." of the eighth creative word whereby humanity is brought into existence (Genesis 1:26–27; cf. Job 38:4–7).[4]

---

[2]   S. Brayford, *Genesis* (Leiden: Brill, 2007); G. von Rad, *Genesis* (London: SCM Press, 1972); E. A. Speiser, *Genesis* (New York: Doubleday, 1964), pp. 11–20; W. Brueggemann, *Genesis* (Atlanta, GA: John Knox, 1982); S. Niditch, *Chaos to Cosmos* (Chico, CA: Scholars, 1985); M. Noth, *A History of the Pentateuchal Traditions* (Atlanta, GA: Scholars, 1981); M. S. Smith, *The Priestly Vision of Genesis 1* (Minneapolis, MN: Augsburg Fortress, 2009); G. J. Wenham, *Genesis 1–15* (Waco, TX: Word, 1987); C. Westermann, *Genesis 1–11* (Minneapolis, MN: Fortress, 1994). Wenham dates P earlier than J, *Genesis 1–15*, pp. xxxi–xxxii, xliii–xlv.

[3]   J. B. Pritchard (ed), *Ancient Near Eastern Texts Relating to the Old Testament* (Princeton, NJ: Princeton University Press, 1969); S. M. Dalley, *Myths from Mesopotamia* (Oxford: Oxford University Press, 2008).

[4]   F. M. Cross, *Canaanite Myth and Hebrew Epic* (Cambridge, MA: Harvard University Press, 1997), pp. 186–90; E. T. Mullen, *The Assembly of the Gods*

While both creation stories have more ancient precursors in ancient Near Eastern mythology, the J account, in which the Garden of Eden represents the climax in God's ordering of the world, is widely believed to have become established in Hebrew tradition at an earlier date.[5] Though lacking the schematization of creation over six days that has become beloved of post-Darwinian fundamentalists, the story is not lacking in sophistication. Man, 'adam, is created from primordial earth, and invigorated with divine breath (Genesis 2:7), and the Garden of Eden planted and provided with waterways (Genesis 2:8).[6] God's creative action in forming the man is analogous to that of a potter, a frequent metaphor of God's creative power.[7] This myth is notable for the formation of the woman from the body of the man (Genesis 2:21–22), as a helper—after the animals created for that purpose had proved inadequate (Genesis 2:18–20).[8] The subordination of woman to man is reinforced, but does not begin, in the story of the consumption of the forbidden fruit, the consequence of which is the expulsion from Eden, imposition of patriarchal social structures and attribution to women of sexual instincts considered dangerous, arduous labour in agriculture and childbirth, and mortality (Genesis 3:1–7,16,17–19).[9] Gender differentiation and the vulnerability of women to male domination are emphasized. Unselfconscious nudity is replaced by clothing, not as a divinely imposed obligation so much as a human reaction to acquiring "knowledge of good and evil".[10] Expulsion from their idyllic existence in the garden, and separation from the tree of life, leads to a lifetime of arduous labour for survival, and mortality. The myth explains the human condition and

---

(Chico, CA: Scholars, 1980); cf. Wenham, *Genesis 1–15*, pp. 27–28.

[5] Wenham, *Genesis 1–15*, pp. xxxvii–xlii, 51–55; Westermann, *Genesis 1–11*, pp. 186–90.

[6] Cf. Genesis 3:9,23; 18:27; Psalms 90:3; 103:14; 104:29.

[7] Job 10:8–9; Psalm 119:73; Jeremiah 18:1–12.

[8] See also Alison Jasper, Chapter 12.

[9] Contra, P. A. Bird, "Sexual Differentiation and Divine Image in the Genesis Creation Texts", K. E. Børresen (ed.), *The Image of God* (Minneapolis, MN: Fortress, 1995), pp. 5–15.

[10] See also Gillies, Chapter 4.

prevailing social customs, a consequence of wilful loss of innocence. The male human being, formed from the earth, is the pinnacle of creation, for whom animal life, including the human female, is created.[11] Nevertheless, whatever God's intention may have been, the divine breath leaves the man, and he will be dissipated into the earth from which he has been formed. The question of continued existence beyond fragile mortality in the present world is not explored further in the creation myth, but was to become the subject of increased speculation during the Second Temple period.[12]

The human being is a quite different figure in the P creation narrative with which Genesis, and the Hebrew canon, begins. Genesis 1:26–27 is, in the view of some interpreters, a later interpolation in the P tradition.[13] Whereas the creation of the cosmos, and of what modern science would identify as botanical and zoological life forms, is effected by divine word (cf. Psalm 8), related in the third person imperative traditionally rendered in English by the "Let there be . . . and there was . . . " formulary, the creation of humanity is effected by divine action, recounted in the first person plural hortatory form, traditionally rendered, "Let us make . . . " This grammatical shift, reflected in the Greek as well as the Hebrew transmission of the text,[14] reflects the language of the heavenly court in ancient Near Eastern mythology.[15] It is an archaism, reflecting the origins of the myth in Mesopotamian polytheism, rather than any resurgent polytheism in the post-exilic Judaism in which this text was incorporated

---

[11] See also Adam, Chapter 10.

[12] P. S. Johnston, *Shades of Sheol* (Downers Grove, IL: IVP, 2002); N. J. Tromp, *Primitive Conceptions of Death and the Netherworld in the Old Testament* (Rome: PBI, 1969).

[13] Westermann, *Genesis 1–11*, p. 143.

[14] J. W. Wevers, *Notes on the Greek Text of Genesis* (Atlanta, GA: Scholars, 1993), p. 14.

[15] Cf. Genesis 3:22; 11:7; Isaiah 6:8. See also Job 1:6–12; 2:1–6. Cross, *Canaanite Myth*, pp. 186–90; Mullen, *Assembly*; Von Rad, *Genesis*; W. Zimmerli, "Der Mensch im Rahmen der Natur nach dem Aussagen des ersten biblischen Schöpfungsberichtes", *ZThK* 59 (1979), pp. 139–58.

into the nascent Pentateuch.[16] Neither the angelology of apocalypticism,[17] nor the notion of divine emanations which later evolved in Hellenistic Judaism,[18] still less later Christian trinitarianism,[19] should be read into this text.[20] Rather, the ancient Near Eastern conception of a heavenly court in which the deities gathered, deliberated, intrigued, fought, and formed the created world from each other's dismembered body parts, should be understood, as depicted in the Babylonian creation myth *Enuma Elish* 6:1–8:

> When Marduk heard the gods' speech
> He conceived a desire to accomplish clever things.
> He opened his mouth addressing Ea,
> He counsels that which he had pondered in his heart,
> "I will bring together blood to form bone,
> I will bring into being Lullû, whose name shall be "man".
> I will create Lullû—man
> On whom the toil of the gods will be laid that they may rest.
> I will skilfully alter the organization of the gods:
> Though they are honoured as one, they shall be divided into two."
> Ea answered, as he addressed a word to him,
> Expressing his comments on the resting of the gods,
> "Let one brother of theirs be given up.
> Let him perish that people may be fashioned.
> Let the great gods assemble
> And let the guilty one be given up that they may be confirmed."[21]

[16] Cf. G. Boccaccini, *Middle Judaism* (Minneapolis, MN: Augsburg Fortress, 1991); Westermann, *Genesis 1–11*, pp. 144–45.

[17] J. J. Collins, *The Apocalyptic Imagination* (Grand Rapids, MI: Eerdmans, 2010).

[18] M. S. Smith, *The Early History of God* (Grand Rapids, MI: Eerdmans, 2002).

[19] G. T. Armstrong, *Die Genesis in der alten Kirche* (Tübingen: Mohr, 1962), p. 39.

[20] Wenham, *Genesis 1–15*, pp. 27–28; Westermann, *Genesis 1–11*, pp. 143–45.

[21] ET W. G. Lambert, Electronic Tools and Ancient Near Eastern Archives. <http://www.etana.org/node/581>, accessed 27 March 2020.

The P creation narrative is a development from this mythology, which does not imply direct dependence on this particular text. The story is retold in monotheistic and also transcendental terms: not only is creation the work of a single god,[22] in whom are concentrated the attributes associated with all the deities of the ancient Near Eastern pantheons, now relegated to a more ambiguous status in the heavenly court.[23] Also, at least as significantly, 'elohim is not part of the created order; none of the heavenly bodies nor the earth or any geographical feature thereon is identified with the creator deity or with any (anthropomorphically conceived) body parts of the said deity, as is common in other ancient Near Eastern creation myths. This aspect of the ancient Near Eastern myth is reflected elsewhere in the biblical tradition, in Psalms 74 and 89, and in Isaiah 51:5, and in the figures of Leviathan and Behemoth.[24]

While God's location is not disclosed, it is implied that God is transcendent, and there is no suggestion that God is present in the world in a form which, if not visible is certainly recognizable, and can move, make objects, and communicate verbally with people (cf. Genesis 3:8–21). God is beyond creation, while human beings, created in God's image, are part of creation, and part of the ecology of the earth. Whereas in the J myth, God is all but anthropomorphic, in the P myth God is transcendent and invisible. The conception of humanity as created in God's image belongs to the P myth, and it is important to recognize that the physical, anthropomorphic depiction of God in the J myth is not that in terms of which the notion of humanity in God's image is to be understood.

The above-mentioned change from third to first person in the P account of the creation of humanity implies that human beings are categorically distinct from other created beings and from the world they inhabit.[25] It

---

22 The plural form of 'elohim (lit. gods) reflects the polytheistic tradition behind the canonical text.

23 Cf. Mullen, Assembly; J. J. Collins & G. W. E. Nickelsburg, Ideal Figures in Ancient Judaism (Chico, CA: Scholars, 1980).

24 Leviathan: Job 41:1; Psalm 104:26; Isaiah 27:1. Behemoth: Job 40:50.

25 E. T. Mullen, Ethnic Myths and Pentateuchal Foundations (Atlanta, GA: Scholars, 1997), pp. 96–98.

is not necessary to speculate as to precisely what action on God's part is envisaged, whether analogous to the physical activity described in the J account or otherwise, to recognize that this distinction may not have been intended when the text was composed. What is distinctive about humanity is that 'adam is created in God's image, tselem (Greek: 'eikon), and likeness, damut (Greek: 'omoiosin), to exercise a particular role in ruling those created beings which modern taxonomy would describe as animals. Whether or not a clear distinction can be drawn between "image" and "likeness",[26] it is clear that humanity represents the presence of a transcendent god within the created order, and for that reason is endowed with a sanctity not shared with other living beings (cf. Genesis 9:6), but is nonetheless created, and neither eternal nor divine. Human mortality is not viewed as problematic; the finitude of the individual is inconsequential, compared with the continuity of the species created in God's image. In the modern world, human domination over creation is taken for granted, but there are serious questions to be asked about ways in which this power has been and continues to be abused, and we are increasingly aware of the consequences of this abuse in environmental degradation and climate change.[27] However, this form of domination cannot be read into the Genesis text, written at a time when human life was very much more fragile, and people possessed relatively little technology, had less capacity to preserve supplies of food and water, less developed weapons for hunting and for defence against human and animal predators, and fewer remedies against disease.

Tselem is used of human beings created in the image of God in the P tradition in Genesis (1:26–27; 5:3; 9:6), and otherwise in the Hebrew Bible only of cultic idols,[28] and in contexts in which contempt for idolatrous

---

26 For discussion of these terms, Wenham, *Genesis 1–15*, pp. 29–32; Westermann, *Genesis 1–11*, pp. 146–47; Wevers, *Notes on the Greek Text of Genesis*, p. 14.

27 Pope Francis, *Laudato Si'* (London: St Paul's, 2015); cf. N. H. Taylor (ed.), *Religion, Ecology, and Justice. Listening: Journal of Religion and Culture* 35.3 (2000).

28 Numbers 33:52; 1 Kings 11:18; 2 Chronicles 23:17; Psalm 73:20; Ezekiel 7:20; 16:17; 23:14; Daniel 2:31–3:15 [Aram]; Amos 5:26.

cults is expressed (1 Samuel 6:5,11).[29] The rendition "image" in English therefore needs to be understood in a quite specific sense, in terms of reflecting or embodying divine presence on earth. The human being is not understood to "look like" God, but rather to embody something of the divine essence, and thereby to make a transcendent god present in the created world.

Both Genesis creation narratives reflect a temple cosmology, in which chaos is brought to order.[30] The garden of Eden in the J account, and the inhabited earth in the P, form a botanical arrangement of sacred space, reflecting the architecture of ancient Near Eastern temples. The human being is, in the P tradition, the image of God placed on earth to represent God's presence in the way a statue or other idol might be placed in a temple as the representation of the deity worshipped there. The centrality of the (male) human being to creation in J is, at least until the expulsion from Eden, analogous but not identical. The prohibition of idolatry in the Decalogue (Exodus 20:4; Leviticus 26:1) reflects the same principle, that the human being—and no carved inanimate object—is the authentic image of God on earth.[31] While consistently denouncing idolatry in the form of graven images, the biblical tradition abounds in anthropomorphic verbal imagery of God.[32] A particularly vivid example

---

[29]   There are two possible exceptions, one in Hebrew (Psalm 39:6) explores the significance of human life, in reflection on Genesis 1:26–27, W. Brueggemann & W. H. Bellinger, *Psalms* (Cambridge: Cambridge University Press, 2014), pp. 192–93. The other, in Aram, refers to the face of Nebuchadnezzar whose idol of himself is ridiculed in the passage (Daniel 3:19).

[30]   A. Sherwood, *Paul and the Restoration of Humanity in Light of Ancient Jewish Traditions* (Leiden: Brill, 2013), pp. 135–41.

[31]   Similarly, Paul's speech on the Areopagus includes the assertion that the status of humanity as children of God implies that God cannot be represented in any crafted image, Acts 17:29. Cf. Hill, *Being Human*, p. 197; Sherwood, *Paul and the Restoration of Humanity*, p. 161.

[32]   Exodus 6:6; 15:6; 33:20–23; Deuteronomy 4:34; 5:15; 7:19; 26:8; 1 Samuel 5:11; 2 Chronicles 30:12; Ezra 7:9; Nehemiah 2:8; Job 2:10; 5:17; 12:19; 19:21; 27:11; 29:4; 40:9; Psalms 44:3; 89:10; 98:1; Ecclesiastes 2:24; 9:1; Isaiah 30:30; 40:10; 52:10; 53:1; 59:1; 63:12. Hill, *Being Human*, p. 198.

of this, and one which informed subsequent Christian imagery, and not only in the apocalyptic tradition, is the "Ancient of Days" in Daniel 7:9, and the one described as *kebar-'enash*, in the likeness of a man, who is presented before the throne of God (7:13).[33]

The image, *tselem*, of the deity is the focus of devotion in a temple, such as those which proliferated in the eastern Mediterranean world and along the Fertile Crescent.[34] That later built in Jerusalem, and its mythical predecessor the tabernacle in the wilderness, conspicuously did not house such an image, or at least it ought not to have done according to the Deuteronomistic and Priestly writers. On the contrary, the introduction of such images by certain of the kings of Judah is condemned as apostasy and idolatry.[35] It has long been recognized that monotheistic Yahwism emerged gradually from ancient Near Eastern polytheism, and that the monarchical period was characterized by monolatry or henotheism in competition with, often diplomatically motivated, polytheism, at least until the time of Josiah, and that radical, aniconic, monotheism prevailed only during the post-exilic period.[36] Persian rule brought Judaean Yahwism into contact with Zoroastrianism, which similarly vacillated

---

[33]   For discussion of this figure, see P. M. Casey, *Son of Man* (London: SPCK, 1979); T. B. Slater, *The Son of Man in Second Temple Judaism* (Macon, GA: Edward Mellen, 2018).

[34]   Sherwood, *Paul and the Restoration of Humanity*, pp. 135–41.

[35]   2 Kings 21:4–6; 23:26–27; Jeremiah 11:9–13; 15:4; Ezekiel 8–11; 20; 23.

[36]   J. S. Anderson, *Monotheism and Yahweh's Appropriation of Baal* (London: Bloomsbury, 2015); J. Day, *Yahweh and the Gods and Goddesses of Canaan* (Sheffield: Sheffield Academic Press, 2001); W. G. Dever, *Did God Have A Wife? Archaeology and Folk Religion in Ancient Israel* (Grand Rapids, MI: Eerdmans, 2005); B. Halpern & M. J. Adams, *From Gods to God* (Tübingen: Mohr Siebeck, 2009); N. MacDonald, "Aniconism in the Old Testament", R. P. Gordon (ed.), *The God of Israel* (Cambridge: Cambridge University Press, 2007), pp. 20–34; P. D. Miller, *The Religion of Ancient Israel* (Louisville, KY: Westminster John Knox Press, 2000); R. Albertz, *A History of Israelite Religion* (Louisville, KY: Westminster John Knox Press, 1994); M. S. Smith, *The Origins of Biblical Monotheism* (Oxford: Oxford University Press, 2003); *Early History of God*.

over the centuries, and in different traditions, between monotheistic, dualistic and polytheistic expressions, and in its depiction or otherwise of Ahura Mazda.[37] Any mutual influence between these movements would not have anteceded the Medo-Persian conquest of Babylonia, c. 540 BCE. Nevertheless, both reflect a tendency towards monotheism and away from anthropomorphic and other visual depictions of God—a process analogous to the development of the Greek philosophical traditions which emerged alongside, but did not supersede, the polytheistic myths and cults of the eastern Mediterranean.

Notwithstanding their complex history, the canon both of the Hebrew *Torah* and of the Christian Old Testament open with the monotheistic redaction of the myth of the creation of the world by a transcendent God. Despite incidental references in the narrative to family deities whose images were used as an aid to devotion (1 Samuel 19:13–16; cf. Genesis 31:34), and the enigmatic account of the image of the serpent erected by Moses in the wilderness (Numbers 21:8), the prohibition of such objects in the Decalogue[38] gradually eclipsed contrary traditions. The account of the golden calf forged by Aaron while Moses was receiving the Decalogue on Mount Sinai (Exodus 32; Deuteronomy 9:13–21), and the deification of what may have been conceived as the mount on which God rode, rather than an object of worship in itself, originated as a polemic against the shrines associated with Jeroboam I at Dan and Bethel (1 Kings 12:26–30).[39] These shrines, and the earlier dynasties of the northern kingdom, preserved more ancient Israelite cultic traditions, suppressed in favour of the temple in Jerusalem in which the Davidic dynasty was sacralized, and condemned by later Deuteronomistic and Priestly writers. According to the dominant narrative in the Old Testament canon, until the Babylonian exile the symbol of God's presence in the temple is the Ark of the Covenant, conceptualized as the throne of God rather than as representing its occupant.[40] In later centuries, the *inner sanctum* stood

---

37   N. E. M. Boyce, *A History of Zoroastrianism* (Leiden: Brill, 1975, 1982, 1991).

38   Exodus 20:4,23; 34:17; Leviticus 19:4; 26:1; Deuteronomy 4:15–19; 5:8; 27:15.

39   Y. H. Chung, *The Sin of the Calf* (London: Bloomsbury, 2019).

40   Exodus 25:22; Leviticus 16:2,13; Numbers 7:89; 1 Kings 8:6–13; Psalm 26:8; 84:1.

empty, as Pompey, among other invading intruders, was to discover.[41] This led to perceptions, or at least polemics, to the effect that the Jews were atheists,[42] or that the god they worshipped was porcine[43] or asinine[44] in form.

While the J creation myth is the more crude in asserting and sacralizing male domination, we should not assume that the P myth presupposes any less patriarchal a society. Nevertheless, the Hebrew 'adam and the Greek 'anthropos are alike generic, and Genesis 1:26–27 is quite explicit that male and female alike are created in the image of God; a god who is transcendent and nowhere depicted anthropomorphically, or for that matter bestially, in the myth, and is therefore not attributed any binary sex or gender identity or role. Sexual differentiation is essential to procreation of the species, but has no other function or significance in the myth, despite patriarchal assumptions and social structures prevalent at all stages in the transmission of the tradition until the formation of the canon and beyond. Nor is masculinity attributed to God in the J myth, notwithstanding the anthropomorphism and the more overt assertion of male priority and dominance.

In both creation myths, humanity has a distinctive role, responsibility and power within creation. In the J myth biological life is created for human benefit. In P, the authority of the human to rule the animal is a function of the divine image, the representation in the human body of God's presence in creation.[45] This rule is implicitly benign, and in both myths a vegetarian diet is imposed on human and animal alike (Genesis

---

[41] Josephus, *Ant.* 14.3.50–53; 4.54–73; cf. also Hecataeus, *Aegyptiaca*, cit. Diodorus Siculus, *Bibliotheca Historica* 40.3.4; Livy, *Scholia in Lucanum* 2.593; aniconic worship mentioned with approval by Cassius Dio, *Historia Romana* 37.16.5–17.2; cf. Tacitus, *Hist.* 5.5.4.

[42] Apollonius Molon, cit. Josephus, *C. Apionem* 2.148; Manetho, *Aegyptiaca*, cit. Josephus, *C. Apion* 2.6; Ptolemy, *Apotelesmatica* 2.3.31.

[43] Petronius, Fr. 35, <http://www.thelatinlibrary.com/petroniusfrag.html>, accessed 15 May 2020.

[44] Mnaseas, cit. Josephus, *C. Ap.* 2.112–14; Apion, cit. Josephus, *C. Ap.* 2.80; Tacitus, *Hist* 5.3.2; Plutarch, *Quaest. Conv.* 4.5.2.

[45] Westermann, *Genesis 1–11*, p. 159.

1:29–30; 2:16). This would seem to imply that human jurisdiction does not extend to a right to kill, even for food; the first allusion to animals being killed is for their skins, by God in anticipation of the expulsion of the first couple from Eden (Genesis 3:21 J). The cultic slaughter of animals is first mentioned in the concluding scene of the J myth, in which the butcher, Abel, is himself violently killed (Genesis 4:1–16). While there is no reason to believe that the societies in which these myths were transmitted were vegetarian in culture, it is nevertheless clear that human dominion over animal life was envisaged as limited.

Our consideration of the human being in the creation narratives of Genesis has said as much, if not more, about God the creator as about the human, and the place of the human in creation. This is appropriate, and not only because the notion in P of the human as created in God's image in itself raises questions about the God reflected and represented on earth by the human being. Increasingly secular societies, in which there has been an implicit tendency towards Deism in much Christian belief and practice over recent centuries, have also been the environment in which responsible stewardship of the earth and its resources has given way to increasingly unscrupulous exploitation of people and of natural resources by the powerful. If Christian witness is to be meaningful and authentic in the face of the prevailing global environmental crisis, then theological claims about the sovereignty of God, as well as the place of humanity in creation, will need to be asserted.

The image of God and human redemption in the New Testament

While the redaction of Genesis is generally ascribed to the post-exilic reconstruction of what became Judaism, a date very much later than popular and traditional conceptions of Mosaic authorship, the intervening centuries brought very considerable developments and diversity to the religiosity of the people for whom the *Torah* gradually became sacred scripture. The encounters with Zoroastrianism in the east and with Hellenism in the West are so sparsely recorded that they are beyond reliable reconstruction.[46] Aramaic superseded Hebrew as the vernacular language of Jews in the Levant and eastwards, and increasingly entered religious discourse. Greek language and culture penetrated Judaism, introducing philosophical concepts and systems in which Jewish beliefs and values were increasingly articulated, and into which the books of scripture were translated, and new books written. It was the Hellenistic influences which were to prove particularly formative for the development of Western Christianity.

The increasing transcendence of God in Jewish thought is reflected in both Aramaic and Greek texts, in both supernatural intermediary figures and in abstract divine emanations. The divine–human relationship is attenuated, and a plethora of mediator figures evolved through the demotion of supernatural figures regarded as deities by previous generations, and the construction of divine qualities or principles which gradually acquired identity. The notion of the human being as created in God's image nonetheless persisted in Judaism.[47] These developments were to influence early Christian beliefs about Jesus rather more than they did messianic ideas in Judaism. For the early Christians, Jesus acquired the ultimate and definitive mediating role between God and humanity, conceptualized not only through the appropriation of traditional messianic motifs, such as those associated with David, but also of figures in apocalyptic myths and divine emanations developed in sapiential speculation. This was to have implications not only for Christology but also for the Christian reconceptualization of humanity in relation to God. This triangulation is reflected not least in the reinterpretation of the creation narratives in early Christian literature, and their appropriation to illustrate aspects of Christology, anthropology, soteriology and eschatology.

The Pauline and Johannine traditions in the New Testament are, for the present purpose, the most significant in their interpretation of the

---

[46]   Albertz, *History of Israelite Religion*; Boccaccini, *Middle Judaism*; P. Sacchi, *The History of the Second Temple Period* (Sheffield: Sheffield Academic Press, 2000).

[47]   *T. Naph* 2.5; *Apoc. Mos.* 10:3; 12:1; 33:5; 35:2; *Vit. Adam & Eva* 14:1–2; 37:3; *4 Ezra* 8:44; *2 Enoch* 65:2.

Genesis creation narratives, and in particular their appropriation of the *'eikon theou* (image of God) motif to Jesus, and its implications for their anthropology. *'eikon theou* is employed both of humanity, in continuity with Genesis 1:26–27, and also, specifically, of Jesus, reinterpreting the relationship of humanity with God so that it is redemption which brings Christians into conformity with God's image in Christ. It is worth noting, before considering some relevant passages, that the notion of *'eikon theou* enjoyed some currency in Hellenistic philosophy, particularly in traditions where philosophical monotheism coexisted with traditional cultic polytheism. Plato regarded the visible, created, world, or world of sense perception, as the image, *'eikon*, of the invisible, uncreated, world of ideas, or even as the image of God (*Timaeus* 92c). Human beings, and particularly kings, are similarly described in texts which antedate the New Testament,[48] and, in modified form, also in the writings of the Jewish philosopher Philo of Alexandria,[49] which are particularly significant for our understanding of Jewish thought in the Hellenistic world. Philo interprets Genesis 1:27 to describe humanity as "moulded after the image of God", and that that divine image is *'o theou logos*, "the *Logos* of God" (*De Opif.* 25; cf. *Q. Rer.* 231; *De Fuga* 101; *De Somn.* 1.239). The *Logos*, identified also as the image of God, is the ideal model of creation, perceptible only by the intellect, and the physical universe, and humanity, are in turn a physical image of the Logos. The human mind, the ruling part of the soul, is made in the image of God (*De Opif.* 69). The *Logos* is the prototype of the human soul; humanity "was made an image and imitation", when the *Logos* breathed the divine breath into his face (*De Opif.* 139; cf. *Leg. All.* 3.96).

---

[48]   P. München, ed. L. Mitteis & U. Wilcken, *Grundzüge und Chrestomathie der Papyruskunde. I* (Hildesheim: Georg Olms Verlagsbuchhandlung, 1963), p. 109; Rosetta Stone, ed. W. Dittenberger, *Orientis Graeci Inscriptiones Selectae* (Leipzig: Hirzel, 1903), p. 90.

[49]   P. Borgen, *Philo of Alexandria* (Leiden: Brill, 2005); M. Hadas-Lebel, *Philo of Alexandria* (Leiden: Brill, 2012); D. Winston, *Logos and Mystical Theology in Philo of Alexandria* (Cincinnati, OH: Hebrew Union College Press, 1985).

In Galatians 3:28, in what may be an ancient formulary associated with baptism,[50] Paul contrasts the Church with human society as experienced in the Graeco-Roman world of his day. In a passage which does not explicitly cite the *'eikon theou* motif, but which does quote the Septuagint of Genesis 1:27 verbatim, Paul identifies Christians as descendants of Abraham and children of God, through Christ. Paul repudiates the distinctions between Jew and Greek, slave and free, *'arsen kai thelu*, the last pairing using the neuter form to refer not to men and women as individuals, but the male and female principles, created in God's image, which constitute the human species.[51] It has frequently been argued, or assumed, that Paul is concerned more, or only, with the first contrasting pair, Jew and Greek, the latter being a metonymy for gentiles generally.[52] While the relationship between Jew and Gentile in Christ, and the enduring relevance of the Mosaic Law, are perhaps the most developed themes in Paul's theology,[53] and it was many centuries before the Church discerned therein any impetus for the abolition of slavery or the ordination of women, these issues are by no means irrelevant to his argument in Galatians. The contrast between slave and free is quite crucial to his relegation of the Law to a more temporary and limited role in Galatians 3:15–5:1, as is also that of gender distinction in questions of inheritance in the household, the dominant metaphor of salvation in Galatians 3–4.[54]

---

[50] N. H. Taylor, *Paul on Baptism* (London: SCM Press, 2016), pp. 25–33.

[51] G. N. Uzukwu, *The Unity of Male and Female in Christ* (London: Bloomsbury, 2015).

[52] Cf. J. M. G. Barclay, *Obeying the Truth* (Edinburgh: T&T Clark, 1988); H. D. Betz, *Galatians* (Philadelphia: Fortress, 1979), pp. 173, 175; J. L. Martyn, *Galatians* (New York: Doubleday, 1997), p. 376; R. N. Longenecker, *Galatians* (Waco, TX: Word, 1990), p. 157.

[53] J. D. G. Dunn, *The Theology of Paul the Apostle* (Grand Rapids, MI: Eerdmans, 1998); N. H. Taylor, "Paul, Pharisee and Christian", *Theologia Viatorum* 24 (1997), pp. 45–65.

[54] N. H. Taylor, "Liturgy and Identity: Conversion-Initiation in Galatians 3:26–29", *Anaphora: Journal of the Society for Liturgical Studies* 6:2 (2012), pp. 1–18; cf. J. D. G. Dunn, *Galatians* (London: Black, 1991); L. A. Jervis, *Galatians*

> Paul's redefinition of sonship and inheritance in a transcendent manner facilitates the termination of this-worldly distinctions of "Jew or Gentile, slave or free, male and female" to define who is in and who is out or to define a relation of advantage and disadvantage.[55]

Humanity in Christ, therefore, knows no distinction between Jew and Greek (Gentile), slave and free, male and female, notwithstanding the complementarity of the last in human reproduction and the socio-economic realities of a highly stratified society in the present order.

In 1 Corinthians 11:7–8, Paul describes the male human being, *'aner*, as the image, *'eikon*, and glory, *doxa*, of God, and relegates the female to being the glory, but not the image, of the male. The context is conduct in worship, and specifically the use of head coverings while praying, which raises issues of cultural convention and symbolic association which can be reconstructed only very incompletely.[56] It has been argued that Paul presupposes, on the basis of Genesis 1:26–27, that women and men alike are made in God's image, and that their interdependence and equality are demonstrated in his contrast between the creation of Eve out of Adam's body (11:12, citing Genesis 2:21–22) and the normal pattern of birth from the body of the woman.[57] Even if Paul is referring specifically to how wives should conduct themselves when accompanying their husbands to a public gathering, rather than to men and women generally, it remains impossible to extract this text from the cultural context in which it was

---

(Peabody, MA: Hendrickson, 1999); B. W. Longenecker, *The Triumph of Abraham's God* (Edinburgh: T&T Clark, 1998); N. A. Meyer, *Adam's Dust and Adam's Glory in the Hodayot and the Letters of Paul* (Leiden: Brill, 2016), pp. 95–102; Uzukwu, *Unity of Male and Female*.

55   Meyer, *Adam's Dust*, p. 102.

56   R. F. Collins, *First Corinthians* (Collegeville, MN: Liturgical, 1999), pp. 396–411; D. B. Martin, *The Corinthian Body* (New Haven, CT: Yale University Press, 1995), pp. 233–49.

57   K. E. Bailey, *Paul through Mediterranean Eyes* (London: SPCK, 2011), pp. 308–10.

written, and the prevailing patriarchal assumptions regarding gender roles.

In a section of 2 Corinthians in which he compares Christ and the Christian experience with Israel at Sinai,[58] Paul alludes to Moses, the mediator of the Law, as being also "mediator of the glory of God" (3:7).[59] Through Christ, described as both *kurios* (lord) and *pneumatos* (spirit), Christians see the glory, *doxa*, of God *katoptrizomenoi*, "as in a mirror",[60] and are transformed into God's image (3:18). Christ is identified explicitly as the *'eikon* of God (2 Corinthians 4:4), compared with whom Christians are the very incomplete, unclear and inadequate mirror image.[61] Rather than its being intrinsic to humanity since creation, it is the Christ event that realizes the image of God, in Christians rather than in all people.[62] This is consistent with the transformation Paul associates with resurrection in 1 Corinthians 15:49, from *ten 'eikona tou choikou*, the image of the earthly one or of dust, to *ten 'eikona tou 'epouraniou*, the image of the heavenly one. The image of Adam, inherited by his descendants (Genesis 5:3), is to be transformed into the heavenly image of the risen Christ.[63]

---

[58] Exodus 32–34. It is recounted that, on his return from meeting God on the mountain, Moses' face reflected God's glory (34:7), instilling fear in the Israelites, so that thereafter Moses veiled his face after meeting God, until the sheen had faded. The apparition, and consequent fear, follow the incident in which Aaron formed the golden calf as a cult object, with its connotations, in the canonical tradition and subsequently, of apostasy and idolatry. The implication is that this incident caused some estrangement from God; hence the perceived danger in seeing God's glory reflected in Moses' face.

[59] J. M. Scott, *2 Corinthians* (Peabody, MA: Hendrickson, 1998), p. 73.

[60] A rather more primitive implement in the ancient world than is taken for granted today.

[61] Cf. Wisdom 7:25–26, R. F. Collins, *Second Corinthians* (Grand Rapids, MI: Baker Academic, 2013), pp. 89–92.

[62] Scott, *2 Corinthians*, pp. 82, 86, associates this manifestation of God's glory with the vision of the *merkabah*, God's throne-chariot, in which God is depicted anthropomorphically (Ezekiel 1:26–27), and argues that Paul envisages Christ accompanying God in the chariot.

[63] Collins, *First Corinthians*, p. 572.

A similar notion of the transformation of Christians into conformity with the image of Christ is expressed in Romans (8:29). It would not be possible to digress into any treatment of the predestinarian motif in this passage,[64] but the connection between creation (of humanity in God's image) and eschatology is important.[65] Christian life, from baptism to its eschatological consummation, is conceptualized as a process of transformation into the image of God's risen son, the *prototokos*, preeminent and archetypal as well as eldest of the new humanity.[66] "According to the divine plan, Christians are destined to reproduce in themselves an image of Christ by a progressive share in Christ's risen life."[67]

This imagery is developed further in Colossians 1:15,[68] which may quote, but also possibly embellish, an earlier hymnic or creedal tradition:[69]

He is the image of the invisible God,

The firstborn of all creation.

This text may have originated in the Jewish wisdom tradition, and been appropriated for Christian use by claiming for Jesus the attributes of *Sophia*, claiming for Christ in particular the relationship of *Sophia* to *Torah*.[70] The identification of *Sophia* with the divine *ˈeikon* is attested in

---

64 Cf. R. Jewett, *Romans* (Minneapolis, MN: Fortress, 2007), p. 529, for a helpful discussion.

65 J. D. G. Dunn, *Romans* (Waco, TX: Word, 1988), p. 495.

66 Dunn, *Romans*, pp. 483–4; cf. J. A. Fitzmyer, *Romans* (New York: Doubleday, 1992), p. 525; Jewett, *Romans*, pp. 528–9.

67 Fitzmyer, *Romans*, p. 525.

68 Scholars are divided as to whether Colossians was written by Paul (L. T. Johnson, *The Writings of the New Testament* [Minneapolis, MN: Fortress, 2010], pp. 347–49); by an associate during his lifetime (J. D. G. Dunn, *The Epistles to the Colossians and to Philemon* [Grand Rapids, MI: Eerdmans, 1996], p. 41), or during the years following his death (G. P. Foster, *Colossians* [London: Bloomsbury, 2016], pp. 80–81; J. L. Sumney, *Colossians* [Louisville, KY: Westminster John Knox Press, 2008], p. 9).

69 Sumney, *Colossians*, pp. 60–63; cf. Dunn, *Colossians*, pp. 84–85.

70 Dunn, *Colossians*, p. 85; Sumney, *Colossians*, pp. 60–61; *contra*, C. Stettler, *Der Kolosserhymnus* (Tübingen: Mohr Siebeck, 2000).

the Jewish wisdom tradition.[71] This assimilation of divine emanations into Christology would be consistent with Paul's approach to scripture, which became increasingly normative in early Christianity, whereby Jesus is, as it were, the lens through which scripture is read and interpreted, and the Christ event the standard by which the Law is measured and the definitive fulfilment of all prophecy.[72] Christ is the ultimate and definitive revelation of God, "the means by which God reveals Godself to the world . . . the knowable and approachable manifestation of God in creation".[73] The invisibility of God is fully consistent with the P creation narrative in Genesis 1, discussed above, and with the religiosity of Israel outside the visionary experiences attributed to Moses (Exodus 33:17–23), and claimed by the prophets (Isaiah 6:5; Ezekiel 1:26–28) and some of their successors in the apocalyptic (Daniel 7:9–12) and *merkabah* traditions; any divine visibility in the J creation narrative would be somewhat anomalous within the tradition. The invisibility of God is consistent also both with the increasing sense of divine transcendence in contemporary Judaism and with the platonic distinction between the visible and invisible worlds, prominent in the writings of Philo noted above.

In identifying Jesus as *prototokos* of creation, Paul claims for him pre-eminence in status and (possibly, though not necessarily) chronological priority in the created order, as well as being its pattern or archetype.[74] The claim is made for *Sophia* in the Jewish Wisdom tradition,[75] and is consistent with the status Paul accords Jesus in the resurrected order (1 Corinthians 15:23; cf. Romans 8:29). Jesus is identified also as the head of a body, indicating the relationship between the risen Christ and the corporate entity formed by the human members of communities of believers. This image conceives of Christians as forming an organic union

---

[71] Wisdom 7:26; Philo, *Leg. All.* 1.43.

[72] Cf. H. Räisänen, *The Torah and Christ* (Sheffield: Sheffield Academic Press, 1992); E. P. Sanders, *Paul, the Law and the Jewish People* (London: SCM Press, 1983).

[73] Sumney, *Colossians*, p. 64.

[74] Dunn, *Colossians*, p. 97–98; cf. Sumney, *Colossians*, pp. 65–72.

[75] Proverbs 8:22; Philo, *Leg. All.* 1.43. Cf. also (of the *Logos*), Philo, *Quod Det.* 118; *De Conf. Ling.* 146.

with Christ, as previously Paul had spoken of union with Christ in his death and resurrection in their baptism (Romans 6:3–4).[76]

Baptism is similarly behind Paul's ethical injunctions in Colossians 3:8–15, a passage which shows continuity with, but also significant deviation from, his earlier letters (Galatians 3:26–29; 1 Corinthians 12:12–31).[77] The distinctions of race and social rank (gender not mentioned) which determine identity and status in the world are abolished in Christ, as Christians put on their new nature *kat' 'eikona tou ktisantos 'auton*, "according to the image of its creator" (3:10). The "new eschatological reality" transcends restoration to the pristine created state reflected in Genesis 1,[78] as Jesus "is associated both with the creation of the world and with God's new creation through his death and resurrection".[79] Humanity attains its full potential through participation in Jesus' death and resurrection in baptism, and in thereafter living as the eschatological body of Christ, in accordance with his formative role in creation and redemption.

In the Pauline tradition, therefore, the tension between humanity collectively created in the image of God and Christ, the unique bearer of the divine image, is resolved in the death and resurrection of Jesus, in which fallen humanity shares through baptism, and thereby comes to share also in the restored and renewed creation in which God's image is realized in all members of Christ's body.

The prologue to the Fourth Gospel is consciously modelled on the opening of Genesis:

Genesis 1:1 (Masoretic Text)
In the beginning God (*'elohim*) created the heavens and the earth.

Genesis 1:1 (Septuagint)
In the beginning God created (the) heaven and (the) earth.

---

76   N. H. Taylor, "Dying with Christ in Baptism", *The Bible Translator* 59 (2008), pp. 38–49.

77   Taylor, *Paul on Baptism*, pp. 76–77.

78   Sumney, *Colossians*, p. 203; cf. Foster, *Colossians*, pp. 336–7.

79   Taylor, *Paul on Baptism*, p. 77.

John 1:1

In the beginning was the *Logos* and the *Logos* was with God and the *Logos* was God.

This statement forms an *inclusio* with the confession of the apostle Thomas on seeing the risen Christ: "My Lord and my God" (20:28).[80] The prologue continues to speak of the *Logos* as God's eternal companion, who shares somehow in God's divinity without thereby being identical with God.[81] Creation was brought about through the *Logos*, humanity uniquely sharing with God in life in its fullest sense, and in the illumination of the mind, i.e. capacity to receive divine revelation, and conscience through the *Logos*, so enabling the divine work of creation to continue through inspired humanity, in particular Moses and the Prophets.[82] John's conscious reinterpretation of Genesis 1 reaches its distinctive and climactic point in stating that "the *Logos* became flesh and dwelt (literally: "pitched his tent") among us" (1:14).[83] This alludes to the Old Testament motif of God's dwelling with Israel, most particularly in the Exodus narratives of the desert wandering, in which the tabernacle, or tent, is the (not exclusive) locus of God's presence, and place where Moses met God when he did not ascend a mountain for that purpose.[84] Here it emphasizes that, in becoming human in Jesus, the *Logos* did not cease to be divine; any dualist interpretation of Jesus is thereby repudiated.[85] It points also to Jesus' proclamation of the replacement of the temple with his (resurrected) body (2:19–22).[86] John interprets the birth of Jesus as

---

[80] R. E. Brown, *The Gospel according to John* (New York: Doubleday, 1966), p. 5.

[81] Brown, *John*, pp. 4–5; F. C. B. Lindars, *The Gospel of John* (Grand Rapids, MI: Eerdmans, 1972), p. 77; F. J. Moloney, *The Gospel of John* (Collegeville, MN: Liturgical, 1998), p. 35.

[82] Lindars, *John*, p. 77.

[83] See also Hart, Chapter 3.

[84] Exodus 25:8; 29:46; cf. 2 Chronicles 2:14. For discussion, Brown, *John*, p. 32; Moloney, *John*, p. 39.

[85] Brown, *John*, p. 32; Lindars, *John*, p. 79.

[86] Cf. Ezekiel 43:7. For discussion, Brown, *John*, p. 32.

revealing the full purpose of God in creation, transcending the revelation through Moses.[87] Humanity, the acme of creation in Genesis, is able to attain sonship of God through the incarnation of the *Logos*, so bringing the eschatological and metaphysical aspects of creation, as interpreted in the prophetic and sapiential traditions of Judaism, to their fulfilment.

John's use of the figure of the *Logos*, usually, but at least potentially misleadingly, rendered "Word", interprets motifs drawn from the Hebrew tradition as well as from Hellenistic philosophy, as had previously been integrated by Philo of Alexandria, particularly in *De Opificio Mundi* ("On the Creation of the Earth"). Philo's integration of the Hebrew *hokmah* / *sophia* with the Stoic *logos* enables him to develop a philosophical system that is not merely theistic, but consistent with Jewish monotheism.[88] Philo interprets Genesis 1:27 to describe humanity as "moulded after the image of God", and that that divine image is *'o theou logos*, "the Logos of God" (*De Opif.* 25; cf. *Q. Rer.* 231; *De Fuga* 101; *De Somn.* 1.239). The *Logos*, identified also as the image of God, is the ideal model of creation, perceptible only by the intellect, while the physical universe, and humanity, are in turn a physical image of the *Logos*. The human mind (*nous*), the ruling part of the soul (*psuche*), is made in the image (*'eikon*) of God (*De Opif.* 69). The *Logos* is the prototype (*paradeigma*) of the human soul; humanity (*'anthropos*) "was made an image and imitation", when the *Logos* breathed the divine breath into his face (*De Opif.* 139; cf. *Leg. All.* 3.96). In another context, ostensibly interpreting the dreams of Joseph, Philo asserts that God "stamped the whole of creation with his image and impression, his own *Logos*" (*De Somn.* 2.65; cf. *De Fuga* 13). Particularly significant for the Johannine prologue is that the *Logos* is identified with human agents, most conspicuously Moses (*Quis Rer.* 182–85).

It is not necessary to argue that John reflects the same degree of erudition as Philo to recognize that, by the time the Fourth Gospel was written, Jewish beliefs had been articulated in the language of Greek philosophy for centuries, and this process had penetrated Judaea and Galilee as well as diaspora Judaism.[89] Nor is there any need to argue

---

87   Lindars, *John*, p. 78.

88   Lindars, *John*, p. 83.

89   Cf. M. Hengel, *Judaism and Hellenism* (London: SCM Press, 1961).

that John was dependent on Philo.[90] That God's creative word, *dabar* (Psalm 33:6–9), has come to be personified or hypostatized, represents a development of some significance, but one widely attested in the extant literature of the period. The same tendency is found in the *Targumim* (the Aramaic rendering of the Hebrew scriptures), where, in a number of passages, *memra'* (word) denotes an intermediary, when, in the corresponding Hebrew passages, God speaks directly.[91] This device both emphasizes the transcendence of God and avoids anthropomorphic depiction of God.[92] The attribution of the status accorded to humanity in Genesis 1, viz. being created in God's image, to a divine manifestation or personified divine attribute, elsewhere described as wisdom, *hokmah / sophia*,[93] significantly relegates humanity in the ordering of creation. This process is attested in some strands of Judaism well before the emergence of Christianity, and we have seen that the status of humanity as created

---

[90] Lindars, *John*, p. 39.

[91] Tg Onq Exodus 4:7; Deuteronomy 33:13. The extant Targumim cannot be dated with precision, but neither Onqelos nor Neofiti (c. IV CE) substantially develops Genesis 1:26–27; the much later ps-Jonathan (VII CE or later) reads:

> And the Lord said to the angels who ministered before Him, who had been created in the second day of the creation of the world, Let us make man in Our image, in Our likeness; and let them rule over the fish of the sea, and over the fowl which are in the atmosphere of heaven, and over the cattle, and over all the earth, and over every reptile creeping upon the earth. And the Lord created man in His Likeness: In the image of the Lord He created him, with two hundred and forty and eight members, with three hundred and sixty and five nerves, and overlaid them with skin, and filled it with flesh and blood. Male and female in their bodies He created them.

<https://www.sefaria.org/Targum_Jonathan_on_Genesis.1.27?lang=bi&with=all&lang2=en>, accessed 15 June 2020.

[92] Lindars, *John*, p. 83.

[93] Proverbs 8:22–31; *Sirach* 24:1–22; *Wisdom of Solomon*. 9:1–2.

in God's image had been redefined prior to the composition of the New Testament documents. Where the Johannine prologue is perhaps distinctive is in its explicit identification within a single passage of the eternal, divine, *Logos*, with a particular historical person, viz. Jesus.[94]

While distancing humanity from God, in continuity with developments wider than Judaism, John also identifies the incarnation of the *Logos* as bringing to fulfilment God's purpose in the creation of humanity. The mission, crucifixion and resurrection of Jesus realize not only the glory of God in Christ, but also the salvation of humanity in and through him. This too is consistent with Philo's exposition of the *Logos*, elsewhere identified as the *'eikon theou*:

> The father of all has bestowed on his chief messenger and first-begotten Logos the special gift, to stand at the border between the creator and the created. This same [Logos] is both suppliant on behalf of distressed mortals to the uncorrupted and ambassador of the ruler to the subject (*Quis Rerum* 205).

Concluding reflections

This treatment of humanity in the biblical tradition has not been comprehensive. There are undoubtedly other images and motifs which would complement and significantly alter the portrayal here, focused as it has been on the notion of the creation of humanity in God's image in Genesis 1, and therefore enjoying a distinctive role and status, somehow representing God in the world. Early Christian writers identify Jesus as uniquely bearing God's image, among the numerous attributes progressively accorded him in early Christology. However, they also teach that Christians, through baptism, can attain to conformity with God's image and share with Jesus in the relationship with God commensurate with this. While the human potential which may be realized through Christian baptism is founded upon the death and resurrection of Jesus, this portrayal is less pessimistic than those which emphasize the

---

94   Lindars, *John*, p. 83.

crucifixion, and the themes of human depravity, judgement and penal substitution developed in Western Christianity since Augustine, and emphasized particularly, and almost exclusively, in some strands of Protestantism. While these rather bleaker assessments of the human condition are undoubtedly rooted in selected passages of scripture, and in particular traditions of their interpretation, there is as venerable, and as deeply rooted in our heritage, a tradition which speaks of humanity as God's creature, made in God's image and in accordance with God's purposes. However human history may be understood—and the "Fall", moral degeneracy and damnation are not the only motifs attested in scripture—there remains, in Christ, the potential for the human being to fulfil God's purposes, and for the divine image, however tarnished or distorted, to be restored. In recognizing the image of God in each human being, and the potential commensurate with this, we may perhaps perceive also something authentic of the God who created us, who intends the loving purposes of creation to be fulfilled in us, and who wishes that potential in us to be realized in Christ.

Questions for discussion

1. If human beings are made in God's image, how are we to understand sin?
2. How do our relationships with other people depend on our recognition of God's image in them?
3. How does recognizing God's purpose in the creation of humanity affect our understanding of God's judgement?
4. Can we perceive God more adequately by recognizing God's image in other people?

Further reading

James D. G. Dunn, *Theology of the New Testament* (Nashville, TN: Abingdon, 2009).

John R. Sachs, *The Christian Vision of Humanity* (Collegeville, MN: Liturgical, 1991).

Udo Schnelle, *Theology of the New Testament* (Grand Rapids, MI: Baker, 2009).

Claus Westermann, *Genesis* (Minneapolis, MN: Fortress, 1992).

Walther Zimmerli, *Man and his Hope in the Old Testament* (London: SCM Press, 2012).

CHAPTER 2

Human being and the praise of God

John Reuben Davies

In praise, the full identity of the human self is reached.
William P. Brown, Psalms *(2010), p. 151.*

At the beginning of the Gospel according to Luke, as the evangelist tells the story of the Son of God's incarnation—a new Genesis, with a new Adam in whom the whole of humankind finds its fulfilment—the human and angelic response to the good news is defined by joy and praise. While still an unborn child, John the Baptist leaps with joy in his mother Elizabeth's womb when the pregnant Mary greets her. Mary's soul glorifies the Lord, and her spirit rejoices in God her saviour. The messenger of the Lord, as he announces to the shepherds the gospel of great joy, the birth of the Saviour, is accompanied by a heavenly army praising God in a hymn of glory and peace. When Mary and Joseph bring the child Jesus to the temple, and Simeon takes the boy in his arms, his first response is to praise God. In the eyes of the evangelist, when God comes to meet us in Christ, the natural response is joy and praise; a response not limited to the highly favoured Mary, to the prophet John, to the faithful Simeon; it is a response that also draws in the unsuspecting shepherds; for the news will be a cause of great joy to all the people.

The Christian experience of God, which Luke markedly and explicitly portrays in the story of God's incarnation—that is, at the annunciation to Mary (Luke 1:26–38)—is that God does not burst into our lives, our hearts and souls and bodies, uninvited. At least, the invitation to share in the life of the Holy Trinity requires a response from us. We are asked for the *fiat* that Mary gave to God's messenger, Gabriel—"Let it be with me according to your word" (Luke 1:38). There is always a call—a call that we freely answer. And that answer leads to praise.

So it is, that when Mary greets her kinswoman Elizabeth on entering the house of Zechariah, the response of Elizabeth and the child in her womb when they recognize the Christ child being carried by Mary is great joy. Mary herself then responds to Elizabeth's joy with a hymn, and her soul extols the Lord (Luke 1:46–55). Mary's response to her calling is in the present continuous tense; it is a steady and sustained song of liturgical praise. Mary's example is likewise followed, at the birth of John the Baptist, by Zechariah's liturgical hymn (Luke 1:68–79) recognizing the fulfilment of the divine promise to save the people of God:

> Blessed be the Lord God of Israel,
> for he has looked favourably on his people and redeemed them.
> He has raised up a mighty saviour for us
> in the house of his servant David.
>
> *Luke 1:68–9*

Luke's vision of the Christian life, as expressed in his "orderly account" (Luke 1:1), culminates in the ascension of Jesus. Having opened the minds of the apostles to understand the scriptures, Jesus is carried up into heaven:

> They worshipped him, and returned to Jerusalem with great joy; and they were continually in the temple praising and blessing God.[1]
>
> *Luke 24:52–3*

Just as Luke's account of the earthly life of the Saviour begins with Zechariah in the temple at Jerusalem, so it concludes by bringing the audience back to the sanctuary as the apostles offer their continual worship of the living God. The evangelist describes for us an experience of God that points us towards—and places us within—the liturgy and the

---

[1]   The Byzantine/Majority Greek text and the Latin Vulgate read "praising and blessing", other sources omit "praising".

liturgical community. That liturgical community is the body of Christ, the baptized community assembled for worship most especially in the eucharistic liturgy of praise and thanksgiving. This is the embodiment of the temple; this is the place where time and eternity coincide—the life of this world, and the life of the world to come. Here, in the liturgical community, we encounter God's salvation, and we meet Christ as the fullness of grace and truth.[2]

Saviours, religion and human societies

Saint Luke's Gospel tells us about people who had been waiting for a saviour, and how that saviour came. Elsewhere in this present volume, David Jasper criticizes those theologians who begin "too far down the line to be any longer heard or understood except by very few people".[3] He laments the kind of pious language which is "good for sermons" but "frankly means very little in a world where elected leaders behave ever more like amoral bullies in the school playground".[4] We may do well, therefore, to halt the train and reverse back up the line in order to consider the secular, post-Enlightenment, Western context in which this chapter is being written. What can the Christian churches say about the human condition amid the coarsened, "post-truth" political discourse of the 2010s and 2020s?

The anxiety of news and social media commentators in the UK and the USA, which accompanied Brexit and the Trump presidency, suggested a crisis in civic society and the body politic; a crisis in which the churches perhaps failed to offer a convincing response. The COVID-19 pandemic, beginning in 2020, intensified the existential dilemma as political systems and ideologies, political parties and leaders that had become the focus for a secular salvation, fell into a pit dug with the spade of their own hubris.

---

[2]   See John Reuben Davies, "Liturgy as a repository of truth", in David Jasper and Jenny Wright (eds), *Truth and the Church in a Secular Age* (London: SCM Press, 2019), pp. 84–101, at p. 86.

[3]   See also David Jasper, Chapter 7.

[4]   See also David Jasper, Chapter 7.

When Barack Obama won the final primary and secured the Democratic Party's nomination for president on 3 June 2008, the rhetoric of his victory speech indicated that if elected, the young senator's effect on the USA, and indeed the world, would be along messianic lines:[5]

> I am absolutely certain that generations from now, we will be able to look back and tell our children that . . . this was the moment when the rise of the oceans began to slow and our planet began to heal; this was the moment when we ended a war and secured our nation and restored our image as the last, best hope on earth.
> (Tuesday 3 June 2008, St Paul, Minnesota)

There was no slowing of the rising oceans: the rising continued to accelerate.[6] North Africa, Iraq and Syria descended into the bloodiest of conflicts, and innocents were murdered from the air as US drone strikes were escalated.[7] But the search for a new messiah continued, and Middle America's response to a two-term Obama presidency was perhaps to choose "what is foolish in the world to shame the wise" (1 Corinthians

---

[5]   See, for example, David Paul Kuhn and Ben Smith, "Messianic rhetoric infuses Obama rallies", *Politico* (9 December 2007; updated 11 December 2007) <https://www.politico.com/story/2007/12/messianic-rhetoric-infuses-obama-rallies-007281>, accessed 28 December 2020; Cheryl K. Chumley, "Barbara Walters admits 'we' thought Obama was 'the next messiah'", *Washington Times* (Wednesday, 18 December 2013) <https://www.washingtontimes.com/news/2013/dec/18/barbara-walters-admits-we-thought-obama-was-next-m/>, accessed 28 December 2020.

[6]   Data from the National Oceanic and Atmospheric Administration, online at <https://www.climate.gov/news-features/understanding-climate/climate-change-global-sea-level>, accessed 29 December 2020.

[7]   "The 542 drone strikes that Obama authorized killed an estimated 3,797 people, including 324 civilians. As he reportedly told senior aides in 2011: 'Turns out I'm really good at killing people. Didn't know that was gonna be a strong suit of mine.'": Micah Zenko, "Obama's final drone strike data", Council on Foreign Relations blog (20 January 2017) online at <https://www.cfr.org/blog/obamas-final-drone-strike-data>, accessed 29 December 2020.

1:27).[8] One hardly needs to say that Christians should be clear: neither Barack Obama nor Donald Trump was a messiah. Yet there are many in the churches who would be prepared to offer evidence that each of these US presidents, in their own way, was doing the Lord's work.

One of the documents in the case might be an executive instrument of 28 December 2020, which gave the US presidency's official capacity to place religion at the heart of public discourse an interesting turn. On the eve of the commemoration of Saint Thomas Becket's death in Canterbury Cathedral at the hands of King Henry II's knights in 1170, President Trump issued a proclamation that 29 December 2020 should be recognized as the 850th anniversary of the martyrdom of Saint Thomas Becket, inviting "the people of the United States to observe the day in schools and churches and customary places of meeting with appropriate ceremonies in commemoration of the life and legacy of Thomas Becket".[9] The aim of the proclamation was to reinforce the USA's prioritization of religious freedom in foreign policy and aid programmes.[10] The Chinese government was a key target: singled out as "tireless witnesses to hope" were Cardinal Joseph Zen of Hong Kong and Pastor Wang Yi of Chengdu. The text went on to state:

> A society without religion cannot prosper. A nation without faith cannot endure—because justice, goodness, and peace cannot prevail without the grace of God.

---

[8] For an account of the religious devotion and messianic hopes directed towards Donald Trump, see Dan Hitchens, "Divine right", *The Spectator* (US edition) (25 December 2020), online at <https://spectator.us/divine-right-trump-religious-leader/>, accessed 29 December 2020.

[9] Proclamation on 850th Anniversary of the Martyrdom of Saint Thomas Becket (28 December 2020); online at <https://www.whitehouse.gov/presidential-actions/proclamation-850th-anniversary-martyrdom-saint-thomas-becket/>, accessed 29 December 2020.

[10] Executive Order on Advancing International Religious Freedom (2 June 2020); online at <https://www.whitehouse.gov/presidential-actions/executive-order-advancing-international-religious-freedom/>, accessed 30 December 2020.

This is a remarkable theological commentary on "America's first freedom"; and the statement as a whole, as we shall see, implies and assumes that the human person is religious by nature.[11]

We must ask, however, what is meant by "religion". During the two decades that straddled the beginning of the twenty-first century, academics in the relatively recent field of religious studies—a subject area that has its focus on religion as a phenomenon and practice, on the human rather than the divine—began to argue from a postmodernist and post-colonialist standpoint that "religion" is a contingent construction of the modern Western imagination. Chief among these writers has been Talal Asad, with his *Genealogies of Religion*, in which he took a critical look at the anthropological idea of religion as a category that can be identified analytically.[12] Religion, in this sense, has an essential quality that can be communicated by symbols across cultures. Based on the observation of Western culture, "religion" (for Asad) is a concept which

---

[11]   Executive Order on Advancing International Religious Freedom, 2 June 2020, section 1. Previous presidents have issued proclamations defending religious freedom, and President Obama referenced Thomas Jefferson's "belief" that "Almighty God hath created the mind free" (Presidential Proclamation on Religious Freedom Day, 13 January 2017; online at <https://obamawhitehouse.archives.gov/the-press-office/2017/01/13/presidential-proclamation-religious-freedom-day-2017>, accessed 31 December 2020). For the theologian, however, it is notable how President Trump's statements have focused on the human person. In 2019, President Trump's proclamation to mark Religious Freedom Day (15 January 2019) stated, without attributing the view to an historical figure, that the right to religious freedom "is innate to the dignity of every human person and is foundational to the pursuit of truth"; text online at <https://www.whitehouse.gov/presidential-actions/presidential-proclamation-religious-freedom-day-2019/>, accessed 31 December 2020.

[12]   Talal Asad, *Genealogies of Religion* (Baltimore, MD & London: Johns Hopkins University Press, 1993).

Western historians and anthropologists have applied as a universal model to understand all human societies.[13]

Central to Asad's thesis is his criticism of Clifford Geertz's well-known definition of religion as a system defined by symbols according to which believers interpret the world and live their lives.[14] Asad viewed Geertz's definition as being essentially too Protestant—it implies a believing individual (the Protestant hero) as the prime locus of religion and ignores the disciplinary practices and systems of institutional authority that are the focus of many (non-Protestant) religions.

Enlightenment liberalism certainly confined religion to a sphere of the private and personal, to the believing individual, and thus opened space for public debate predicated on "universal reason". In the modern West, most of us seem to have accepted, and certainly live with, the notion of an inner, private world of emotions or feelings, which may or may not be linked to religious faith, and an outer, public world of symbolic ritual. Asad's work has argued that anthropologists tend to adopt symbolic models of ritual behaviour in order to privilege their own explanations over those offered by indigenous discourses, so that, for example, those working within that anthropological tradition today tend to label as "fundamentalist" or "traditionalist" religious institutional forms of reasoned criticism found in non-Enlightenment societies.

We may, perhaps, be witnessing an emerging scenario in the postmodern West—in the United States and, for example, in Poland and Hungary as well—where religious faith, which works itself out both in political organization and through the organs of government,

---

[13]   Christian Smith has also drawn attention to Russell McCutcheon (*Manufacturing Religion* 1997), Tomoko Masuzawa (*The Invention of World Religions* 2005), Daniel Dubuisson (*The Western Construction of Religion* 2007); see Christian Smith, "Are human beings naturally religious?", in Timothy Samuel Shah and Joack Friedman (eds), *Homo Religiosus? Exploring the Roots of Religion and Religious Freedom in Human Experience* (Cambridge: Cambridge University Press, 2019), pp. 35–54, here at p. 37.

[14]   See Clifford Geertz, "Religion as a cultural system", in Michael Banton (ed.), *Anthropological Approaches to the Study of Religion* (London: Tavistock, 1966), pp. 1–46.

is re-emerging from its Kantian private and personal confinement, and finding its way back into the body politic as a recognized mode of institutional discourse.[15]

As we make this observation, we can also observe that religious faith in general is not fading away in the modern world as a whole. "Even the most determined attempts by powerful states to repress and extinguish religion", remarks Christian Smith, referencing Revolutionary France, Stalinist Russia and Maoist China, "have been at least partly unsuccessful."[16] Indeed, Christianity is the fastest-growing religion in the People's Republic of China.[17] In the end, as he makes his arguments about religion and human nature, Smith comes to the conclusion that total irreligion and complete secularity appear to be impossible among humans at the level of society.

This observation, however, does not necessarily mean that humans are naturally religious. Smith's critical-realist approach leads him to argue that all human persons are naturally religious in possessing "a complex set of innate features, capacities, powers, limitations, and tendencies" that enable them to be religious, and which, "under the right conditions, tend to predispose and direct them towards religion".[18] For Smith, we are not constantly supressing a religious urge, but humans do have an innate

---

[15]   A significant shift maybe signalled in US presidential rhetoric, from President Obama's reference to the "freedom to worship as we choose", to President Trump's re-emphasis of the constitutional phrasing of the "free exercise" of religion.

[16]   Smith, "Are human beings naturally religious?", p. 38. Christian Smith is (at the time of writing) William R. Kenan Jr Professor of Sociology at the University of Notre Dame, Indiana, and writes from an explicitly Catholic standpoint.

[17]   "Protestant Christianity is booming in China", *Economist* (15 September 2020), online at <https://www.economist.com/graphic-detail/2020/09/15/protestant-christianity-is-booming-in-china>, accessed 29 December 2020.

[18]   Critical realism is the view that our theories do "map onto" an external reality (they are not simply mental constructs), but that those theories are always corrigible in the light of new evidence, so that our knowledge of reality is never complete.

capacity to be religious—that is, we have an innate capacity to believe. Our condition is fundamentally one of believing rather than knowing, because all knowledge is built on propositions, or chains of propositions, that in the end rely on something that is given. Smith therefore argues that insofar as religion is natural, and thus fundamental to human experience, governments which profess a commitment to the values of liberty, equality and human flourishing must also be prepared to protect religious freedom. To do otherwise would be to restrict our capacity to be fully human.

Behind President Donald Trump's proclamation of 28 December 2020, therefore, is the understanding that, at the beginning of the twenty-first century's third decade, religion and faith are still understood in the West's dominant culture as natural to being human. Whether this is a rekindling of a smouldering fire or the temporary glow of dying embers, this means from a Christian perspective that the churches have a responsibility to speak and act in the public as well as the private sphere.[19]

Homo religiosus

Since the eighteenth century, philosophers of religion have been proposing that religion is natural to human beings and that we are inherently religious creatures. The underlying idea was principally worked out by Friedrich Schleiermacher (1768–1834), Georg Wilhelm Friedrich Hegel (1770–1831), Søren Kierkegaard (1813–55), William James (1842–1910), Rudolf Otto (1884–1939), and Paul Tillich (1886–1965), among others.[20]

---

[19] There are those who would argue that the Trump administration's commitment to religious freedom has been selective, especially when it comes to Islam, as well as those who would argue that the proclamation of 28 December 2020 was little more than another stick with which to beat China. I am interested here only in what the text implies.

[20] Friedrich Schleiermacher, *Über die Religion: Reden an die Gebildeten unter ihren Verächtern* ["On Religion: Speeches to its Cultured Despisers"] (Berlin: Johann Friedrich Unger, 1799), tr. Richard Crouter (Cambridge: Cambridge University Press, 1996); Georg Wilhelm Friedrich Hegel, *Phänomenologie*

Mircea Eliade (1907–86), however, was the first to employ the phrase *Homo religiosus* to express the concept of a human person who sees the world in a "religious" way.[21]

James, Otto and Eliade in particular argued that humans are born not only with an awareness of, but also with a strong pull towards, encounters with the holy. The thinking of these philosophers focused on hierophanies, manifestations of the sacred, what Otto defined as the "numinous", the profound emotional experience of the other which inspires wonder, awe and irresistible attraction. In other words, their view was that humans are drawn to the sacred, to ultimate concerns, through observation, awareness, insight, personal contact and exposure. The innate quality of religion, for these philosophers, was therefore to be found in the subjective experience of human beings—the "chains of propositions" that Smith has identified as the "given" that we rely on.

Joseph Ratzinger (Pope Benedict XVI), in attempting to locate the origin of human religious experience, has looked to the very experience of our own existence. He argued that the experience of the absolute happens in two ways.[22] First, when we recognize and push out the boundaries of our own human powers and yearn to go beyond the limits of our own human experience, we recognize and seek that which is other. Secondly,

---

des Geistes ["Phenomenology of Spirit"] (Bamberg and Würzburg, 1807), tr. Terry Pinkard (Cambridge: Cambridge University Press, 2017); Søren Kierkegaard, *Frygt og Bæven* ["Fear and Trembling"] (Copenhagen, 1843), ed. and tr. Howard V. Hong and Edna H. Hong (Princeton, NJ: Princeton University Press, 1983); William James, *The Varieties of Religious Experience: A Study in Human Nature* (New York, NY: Longmans, Green, 1902); Rudolf Otto, *Das Heilige: Über das Irrationale in der Idee des Göttlichen und sein Verhältnis zum Rationalen* ["The Idea of the Holy: An Inquiry into the Non-Rational Factor in the Idea of the Divine and its Relation to the Rational"], tr. John W. Harvey (Oxford: Oxford University Press, 1923; 2nd edn, 1950); Paul Tillich, *The Courage to Be* (New Haven, CT: Yale University Press, 1952).

21   Mircea Eliade, *The Sacred and the Profane: The Nature of Religion*, tr. Willard R. Trask (New York, NY: Harper and Row, 1959).

22   Joseph Ratzinger, *Introduction to Christianity*, tr. J. R. Foster, rev. edn (San Francisco, CA.: Communio Books, 2004), pp. 104–7.

our human quest for and encounter with God has sprung from both loneliness and the need for security.

For Ratzinger, the human as a person experiencing solitariness also experiences how much the whole of human existence "is a cry for the 'You' and how ill-adapted he is to be only an 'I' in himself".[23] (Even the narcissist, in a misordered way, yearns for the other.) But in finding one another, in the fulfilment of love, we become aware of something greater than the sum of the parts; in this finding of another in love, we receive more than either party could contribute. When we experience the fulfilment of love in this way, the experience of God comes out of the joy of security:[24]

> The brightness and joy of finding one another can point to the proximity of absolute joy and of the simple fact of being found that stand behind every human encounter.[25]

In each case, there is the imperative to go outside oneself and to move towards that which is infinitely greater.[26]

Ratzinger's expression of the position that human identity in its fullness is only achieved by going outside the self alludes to the thought of Dietrich Bonhoeffer (1906–45) and Friedrich Nietzsche (1844–1900).[27] Bonhoeffer reflected from prison in Nazi Germany that we should find God in the fullness of our earthly life rather than at times of need and failure. He rejected the understanding of God as an escape, a refuge only in times of need, a construct of necessity which we can abandon, or which becomes redundant and dispensable as we enlarge and reach beyond the bounds of our potential:

> God is not a stopgap. We must recognize God not only where we reach the limits of our possibilities. God wants to be recognized

---

[23]   Ratzinger, *Introduction*, p. 106.

[24]   Ratzinger, *Introduction*, pp. 106–7.

[25]   Ratzinger, *Introduction*, p. 107.

[26]   Ratzinger, *Introduction*, p. 106.

[27]   Ratzinger, *Introduction*, pp. 105–6.

in the midst of our lives, in life and not only in dying, in health
and strength and not only in suffering, in action and not only
in sin. The ground for this lies in the revelation of God in Jesus
Christ. God is the centre of life and doesn't just "turn up" when
we have unsolved problems to be solved.[28]

In other words, there is no "God-shaped hole". Christ is the principle on
which the whole of creation and of human life are organized.

Ratzinger did not see a tension here between a God who is recognized
in the poverty of human existence and a God recognized in its fullness.
Both conditions direct us towards God. Where the experience of humans
has been one of fullness—the beauty and richness, the splendour and
magnificence of existence—Ratzinger asserted that "this existence is an
existence for which they owe thanks":

> precisely in its brightness and greatness it is not what I myself
> have obtained but the bestowed that comes to meet me, welcomes
> me with all its goodness before I have done anything, and thus
> requires of me that I *give* a meaning to such riches and thereby
> *receive* a meaning.[29]

Here Ratzinger expresses the Christian principle that grace comes first.
And this grace draws out a human response. For—we may add—grace
(Latin *gratia*) prompts gratitude (*gratus*); and *gratia* and *gratus* are
etymologically derived from (Greek) *charis* "grace", *chairō* "rejoice, be
glad", *charma* "source of joy, delight". And it is this relationship between
grace, gratitude and joy which leads us in an extraordinary way to
Nietzsche, who perhaps most famously links joy and woe, the unbounded
and the limited, in human experience:

---

28   Dietrich Bonhoeffer, Letter to Eberhard Bethge (29 May 1944), in *Dietrich
     Bonhoeffer: Letters and Papers from Prison*, ed. John W. De Gruchy, tr. Isabel
     Best et al., Dietrich Bonhoeffer Works 8 (Minneapolis, MN: Fortress, 2010),
     pp. 406–7.

29   Ratzinger, *Introduction*, p. 105.

Have you ever said Yes to a single joy? O my friends, then you said Yes to *all* woe as well. All things are chained and entwined together, all things are in love; if ever you wanted one moment twice, if ever you said: "You please me, happiness, instant, moment!" then you wanted *everything* to return![30]

In other words, "all pleasure yearns for eternity and yet experiences itself as a moment".[31] In the second half of an extraordinary sentence, Ratzinger concludes:

this simultaneity of being limited and of yearning for the unbounded and open has always prevented man from resting in himself, made him sense that he is not self-sufficient but only comes to himself by going outside himself and moving toward the entirely Other and infinitely greater.[32]

This relationship between joy and woe, praise and fear, the limited and the unlimited, is further and wonderfully expressed in Yann Martel's novel, *Life of Pi* (2002). Pi is a boy who, like Job, has lost a whole family in the space of a day, and is now adrift at sea with a Royal Bengal tiger. Pi is "thrust into a state of exalted wonder" as he experiences a thunderstorm, and a bolt of lightning strikes the water near his boat. The connection between joy and woe expressed by Nietzsche, and the fleeting nature of earthly joy, is captured as the lightning penetrates the ocean. "Everything was pure white light or pure black shadow . . . As quickly as it appeared, the bolt vanished" (p. 233). The boy is dazed and thunderstruck, "But not afraid". In that simple phrase, "But not afraid", Martel points us

---

[30] Friedrich Nietzsche, *Thus Spoke Zarathustra*, tr. R. J. Hollingdale (Harmondsworth: Penguin, 1969), p. 332.

[31] Ratzinger, *Introduction*, pp. 106. The yearning of all joy for eternity, "deep, deep eternity", is repeatedly expressed in Zarathustra's "Rundgesang" (Nietzsche, *Thus Spoke Zarathustra*, tr. Hollingdale, pp. 244, 245, 247, 289, 329).

[32] Ratzinger, *Introduction*, p. 106.

towards the two Gospel stories involving boats and storms.[33] In each case, fear in the midst of the storm is linked to lack of faith; and the imperative, "Be not afraid", always accompanies biblical manifestations of the divine. Pi's instinctive response of praise in the midst of the thunder and lightning is a signal of his faith, a reaction to his recognition of the divine, of the fullness of God's power in the face of his "limited mortal ways". At first, he only mutters—"Praise be to Allah, Lord of All Worlds, the Compassionate, the Merciful, Ruler of Judgment Day!"[34] But then his perception of God in the storm leads Pi fully out of himself, and he shouts to the tiger cowering on the floor of the boat, "Stop your trembling! This is a miracle. This is an outbreak of divinity." The tiger in the story is the mortal and animal-survivalist element of Pi's nature, while the boy represents Pi's true and eternal identity (Pi is a number that "runs on for ever", p. 285). While the tiger trembles at the destructive power of the storm and the lightning—even at the manifestation of the overwhelming divine power—the boy comes out of his limited human self and praises the Lord of All Worlds.

This idea of the human person going outside the self and moving towards the divine is key to the rest of my argument in this chapter. This going outside of self requires movement; movement towards God; a movement that is a response in joy and thanksgiving to the creator. This response of thanksgiving is to be found in the Christian life in our liturgical response to God; a response most perfectly embodied in the defining action of the Christian life, the Eucharist. And at the heart of the word, eucharistia—literally "giving of thanks"—we again find joy, charis; the joy which has sprung forth from suffering and sorrow.

This going outside of the self must also imply relation, then; and we are reminded that the opposite of the individual is not the community but the

---

33 Jesus calms the storm (Matthew 8:23–7; Mark 4:35–41; Luke 8:22–5); Jesus walks on the sea (Matthew 14:22–34; Mark 6:45–53; John 6:15–21).

34 These words are from the opening of the Quran. During his childhood, Pi's deeply religious but unconventional spirituality has reconciled Hinduism, Christianity and Islam. It is noteworthy that in Ang Lee's film adaptation (2012), Pi lifts and spreads out his arms in a gesture of praise, yelling his words to the heavens above the sound of the storm.

person.[35] The ultimate nature of reality is personal rather than impersonal or individualistic, because the Christian experience is that we have been created by a personal God for interpersonal communion. The person is therefore "the kind of being which can partake in communion".[36] The assumption that lies behind all this, that "before anything or anyone is in relation with anything or anyone else, it's in relation to *God*", can be traced back at least as far as Saint Augustine of Hippo.[37] Sarah Ruden's most English of translations expresses Saint Augustine's meditation on the human's relation to God, at the opening of the *Confessions*, in this way:[38]

> You are mighty, Master, and to be praised with a powerful voice: great is your goodness, and of your wisdom there can be no reckoning. Yet to praise you is the desire of a human being, who is some part of what you created; a human hauling his deathliness in a circle, hauling in a circle the evidence of his sin, and the evidence that you stand against the arrogant. But still a mortal, a given portion of your creation, longs to extol you. In yourself you rouse us, giving us delight in glorifying you, because you made us with yourself as our goal, and our heart is restless until it rests in you.
>
> *Augustine of Hippo,* Confessions *I.1*[39]

From Saint Augustine onwards, says Rowan Williams, the Christian tradition has understood that, "before anything else happens I am in relation to a non-worldly, non-historical everlasting attention and love, which is God".[40] To experience the ultimate fulfilment of love, therefore, one must experience relationship with God. And Saint Augustine

---

[35] Rowan Williams, *Being Human: Bodies, Minds, Persons* (London: SPCK, 2018), p. 36.

[36] Charles Taylor, *A Secular Age* (Cambridge, MA: Belknap, 2007), p. 278.

[37] Williams, *Being Human*, p. 36.

[38] *Confessions*, tr. Sarah Ruden (New York, NY: Modern Library, 2017), p. 3.

[39] Ed. Carolyn J.-B. Hammond, Loeb Classical Library 26 (Cambridge, MA: Harvard University Press, 2014), p. 2.

[40] Williams, *Being Human*, pp. 36–7.

recognized from the very beginning that this relationship involved the desire to praise God.

Homo orans

The journey outside the self, which seeks to experience the relation with God, can be made by means of another quality that may define us as a species, namely prayer. Hans Urs von Balthasar (1905–88) provided the explanation.[41] The foundations of von Balthasar's philosophical anthropology, which underlies his whole theological endeavour, are set out in *Das betrachtende Gebet* (literally "Contemplative Prayer", but known just as *Prayer* in its English edition). Here von Balthasar laid out an argument for "the necessity of prayer" or "contemplation".[42] The human person meets God in praying, and through this meeting one can reach a fulfilment and an authentic identity. By listening to God's "Word", humans can be truly themselves. Von Balthasar's theological and philosophical anthropology therefore points towards a conception of what Victoria S. Harrison has identified and defined in his (von Balthasar's) work as *homo orans*, the "praying human".[43]

---

[41] Von Balthasar was a Swiss Catholic theologian who, with Joseph Ratzinger and Henri de Lubac, in 1972 founded the theological journal, *Communio*, which "stands for the renewal of theology in continuity with the living Christian tradition", see <https://www.communio-icr.com/about>, accessed 17 December 2020.

[42] "Die Notwendigkeit der Betrachtung": this is the title of chapter one in Hans Urs von Balthasar, *Das betrachtende Gebet* (Einsiedeln: Johannes, 1955); *Prayer*, tr. A. V. Littledale (London: Geoffrey Chapman, 1961) and Graham Harrison (San Francisco, CA: Ignatius, 1986).

[43] Victoria S. Harrison, "*Homo Orans*: Von Balthasar's Christocentric Philosophical Anthropology", *Heythrop Journal* 40 (1999), pp. 280–300; see also Victoria S. Harrison, *The Apologetic Value of Human Holiness: Von Balthasar's Christocentric Philosophical Anthropology*, Studies in Philosophy and Religion 21 (London: Kluwer Academic, 2000), pp. 25–35.

Again, we can turn to Rowan Williams for further elucidation. Williams, whose theology, like Ratzinger's, has been influenced by von Balthasar, points out that Christians do not encounter God or grow into the divine life in some general sense; rather we grow into "the particular form of divine life represented by the 'Word', the 'Son', the offspring of the eternal source".[44] Our human identity grows and develops into one in which we acknowledge, through prayer, the kind of dependence that, as adopted children, we have to the one whom Jesus calls, and has taught us to call, "*Abba*, Father".[45]

If one accepts the line of reasoning, however, that humans must go outside themselves and move towards God in order to come to their true selves, one may then go on to ask whether the concept of *homo orans* discerned in the theology of von Balthasar—even if focused entirely on the person of Christ—is too susceptible to a mode of stasis to represent the most fundamental and innate aspect of the human response to God. Not only does *homo orans* have the potential to be a somewhat static and self-contained creature, but the nature of prayer, especially contemplative prayer, is the product of culture, of learnt behaviour, of discipline or asceticism. Contemplative prayer, although a necessary part of the fulfilment of human potential and relation to God—necessary for humans in order to discover the truth about themselves, and necessary to a Christian's mission—is not necessarily an innate or instinctive response to God's initiative.

In fact, von Balthasar's conception of prayer recognizes this. His view is closely related to the eastern Fathers' theological method, which might be characterized as understanding the practice of theology as "a personal communion with *Theos*, the Father, through the *Logos*, Christ, in the Holy Spirit—an experience lived in a state of prayer".[46] Doing theology

---

[44]   Williams, *Being Human*, p. 72.

[45]   Williams, *Being Human*, p. 72.

[46]   Thomas Spidlik, *The Spirituality of the Christian East* (Kalamazoo, MI: Cistercian, 1986), p. 1.

was therefore understood as direct communion with God in pure prayer, and to do theology was to pray in spirit and in truth.[47]

In von Balthasar's theological and philosophical anthropology, in order for the human person really to "hear" Christ through the scriptures, an attitude of reverence is necessary; and he prefers to call this attitude *Anbetung*, "adoration". Von Balthasar rejected the view that one can meet God in Christ simply by reading and studying the scriptures; that it is an encounter which can be made at the desk of the scholar, or the armchair of the idle reader. Rather, such reading or studying can only become real contemplative hearing when permeated and suffused by an attitude of adoration. The very heart of contemplative prayer, for von Balthasar, is this attitude of adoration. We come to know Christ on our knees, as it were, and not in the library.[48]

Homo adorans

With this shift towards the attitude of adoration, we are prompted to move into the realm of worship and liturgical theology to search for some further answers. In fact, with Alexander Schmemann (1921–83) and Aidan Kavanagh (1929–2006), who broke new ground in the field of liturgical theology, we could say that in the context of prayer and adoration it is in fact the liturgy which is the ontological condition of theology and that there is no theology without liturgy. Liturgy forms the essence and nature of the way we come to know God; and liturgy is the way we engage both with God and with the world.[49]

---

[47]   See George Berthold, *Maximus Confessor: Selected Writings* (New York, NY: Paulist, 1985), p. 92.

[48]   Harrison, "*Homo orans*", p. 282.

[49]   See Jacob Vellian, "Theological dimensions of liturgy", *Studia Liturgica* 30 (2000), pp. 1–13; Alexander Schmemann, "Theology and liturgical tradition", in Massey H. Shepherd (ed.), *Worship in Scripture and Tradition* (Oxford: Oxford University Press, 1963), pp. 165–78, at p. 175; Aidan Kavanagh, *On Liturgical Theology* (New York, NY: Pueblo, 1984), p. 75.

Schmemann, a theologian of the modern Orthodox tradition, proposed a new expression to define the nature of the human response to God. For Schmemann, *homo adorans* ("the worshipping human", or "human as worshipper") describes the liturgical actor or participant. Schmemann's classic work, *For the Life of the World*, popularized the term among liturgical theologians. Here he argued that our human nature is to respond to God's blessing with our own blessing; for "in the Bible to bless God is not a 'religious' or 'cultic' act, but the very way of life".[50] Schmemann explained (using the generic "man" and masculine pronouns):

> All rational, spiritual and other qualities of man, distinguishing
> him from other creatures, have their focus and ultimate fulfillment
> in this capacity to bless God, to know, so to speak, the meaning
> of the thirst and hunger that constitutes his life. "Homo sapiens",
> "homo faber" . . . yes, but first of all, "homo adorans". The first
> and basic definition of man is that he is the priest. He stands at
> the center of the world and unifies it in his act of blessing God,
> of both receiving the world from God and offering it to God.[51]

David W. Fagerberg has taken up this concept of *homo adorans*, linking it to a view of the human person as *homo viator*—a being on the way, moving beyond the self towards the likeness of God. "*Anthropos* is a verb (a human *being*)", he has written, "until he or she becomes a noun (saint)."[52] In a train of thought which extends out of Saint Augustine's meditation at the opening of the *Confessions*, Fagerberg lays out a theology in which we were created for communion with God, and for this reason only the Eternal, the Immortal One, is able to satisfy our yearning. For this reason, the "liturgical posture of *homo adorans* is even

---

50   Alexander Schmemann, *For the Life of the World: Sacraments and Orthodoxy* (Crestwood, NY: St Vladimir's Seminary, 1973), p. 15.

51   Schmemann, *For the Life of the World*, p. 15.

52   David W. Fagerberg, "Liturgical Asceticism: Enlarging our Grammar of Liturgy", *Pro Ecclesia* 13:2 (2004), pp. 202–14, here at p. 208.

more basic to *anthropos* than *homo erectus*: happiness will elude us until we stand aright in our vocation as liturgical beings".[53]

Fagerberg, in his extension of Schmemann's liturgical theology, has also offered us a consideration of *homo adorans* as the liturgical ascetic.[54] He sees liturgy as a "substantially theological enterprise", and here *ascesis*—or discipline, practice, exercise—relates to and interpenetrates with theology and liturgy to become a "product and prerequisite for Christian liturgy".[55]

Yet we might contend with Fagerberg, and object that we do not need to be "liturgical ascetics" before we can be "liturgists" in the true sense that Fagerberg proposes.[56] Instead, the instinct, our innate urge, to praise God precedes our participation in the liturgy; and the discipline or *ascesis* of being liturgical, of participation in the liturgical life of the Church, is a result of our first impulse to praise—the impulse described by Saint Luke.

The starting point has to be that Christ is the only authentic "liturgical ascetic", for the Letter to the Hebrews presents Christ as the only authentic priest of the New Covenant (Hebrews 4:14–16). Just as we are priests only by virtue of Christ's high priesthood, so we are liturgical ascetics only by participation in Christ's liturgical asceticism. This participation, from the point of view of our daily lives, involves the *ascesis* of sacrifice, the giving up of one's own time and gifts and self-absorption to the greater pattern of praise and worship. At the same time, the discipline of the liturgy leads us to participation in the priesthood of Christ, and his sacrifice. By uniting ourselves to Christ's sacrificial offering, by offering our hearts to God, the Spirit is manifested and "introduces the human being into the eternal circulation of love between the Father and the Son". All our liturgical

---

53   Fagerberg, "Liturgical Asceticism", p. 208.

54   Fagerberg's initial essay, "Liturgical Asceticism", was developed into an extended treatment, *On Liturgical Asceticism* (Washington, DC: Catholic University of America, 2013).

55   Ian Coleman, review of David W. Fagerberg, *On Liturgical Asceticism* (2013), *Ecclesiology* 11:3 (2015), pp. 383–6.

56   "If 'liturgy' names an action, then 'liturgists' ought to direct us to the ones who do that action. Liturgists make up the church and the church is made up of liturgists" (Fagerberg, "Liturgical Asceticism", p. 202).

actions will ultimately be taken up into what Maximus the Confessor (*c.* 580–662) and others called the "perichoresis" of the Holy Trinity—the "dance of love" and "mutual indwelling by the three persons of the Holy Trinity"—which exists beyond all time.[57]

Homo laudans

The "drumbeat of the psalter" (as Jacqueline E. Lapsley puts it) is praise: the human being's vocation in the psalms is to praise God—and not only humans, but the animals are called to praise God too.[58] Since the time of the desert fathers in the third and fourth centuries, the Psalter has been taken as a single entity and understood as an analogy of the whole of humanity.[59] Indeed, the practice of continuous recitation of the Psalter, which is their legacy through the monastic office of East and West, has therefore been received as a spiritual exercise or discipline, the basis of liturgical worship, and a form of contemplative prayer.

The understanding of the Psalter as an analogy of the whole of humanity also points us towards an apprehension of the fullness of human identity. "In the psalms of praise", says William P. Brown, "dependency and dignity mark the human condition."[60] The self-abasement which characterizes the

---

[57] Fagerberg, "Liturgical Asceticism", p. 214 (quoting Paul Evdokimov); Fagerberg, *On Liturgical Asceticism*, p. 8.

[58] See Jacqueline E. Lapsley, "Ethics and creational dignity in the Old Testament", in Louis Jonker, Gideon Kotzé and Christl M. Maier (eds), *Congress Volume Stellenbosch 2016, Vetus Testamentum* Supplements 177 (Leiden/Boston: Brill, 2017), pp. 93–114, here at p. 106: "The end of the Psalter unrelentingly presses for unified praise by the entire created order, with its last line discharging a final exhortation: 'Let all that breathes praise the Lord. Hallelujah!' (Psalm 150:6; cf. 145:21)."

[59] See John Wortley, "Prayer and the Desert Fathers", in Carlos A. Segovia and Basil Lourié (eds), *The Coming of the Comforter: When, Where, and to Whom?*, *Orientalia Judaica Christiana* 3 (Piscataway, NJ: Gorgias, 2012), pp. 109–29, esp. pp. 119–22.

[60] William P. Brown, *Psalms* (Nashville, TN: Abingdon, 2010), p. 151.

psalms of complaint is entirely lacking, to be replaced by what he calls "a self-abandoning exuberance that focuses resolutely on God".[61] This self-abandonment (so beautifully captured by Yann Martel) in which the human heart and mind, body and soul, are entirely concerned with the praise of God now brings us to the picture of man and woman—*adam*, *anthropos*, *homo*—that we have been searching for: a portrait in which the human being leaves self behind and moves towards God. In this way, says Brown, the psalms of praise "profile the human as *Homo laudans*, 'the praising human', and in praise, the full identity of the human self is reached".[62]

Indeed, *homo laudans* ("the praising human" or "human as one who praises") presents a wider scope for consideration and comprehension of the human being in relation to the act of liturgy. By contrast with *adoratio*, adoration, the outflowing of praise is not capable of being held within oneself in the silence of one's heart. This seems a better way of understanding the liturgical action; and the *ascesis*—the spiritual discipline or training—of the liturgical participant could then be considered in terms of "going beyond oneself". Adoration is too susceptible to "remaining within oneself". In our response of praise and thanksgiving to God, we are called out of ourselves and into the liturgical discipline of the Church.

The terms *homo religiosus*, *homo orans* and *homo adorans*, if not necessarily suggestive of an inward-looking mode or attitude, at least describe a way of being liable to stasis, passivity and remaining within oneself. My argument, in the end, hinges on the proposition that it is the urge and desire to praise God which comes first. If we have (as Christian Smith has argued) only the natural capacity, rather than the natural impulse, to be *homo religiosus*, then we must respond to God's call with an act of free will; and before anything else, God's call is to praise him; before anything else, therefore, when we respond to God's call, we are *homo laudans*.

We have seen that, going back at least to the time of Saint Augustine of Hippo, the Christian theological tradition has been based on the

---

61   Brown, *Psalms*, p. 151.

62   Brown, *Psalms*, p. 151.

assumption that the primary relation of anything or anyone is to God. We have been created with God as our goal, and so we delight in glorifying God. Before all else, this outward movement of praise is what leads us to participation in the liturgy. The discipline of *homo orans* or *homo adorans* is not required before we can be *homo laudans*. Praise is our first response as we recognize Christ. Rather, it is *homo laudans* who lies at the heart of what others have identified as *homo religiosus*; and *homo laudans* who comes before *homo adorans* and *homo orans*. The response of praise leads us to the liturgical action of the Church, most perfectly embodied in the defining action of the Christian life, the gift of the Eucharist, the sacrament of Holy Communion, where we learn in time how to live both in the world and in the divine life of the Holy Trinity that exists beyond all time.

We can therefore see at the beginning of Luke's Gospel, as the Evangelist describes the inception of the new order—as the new Adam comes into the world, in whom the whole of humankind discovers its fulfilment—how the response of the faithful to the good news of the redeemer is expressed in joy that leads to praise. This praise, however, is not just characterized by a spontaneous outburst of joy; those who recognize the saviour move into a new mode of continual praise and blessing; there is a liturgical quality to their praise. The evangelist describes for us an experience of God that points us towards, and places us within, the liturgy and the liturgical community. We have been made for relation in a community of universal recognition, and our response of praise to the recognition of the Saviour happens in the community and through the liturgy.

In our secular lives, we must ask ourselves whether the Eucharist is the real source and summit of our life as *homo adorans* and *homo orans*. For this is where our salvation is to be found, this is where the life of the world is to be found, this is where Christ is to be found.

In praise, and through a liturgical life—as liturgists in the true sense—Christians come to the fullness of human identity. We look to the scriptures to show us the truth about the world, and we interpret that vision in the liturgical assembly, and above all in the context of the Eucharist.

Dietrich Bonhoeffer saw that the Church, separated from the world, becomes nothing more than a religious club or society, with only spiritual authority, its individual members pursuing lives of personal piety. The Church, correctly understood, is the world redeemed by God through Jesus Christ, and this is what the Eucharist presents to us. The Church therefore exists to serve the world by witnessing to Jesus Christ both in the liturgy and in the world. When Church and state become autonomous, thought Bonhoeffer, the Church abdicates its responsibility for the fallen world, while the state is free to become idolatrous.[63]

At the end of the Gospel according to Luke, we are given a vision of the apostles, who have received the true interpretation of the scriptures, returning to the temple to engage in liturgical praise. But the natural result of liturgy is to be sent out into the world, to live out the truth of the good news, "to be Christ's body in the world".[64] And the second part of Luke's account, the Acts of the Apostles, begins that story of sending out.

Questions for discussion

1. Can you think of times when prayer and/or praise have come naturally or spontaneously?
2. Where do contemplative prayer and public worship connect in your own life?
3. In what ways do you bring your life experiences to personal prayer and public worship?
4. Thinking of Fagerberg's definition of "liturgist" (see p. 50), how might you live a more liturgical life (and how might this affect your everyday life)?

---

[63] See, for example, Dietrich Bonhoeffer, *The Cost of Discipleship*, tr. R. H. Fuller (London: SCM Press, 1959), esp. pp. 163–233; *Life Together*, tr. John W. Donbertsien (London: SCM Press, 1954), esp. pp. 15–26; Ferdinand Schlingensiepen, *Dietrich Bonhoeffer 1906-1945: Martyr, Thinker, Man of Resistance*, tr. by Isabel Best (New York, NY and London: Continuum, 2010), p. 117.

[64] Eucharistic Prayer I, *Scottish Liturgy 1982*.

Further reading

Aidan Kavanagh, *On Liturgical Theology* (New York, NY: Pueblo, 1984).

Yann Martel, *Life of Pi* (Edinburgh: Canongate, 2002).

Timothy Samuel Shah and Joack Friedman (eds), *Homo Religiosus? Exploring the Roots of Religion and Religious Freedom in Human Experience* (Cambridge: Cambridge University Press, 2019), especially Christian Smith, "Are human beings naturally religious?", pp. 35–54.

Rowan Williams, *Being Human: Bodies, Minds, Persons* (London: SPCK, 2018).

CHAPTER 3

"A little lower than the angels": The riddle of humanity in Christian theology

Trevor Hart

"What is man, that thou art mindful of him?"[1]

Who on earth do we think we are?

It was the mid-1970s, and I was a teenager supposed to be spending a night under canvas in North Wales. But it was July, the sky was cloudless, and the campfire we had lit earlier had already settled down to become a welcoming bed of embers. So, we decided to drag both groundsheet and sleeping bags out of the tent and spend that particular night instead under a night sky entirely unpolluted by artificial light and, as our eyes adjusted and we gradually called a halt to the flow of meaningless teenage chatter, were treated to a display of *son et lumière* quite unrivalled in proportion or magnificence. And we wondered.

The psalmist's question, inspired, we must suppose, by some such encounter with the sublime as this, still resonates with us today, even though for many the question is unlikely to be directed with any confidence to the heavens, let alone expect an answer from there. And in

---

[1] "When I consider thy heavens, the works of thy fingers, the moon and the stars, which thou hast ordained; what is man, that thou art mindful of him? and the son of man, that thou visitest him? For thou hast made him a little lower than the angels, and hast crowned him with glory and honour" Psalm 8:3–5 (KJV).

all probability, therefore, were we inclined to supply an answer ourselves, being informed by the "story" of the cosmos as told by any number of the paperback "popularizers" of science, it might well be a rather different sort of answer than that which the psalmist gives. For him (or her), the enormity and splendour of the "jewelled tent" which the ancients beheld as they gazed upwards, when compared with the mundanities of everyday human living, provoked both wonder and incredulity ("what [by comparison with all this] is *man*, that thou art mindful of *him*?"); yet in framing an answer, of course, the poet draws not on evidence and common-sense inference alone, but on a story which, in this respect as, no doubt in many others, denies and even contradicts the shape of experience. "You have made (humans) a little lower than the angels,[2] and crowned them with glory and honour" (Psalm 8:5). Even in terms of biblical cosmology this was a remarkable claim, angels being part of the "heavenly host" in the divine court, and the highest among God's creatures. To be created only "a little lower" than the angels, therefore, was to be called to enjoy a status and significance that cast the heavenly bodies of moon and stars themselves into the shade in terms of God's creative purpose, fly as it may in the face of all appearances! The twenty-first-century stargazer, displaced by post-Copernican cosmology from the physical centre of "outer space", and confronted both by its vertiginous depths and the galactic timescales projected in order to chart its regular workings, is even more likely to stumble over the claim, having long since been taught to think of human life on our planet as an infinitesimal speck hardly registering at all on the radar of "reality".[3] That there is no logical connection whatever between this observation and judgments about the relative *significance* of this infinitesimal speck, whether judged theologically or in other terms, rarely troubles those who proceed confidently to the conclusion that, being little more than the fleeting product of a biological accident occurring nowhere in particular and lasting little more than the blink of an eye, the existence of the human species matters little at all to anyone other than humans themselves. There

---

[2]   Or, in more recent translations, "little lower than God", which simply sharpens rather than lessens the point. Cf. Hebrews 2:6.

[3]   See also Fuller, Chapter 8.

is, of course, a certain cognitive dissonance (and, indeed, a degree of logical conundrum) involved in human beings themselves concluding such things, but it cannot be doubted that many of them nowadays do.

Christian theology over the centuries has rarely, if ever, come close to entertaining such reductionist and relativizing ideas. In fact, if anything its errors have lain in the other direction, placing rather too much emphasis on finite human beings within the infinite project of God's creation, and sometimes doing so in a manner detrimental to our appreciation of other species and the material environment in which we find ourselves, and not infrequently detrimental to the wellbeing of both. But Christian accounts of humanity, like those to be found in the canon of scriptural texts that Christian theology is compelled to grapple with in every time and place as its primary source and authority, are certainly not uniform and far from straightforward. Insignificant, Christians may properly never suppose God's human creatures to be; but the nature and implications of their creaturely *significance* is presented as a complex rather than a simple matter. It contains at its heart a series of apparent tensions which, if too quickly or inappropriately resolved, may easily lead (and sometimes have led) to unduly exalted and self-important accounts of human capacity and destiny on the one hand, or (as though by way of compensation) excessively demeaning and self-diminishing accounts on the other.

Christian visions of humanity have thus encompassed everything from the unqualified humanism of the Renaissance, of humankind as God's "godlike" progeny, endowed with unrivalled intellectual, moral and spiritual prowess and summoned to exercise autonomous "dominion" over the rest of creation,[4] to the equally unqualified depiction of us, in some strands of Protestantism in particular, as "totally depraved" denizens of a world alienated from God and, whether as devoted antagonists or pathetic wastrels unable to resist the "powers and dominions" of evil,

---

[4]   See helpfully Cameron Wybrow, *The Bible, Baconianism, and Mastery Over Nature: The Old Testament and its Modern Misreading* (New York: Peter Lang, 1991). Richard Bauckham, *The Bible and Ecology: Rediscovering the Community of Creation* (Waco, TX: Baylor University Press, 2010), Chapter 2.

bereft of any remaining shred of created goodness.[5] These are indeed extreme visions. But the key word for our purposes is not so much "extreme" as "unqualified". We have already considered the testimony of Psalm 8:5–6, a text much cited by Renaissance theologians as we might reasonably expect; but both views, extreme though they are, can find warrant in the rich imaginative resources of scripture as a whole. The temptation will no doubt be to suppose that theologically responsible treatment in this circumstance must lie in the direction of balance or compromise, each set of texts being permitted effectively to temper the edge of the other. This would, I think, be a mistake, simply another way of resolving the tension between them prematurely rather than holding it awkwardly in play, and so missing its real suggestion—namely, that it is not despite but precisely *because of* and *in direct proportion to* our creaturely capacity for godliness, goodness and glory that those created in the "image and likeness" of the Creator[6] must be weighed, and the scale and seriousness of their various entanglements with godlessness judged and measured. It is no coincidence that the embodiment of creaturely evil in biblical and theological narrative is "Lucifer", an angel of light: the first and "highest" of all God's creatures, such depictions acknowledge, is precisely by virtue of this distinction capable of becoming the foulest and most malevolent opponent of all that God is.[7] A Christian account of our humanity, though, can really neither begin nor end with such observations alone, no matter how biblical they may or may not be.

---

[5] See also Adam, Chapter 10.

[6] See, e.g., Philip Edgcumbe Hughes, *The True Image: The Origin and Destiny of Man in Christ* (Grand Rapids, MI: Eerdmans, 1989). "Creator" is a notoriously difficult notion to pin down in doctrinal terms, but the broad indication that human beings are created in some way to reflect rather than contradict the character of God is sufficient here.

[7] See, Isaiah 14:12; Luke 10:18; John Milton, *Paradise Lost* (1667).

How can we discover what we are?

Where, then, ought we to begin? And, do we really need to "discover" (in the words of our subtitle) who and what we are at all? Do we not already *know*, by virtue of *being* human in the first place? It may seem common-sensical to suppose so. After all, we are the ones who actually know what it is *like* to be human, having known little else, in fact, from moment to waking moment of our lives. Are we not bound, therefore, to be the unrivalled experts on this particular topic, in the same way that even young children are acknowledged already to be "expert" speakers of their native tongue, its patterns and peculiarities being "second nature" to them, woven together inextricably as these are with children's indwelling of the world around them? Is "human nature", being not *second* nature to us but precisely our *first*, antedating our acquisition of language and surviving, we might wish to insist, even in its absence, not something we already know inside out and have no need of anyone to tell us what it is? Who better than we ourselves, we might reasonably enquire, to speak authoritatively on the subject?

We might well suppose so. And we would naturally be irate were it to be suggested that our testimony on this were neither relevant nor worth taking carefully into account. Fortunately, there is no need to be as perverse as that; but there are many reasons for suggesting that our "insider" view cannot be the only one to be heard, nor even the view permitted to weigh most heavily in answering the question.

To begin with, while testimonies to what it is like to be human or to experience the world humanly are not difficult to find, they are also remarkably varied in substance and shape. Significantly, such testimonies vary not just from one time and place to another but from one contemporary and geographically/culturally contiguous group to another, and even one member of any given human group to another. This undeniable plurality of perspectives (all offered as "insider" accounts of the matter) has led in recent decades to the intellectually fashionable suspicion that there may, in reality, be no such thing as a shared "human nature" at all. Nothing, that is to say, that *all* human beings share identifiably in common and experience in more or less the same way, unmodified by the particularities of circumstance and, to all appearances, essentially unmodifiable. Things that, if we are human at all, simply come as part of the package.

Without wishing in any way to override or undervalue all the exciting things that distinguish us from one another as the particular persons we are, though, it must be admitted that this suspicion is at best counter-intuitive if pushed too far. If the testimony of individuals and cultures spanning centuries and continents alike is to be taken seriously, there seem at the very least to be things about our species being that crop up as "recurrent features . . . however variously they may be represented",[8] and however much our experience of them may be modified or coloured by the accidents of particular time and place. The examples that jump most immediately to mind tend to be ones involving forms of suffering or the potential for suffering, being bound up in one way or another with the constants of our physiology and its fragility.[9] Suffering, Terry Eagleton suggests, thus provides an exceptionally powerful common language, reaching easily across the boundaries that mark out our human particularity, no matter how far removed from one another in time, space or outlook we may otherwise be.[10] This is no doubt why we find various cultural representations of human experience so powerful and important, sometimes affecting us deeply, and in ways that enhance our understanding not just of others but of ourselves too. If we are moved to pity or "catharsis" by watching the tragic fate of Oedipus or King Lear unfold on the stage, or left stunned and horrified by the senseless violence and trauma depicted in the opening sequence of *Saving Private Ryan*, or even (since pain does not, of course, have a monopoly on all this) find ourselves wiping away an unbidden tear as the latest "feel good" movie reaches its sentimental denouement, it will be because what we have been shown, even though it may be shot through with all sorts of things unfamiliar to us, draws from us nonetheless the peculiar pleasure and pain involved in imaginative *recognition*. Its appeal is to our ability, as we say, to "identify with" something being played out before us, and to

---

[8]   Terry Eagleton, *Sweet Violence: The Idea of the Tragic* (Oxford: Blackwell, 2003), p. xiii.

[9]   See also Fuller, Chapter 8.

[10]   Eagleton, *Sweet Violence*, p. xiii.

know that, in some (often unspecifiable) sense, despite the undeniable differences with our own particular circumstance, we are bound up with the action by virtue of equally undeniable undercurrents of something shared. Its supposition is precisely the existence of something that binds us *as human beings*, placing us, perhaps, under some form of obligation to respond well to fellow sufferers not only on the screen or in literature but in life too.[11]

This interplay between what is "part of the human package" and all the things that make us different from one another is vital to our imaginative life, of course. A good story, for example, in whatever medium it comes to us, will always rely on both. Without a fairly high degree of "recognition" of things familiar to us, things that in some sense we already know or that are similar or close enough to things or people that we know for us to be able to get a handle on them, we would not be able to enter into a story imaginatively at all. An undiluted torrent of things entirely unfamiliar to us, unrecognizable as having anything much in common with anything we already know, would be impossible for us to make much sense of, let alone enjoy. Yet none of us, of course, would be likely to bother much with a story composed almost entirely of things we already know and don't need to be told. If stories are to grab our attention and hold it, and if in doing so they are to impart some fresh understanding of something, then they must certainly tell us about things, places, people, events that differ and perhaps differ quite markedly from what we already know, or at least show us what we *suppose* we already know from a quite different perspective. This "enlarging of our soul", as the great medieval theologian Thomas Aquinas refers to it, by imaginative engagement with

---

11 Correspondingly, of course, the denial of such commonality or its deliberate reconfiguration to exclude (and thereby "dehumanize") others has often been undertaken in order to justify their maltreatment. Slaves in ancient Greece were not considered to merit treatment as human beings, and the propaganda machines of various modern societies have been deployed deliberately (sometimes explicitly, sometimes tacitly) to reclassify particular groups on the basis of race, sexual orientation, disability, and other markers of significant difference to claim putative warrant for inhumane social, economic and military policies.

whatever is different from or other than ourselves is not, we might note, vital to our satisfactory engagement with cultural products—novels, plays, movies, docudramas, poetry and others—alone. It is also, as philosopher and novelist Iris Murdoch reminds us, the very heartbeat of our relationships and dealings with other people. Love, she observes, begins with *curiosity*,[12] the arousal of our interest by someone sufficiently different from ourselves to arouse it and hold it, but having sufficient in common with us for a depth of mutual understanding gradually to develop and flourish.

In all this, the universal and the particular are not best thought of as two distinct quantities or sets of qualities, capable of being disentangled from one another and tabulated in different columns. And nor, therefore, should we see the relationship between them as a zero-sum game in which more of the one *by definition* involves less of the other. It is not like that at all, not in our day-to-day experience of things, nor even in our subsequent reflection and attempts to make sense of them. Rather, as I have already suggested, we typically find ourselves encountering both at once, and recognizing something "essentially human" only as we glimpse it shot through concrete instances, and in such a way that the fusion between universal and particular is vital to the existence of each. This means that "universally significant" things are often so precisely as we grasp and attend to them in their particular form rather than despite it, or only once particularity has been stripped away to reveal some putative naked "essence". Christians have every reason to insist on this, believing as they do that God, in Christ, has acted in a universally significant way in and through the particularities and contingencies of our flesh-and-blood human existence. In the incarnation, the eternal Son did not become "human" in some abstract sense, but entered history to live the life of a particular man, a man who, like all human beings, did and said and suffered very specific things. And it is not despite these things that Jesus is held to be a Saviour for all, but precisely because of them, his differences

---

12   See, e.g., Iris Murdoch, *Existentialists and Mystics* (London: Penguin, 1999), pp. 215–16.

from all others being every bit as vital to his redemptive significance as whatever he shared in common with us.[13]

While, therefore, we may properly hold that aspects of a shared "humanity" are indeed glimpsed as we go about our particular lives, they arise and are presented to us in a host of different ways, concrete incarnations from which they cannot readily be stripped or separated. Like some other very important things, we recognize them when we see or are shown them, but they do not lend themselves to the convenience of abstract collation or formulaic definition. That, no doubt, is why we resort to their rather messier and imprecise embodiments in the particular flesh of stories, and one reason why stories—about ourselves, or about others—matter to us quite as much as they do. The "insider" view of our humanity, then, may give us much food for thought when it comes to answering the question "who or what are we?" as human beings, and its testimony (which remains plural even where different strands converge suggestively) must clearly be heard; but it cannot supply us with a definitive or authoritative pronouncement on the subject.

At this point, we can usefully pause to reckon with another reason why this may be so and why the "insider" perspective on anything is bound, in fact, to fall short of an answer to questions about the "nature" of that thing ("what *is* it?"). In the title of a celebrated essay first published in 1974, the philosopher Thomas Nagel posed the intriguing question "What is it like to be a bat?"[14] His answer, unsurprisingly, was we don't know, and in fact we cannot know. Not because there aren't lots of things we can say about bats. There are: from their association in folklore with vampires, their appetite for small flying insects, their peculiar habit of sleeping upside

---

[13] On the relationship between universal and particular from a theological perspective, see helpfully Colin E. Gunton, *The One, the Three and the Many: God, Creation and the Culture of Modernity* (Cambridge: Cambridge University Press, 1993). On the issues as they arise in Christology, see Trevor Hart, *In Him Was Life: The Person and Work of Christ* (Waco, TX: Baylor University Press, 2019), Chapter 13.

[14] Thomas Nagel, "What is it like to be a bat?", *Philosophical Review* LXXXIII (October 1974). Republished in Thomas Nagel, *Mortal Questions* (Cambridge: Canto, 2015), pp. 165–80.

down, to their virtual blindness and their reliance on sonar signals for navigation. We know and can say such things and many more besides, based on our observation of these oddest of creatures. But none of that is relevant at all by way of an answer to the question as posed. For there is a fundamental distinction to be drawn, Nagel observes, between what a thing *is* (its "nature" as we typically say) and what, on the other hand, it is like *for the thing itself* to *be* that thing. The latter is a question about the subjective character of creaturely experience, about how, being conscious as both humans and bats are, each experiences the world. And the point Nagel makes is that what it is like for a bat to be a bat is something only a bat can actually know, since the shape and substance of the relevant conscious experience is bound to be dependent from first to last on the specific ways that bats themselves are adapted and equipped to experience things. Our human physiology, sensory and neurological apparatus and, of course, powers of thought, speech and imagination, likewise determine what it is like to experience the world humanly. And the distinct points of view (if, given bats' blindness, this is not already a misleading metaphor) granted by the capacities and limits of these two respective organic systems are so radically far apart as to make meaningful analogy between them more or less impossible. We may well be able to imagine ourselves flapping elastically around a church spire eating flies at midnight; but this, as Nagel observes, is merely to imagine what it might be like for me (with all the capacities and limits of a human way of experiencing things) to behave as a bat behaves. No doubt there is a lot of fun to be had in such imagining, but it can tell us nothing of what it is like for a bat to engage in such behaviour.

Imagination can accomplish great things by modifying human experience, in enabling us to put ourselves, as we say, in someone else's shoes or see things through their eyes. Even this can be a stretch, though, and we frequently fail to do it well, the differences between us placing a barrier or stumbling block in our way. When it comes to exchanging some human way of experiencing things for a non-human way of experiencing them such as that of the bat, however, the remoteness of the two points of view is of a different order altogether, and not even the liveliest imagination can make the leap. Unable to prescind from the world as it is presented to us by our own creaturely make-up, the remoteness of that experience from our own leaves it inaccessible and beyond our reach. We may, as we suppose, be altogether more intelligent than a bat, but we can no more fathom what it is like for a bat to be a bat than a bat can know what it is like for us to be human. It's not a matter of intellect or imagination, but of our inability to choose at this late stage to have been born as a member of a species other than our own. There are just some things which, as human beings, we were not created in such a way as to be able to know. Unfair, no doubt, and inconvenient for the pathologically curious; but there it is.[15]

The thing is, however, that we can immediately turn this same observation on its head. If there are things about bats that only a bat can possibly know, so, too, there are things about bats that, precisely because they are bats, bats themselves cannot possibly know about themselves. No bat, we may take it, has ever heard of sonar, let alone vampires. We can know these things, because they are available to our human perspective on the world, including its bats—precisely an "outsider" perspective, but one that has its own distinctive and important insights to offer. In other words, the "insider" perspective is precisely that, a perspective, and one from which all sorts of things are necessarily hidden or unavailable to experience. Leaving bats safely (and happily) behind now, we are well aware of this from analogous circumstances in everyday human life. The person who walks into a smoke-filled room notices what those who have happily been filling it with smoke for several hours have long since lost sight (or smell) of. We typically dislike seeing or hearing ourselves on recordings, the person who appears before us there being in all sorts of

---

15   The very same point can be made, of course, about the challenges presented by the many things that differentiate us from one another humanly, affording us each what is strictly speaking a unique standpoint from which to experience the world, whatever we may also be taken to share. Such differences and the limitations imposed by them on our imaginative lives can be either understated or overstated in unhelpful ways. My supposition here, though, is that they are in any case of a different order of magnitude to the challenge which Nagel's essay identifies. See further Trevor Hart, *Faith Thinking: The Dynamics of Christian Theology*, second edition (Eugene, OR: Wipf and Stock, 2020), pp. 243–69.

ways strange to us. Surely, we know ourselves best? What right has this imposter to claim to represent us? And yet, traditions of human wisdom tell us, there is actually no greater gift than that of being shown how we and our behaviour appears to other people—from an "outsider" rather than our own "insider" perspective. We may be the only person to know precisely "what it is like to be me"; but there's more to me and you than this unique perspective typically affords. What it is like to have to put up with me is also part of the larger reality of things, and for those concerned (whose perspective grants them access to that particular version of "me") it will no doubt have a significant claim on the truth of the matter.

This, of course, is precisely why in their quest for truth, the natural sciences undertake the highly imaginative exercise of seeking to bracket out as much of the human perspective (and any *particular* human perspective on things as possible, or, we might say, by supplementing it to correct the ways in which it might distort or colour our knowledge of things in an unhelpful manner. In other words, science typically seeks an "outsider" perspective on things (including our own humanity) or, better, a "perspectiveless" perspective, a "view from nowhere" as it has been called[16] or a "God's-eye view" of the cosmos, which might enable a purely "factual" and "objective" approach to the reality or "nature" of things. As imaginative projects go, there can be no doubt that this one has, over the past four hundred years or so, proven to be extremely useful in all sorts of ways, by acknowledging and seeking to compensate for the shortfalls of "what it is like" to experience the world humanly, aspiring to a fuller and deeper knowledge of reality than that perspective typically grants us. As a result, we certainly know and understand far more about all sorts of things than we otherwise should.

But there are limits and losses attendant on the project too, and they are not always acknowledged honestly. For, of course, while its ideals and aspirations may be laudable and its gains undeniable, the fact remains that science can never actually succeed in the task it sets itself—not, at

---

[16] See, e.g., Thomas Nagel, *The View from Nowhere* (Oxford: Oxford University Press, 1986).

least, while ever it is practised by human beings.[17] Its imaginative venture can strip away only so much of our distinctly human perspective on the world; and when it has done so to its best ability, what remains is precisely the result of what human imagining is capable of, and to that extent itself a thoroughly human perspective, from which all sorts of things remain hidden or obscure, and will always be so. Despite our aspiration and desire, *we are not made in such a way as to experience everything there is.* (Our Border Terrier hears all sorts of things lying well beyond the range of frequencies available to my human ears, and that is not only the result of middle-age diminishment of capacity! It is because she is a dog and I am not, and there are realities I cannot and do not register, because, I take it, being human I was not, unlike her, ever intended to do so.) Furthermore, to the extent that science pares away at the layers of our sensory and neurological and other interfaces with reality, its imagining of things (its grasp on "reality") rules out of consideration, and so loses sight of, all sorts of things that, in the ordinary run of affairs, we take ourselves to "know" the reality of with sufficient assurance, so that to doubt their existence or behave as though they were unreal (something which "scientism" if not science itself has often done) would be ludicrous—inhuman, in fact.[18]

---

[17]   As the research chemist and philosopher of science Michael Polanyi observes, even the most "objective" of scientific achievements remains grounded finally in the particularities of some human take on things. As the product of the sorts of experience, reasoning and imagining that humans happen to be capable of, it is also a product of particular time and place, and of irreducibly personal acts of knowing. Michael Polanyi, *Personal Knowledge* (London: Routledge and Kegan Paul, 1958).

[18]   Such reductive tendencies were central to the philosophical movement known as Logical Positivism that enjoyed a period of dominance in the middle of the twentieth century. Elevating the sort of knowledge proper to the natural sciences as the only sort really worth having, members of the so-called "Vienna Circle" (Moritz Schlick, Rudolf Carnap and others) insisted that statements were only meaningful in so far as their truth or falsity could be demonstrated either on the grounds of pure logic (tautologies or analytic statements) or by appeal to the evidence of sense-experience. This ruled out of court not

To deny the gains of science, though, would be as ridiculous as supposing that it can tell us everything about everything in some authoritative manner that trumps all other perspectives. Yet those gains, to repeat, are had by the acknowledgement that reality is bigger, deeper and more mysterious than "what it is like to experience it humanly" alone can ever tell us. Even when it comes to our own humanity (since it is part of this same "reality"), every "insider" perspective is at best incomplete and can be misleading, craving other perspectives to supplement and correct it, insofar as these are available or imaginable. We are not, that is to say, best placed to answer the question "what is humanity?" based on the knowledge of what it is like to be human. Just as other people can help us see and understand ourselves more fully by offering us a valuable corrective to our personal "insider" view of ourselves, so, as a species, we might say, there is a sense in which in order to answer that question we need to be told or shown how it might be answered from a point of view other than our own; ideally, a bigger, more complete perspective on the reality of things than we either have or are capable of obtaining for ourselves. Christians might naturally suppose that, if such a perspective exists, then a "God's-eye" point of view is precisely where we might reasonably expect to find it. If, in other words, we were to answer the question of who and what we are as human beings in the world, as well as reckoning with the testimony of our own human experience we should properly expect at the last to have to be shown and told, were God willing to grant us that gift—of seeing ourselves as God sees us.

---

only the metaphysical claims of religion, but statements about morality, aesthetics and a good deal else besides. All this was to be relegated as strictly meaningless and, by inference at least, lacking in the sort of "reality" worthy of serious consideration. Much ink was spilled seeking alternative grounds for the meaningfulness of talk about God, good and evil, beauty and so on, until it was observed that the Logical Positivists' "principle of verification" was itself neither logically necessary nor empirically demonstrable, and therefore hoist with its own petard! In the English-speaking world Logical Positivist doctrines were popularized by A. J. Ayer, *Language, Truth and Logic* (London: Victor Gollancz, 1936).

At this point, though, the attentive reader might spot an apparent problem, based on the foregoing. Surely, it might be asked, even God is in no position to offer a full answer to the question? For, no matter how much knowledge God, as our creator, may be supposed to have of human beings, God's view can, precisely as God's view, only ever be that of an outsider. In this respect, it might be enquired, is God any better off than we are when we crave knowledge of what it is like to be a bat? If this can indeed only be known from the inside, then precisely because God is God, creator and not creature, must we not suppose it to be something lying beyond even the impressive scope of divine knowing? There are almost certainly all sorts of ways of exploring an answer to this question; but I want simply to take it as an opportunity to draw attention to the fact that what it is like to experience the world *humanly* is, according to the pattern of Christian believing, not beyond the reach of God's own experience at all, but (and even faith stumbles here to express the matter well) exactly what occurs when, as the Gospel of John says, the creative Word of God himself "takes flesh" and dwells among us as—we cannot put the matter any less awkwardly—one of his own human creatures. The logic of the doctrine of the incarnation, in other words, insists that God's knowledge of our humanity is a knowledge won from within as well as owned from without, which suggests all the more reason for attending to the perspective it offers, literally "fleshes out" or "bodies forth", and shows us. The incarnation is, though, Christians believe, far more than an elaborate teaching aid. In it, the tradition holds, our humanity is laid hold of by God and made God's own, not as a temporary measure, but permanently, becoming part of God's own life and sharing now in God's glory, a transition and transformation that demands and is accomplished, nonetheless, only via a process of suffering, death and resurrection to new life of which God himself, in the person of the Son, is the personal subject. This is a remarkable claim, of course, and to take it seriously at all is to admit that the intentionality of this radical "economy" of action and passion undertaken by God itself tells and shows us something about our humanity, something that may and must underpin and provide the context for whatever else we have to say on the subject: namely, that God places so high a value on it as to immerse himself in and identify himself with it in this way, and that, whatever appearances and the weight of experience may suggest, *this*—this dwelling in union with God, sharing the Son's life with the Father in the power of the Holy Spirit—is, in God's hands, its true creaturely capacity and its intended end. We shall return to this claim again before the chapter ends.

Some predicaments of being human

There are certainly challenges in the fact of being human, whatever "being human" means. It is interesting, though, that some serious treatments of our humanity (some of them theologically informed, some not obviously so) have chosen to characterize it not, say, as a blessing, or for that matter a curse, but instead as a state that places us in a *predicament*.[19] To be human, they suggest, is to find oneself constantly tugged in two opposing directions at once, as though—simply by virtue of the sorts of beings we are—we are called to hold together in ourselves and wrestle with various sorts of realities that sometimes seem to be equally but oppositely matched and locked, as I suggested earlier, into a contest that is to all intents and purposes a zero-sum game. This perception is closely linked to what I said at the outset of this chapter, namely, that certain key features of our humanity—whether they are ones known to us from within the experience of being human itself or things shown or told (in theological terms, "revealed to") to us or, perhaps, some constructive mixture of the two—present themselves most naturally and immediately in the guise of tensions to be negotiated, though on closer inspection they may prove not to be simple binaries one term of which threatens to cancel out the other.

We have, in fact, already dealt fairly thoroughly with one of these tensions; namely, that tension between purported universal and identifiably particular aspects of what and who we are humanly. Or, expressing the same point differently by alluding to specifically theological uses of terms, between *what* we are as humans (the shared "nature" that marks us out from other species) and *who* we each are (as "persons"

---

19 So, for instance, David Jones, *Epoch and Artist* (London: Faber & Faber, 1959) pp. 143–79, esp. 166; Brian Magee, *Ultimate Questions* (Princeton: Princeton University Press, 2016), pp. 33–57.

whose particular way of being human is unique and differentiates us from one another even as it locates us as particular nodal points in a web of relationships to one another). I argued, however, that far from cancelling one another out, the universal and the radically particular are woven together in the actual substance of "reality" as we encounter it, so closely as to permit no meaningful disentangling of them without breaking faith with reality itself, exchanging our flesh-and-blood dealings with it for a set of wraithlike abstractions.

Mention of flesh and blood points us helpfully to another apparent tension confronted by the human creature; namely the fact that we both appear to ourselves and are encouraged by scripture and tradition to suppose that we dwell in two different dimensions or zones of reality at once. We are conscious of being animals, biological organisms embedded and keyed into a material world by our bodies and subject to its regular processes and laws; but we know, too, that we live and move and have our being in a reality that cannot be reduced to materiality, a world of rich significances—meanings, values, feelings, relationships, ideas, hopes, fears, intentions, all the things that make our lives in the world *significant* in one way or another, but certainly do not lend themselves to being weighed, measured, or analysed exhaustively in terms of the play of atoms.[20] So, while matter *matters* for creatures like ourselves, the very fact that it matters, that we grasp it as laden with *significance*, depends wholly on the fact that it is not the whole "caboodle". We are more than our bodies alone. And this presents us with a particular challenge, because the realities of this "more than", being precisely non-material, cannot be grasped in the way that we reach out and grasp the solid objects lying to hand all around us; they cannot be seen or heard directly, and in "grasping" them and expressing them and pointing to them, therefore, we are constantly obliged to hold them together within the complexity of our own creaturely existence, mediating the realities of each to and through the realities of the other. David Jones, the Welsh poet-painter, refers to this distinctive human activity as "sign-making", the way in which the solid things of sensory experience become significant for us—that is, become for us the incarnations of things that they themselves otherwise

---

[20]　See also Reid, Chapter 9, and Harries, Chapter 6.

are not—black marks on a piece of paper are apprehended as words, a hand gesture is grasped as "angry", a rose as a token of love, or the bodily consumption of bread and wine as laden with meaning to do with our relationship with God. In all these and a myriad of other instances in our daily, minute-to-minute engagements with reality, as Rowan Williams (drawing on Jacques Maritain) puts it, "the flesh is more than it is, gives more than it (as flesh) has".[21] Matter matters, and for that reason we know the world to be more than matter alone. This is a demanding fact, because "making sense" of things is never straightforward, and we frequently get it wrong; but if it places us in a perpetual predicament, it is nonetheless the fact about us upon which all that truly matters humanly relies. That the discernment of the significance of things is not an easy but shallow one-to-one correspondence in which they simply are what they are and mean what they mean, but a far more mysterious business in which meaning often opens up and multiplies beneath surface appearances, can no doubt be difficult and sometimes even dangerous; but it is also the source of the greatest blessings to be had in our shared indwelling of creation.

None of this requires a specifically theological account as such; it is something which anyone might have their attention drawn to, if they had not already noticed and felt the tension for themselves. For that reason, I have thus far avoided theologically charged language such as that of "soul", "spirit" and "spiritual", the latter in particular being vague and loosely used in our day, and likely to raise rather more questions than it answers. But, of course, the account I have given fits well with the sorts of creatures scripture and tradition consistently encourage us to suppose ourselves to be;[22] far more than *animals* alone (though let's not fall into the "exceptionalist" trap of speaking as though we know what it is like for a bat to be a bat, a cat a cat, or a dog a dog!), yet distinguished equally clearly from *angels* by our embeddedness through the body in the space–time of the material cosmos.[23] More than this, the thrust of

---

[21] Rowan Williams, *Grace and Necessity: Reflections on Art and Love* (London: Continuum, 2005), p. 61. The allusion is to Jacques Maritain, *Art and Scholasticism* (London: Sheed and Ward, 1930).

[22] Jones, op. cit.

[23] Ibid., p. 178.

a theological account of our humanity is to suggest that we are created, called and intended by God for "something better than a purely human life" alone,[24] approaching the matter of our "nature" not so much in terms of what we currently *are* but of what God has promised we *shall be*. In words redolent of the theology of Thomas Aquinas, David Jones sums this up by saying that we are creatures who, by virtue of their nature, are "naturally" directed by God to a "supernatural end". In more directly biblical terms we might say instead that to be human is to be a creature whose very constitution is equipped, intended and called not to be closed in upon itself,[25] but to be open to that promised dwelling together of heaven and earth, God and God's creation, that is a fundamental part of biblical hope, foreshadowed already by the ancient tabernacle, the Ark of the Covenant, and the temple, and fulfilled proleptically by the coming of God himself in the person of the Son to "tabernacle" or "pitch his tent" among us[26] on earth in creaturely form—specifically, that form proper to human being.[27] Humans, in other words, are creatures created for the goal of their active sharing in God's life when, in Christ and finally in the new creation, God fulfils God's promise to bring heaven down to earth and suffuse the world with God's presence and glory.

---

[24]   Jacques Maritain, *True Humanism* (London: Geoffrey Bles—The Centenary Press, 1938), p. xi.

[25]   Being "closed in" or "curved in" upon ourselves actually arises as a powerful image of our human alienation from God in the writings of theologians such as Augustine of Hippo, Martin Luther and others.

[26]   The Greek verb *'eskenōsen* (generally translated "dwelt") in John 1:14 bears these more theologically precise meanings, which make better sense of the specific allusion that follows immediately to the presence of God's glory (which dwelt in both tabernacle and temple).

[27]   Philippians 2:6–8.

Putting us finally in our place

This, however, is to get too far ahead of ourselves. And, if we return to reckon with present rather than future reality, to our condition *in via* rather than at the promised *end* towards which we are supposedly directed, then we find ourselves compelled to face something that actually seems to point in a different direction altogether. I am thinking, of course, of yet another "tension" that we seem, as human beings, to live in and have to wrestle with, namely, that between good and evil, obedience and sin. Our awareness of this tension in ourselves is probably already sufficient to indicate that our route to our creaturely end is bound to be anything but straightforward—a matter not of gradual ascent or consistent progress, but a far more messy, broken and stuttering journey, one involving suffering and death associated not just with our biological mortality, but with our being keyed in to a reality that is at once moral as well as physical, a world where the "hallowing of God's name" can only finally occur by the judgement upon, and putting to death of, whatever in us is inclined instead to godlessness and the darkness of evil.

This is not, to be sure, a struggle and self-denial that we are compelled or in any way able to undertake on our own. That would be the worst of bad news rather than gospel! For what is shown us of our human predicament by God's dealings with us in Christ, as distinct from the self-knowledge available to us as "insiders" to the circumstance, is its sheer scale and seriousness. The theological language of "sin" has a limited purchase in the wider vocabularies of our day, and its unashamed public use is likely only to mislead rather than illuminate. If we wish to convey something of its actual sense and scope, therefore, Francis Spufford suggests, we could do worse than substitute for "sin" the acronym "HPtFtU" (the "human propensity to fuck things up"), something that is part of almost everyone's normal human experience and identifiable, therefore, as one of the basic truths about ourselves, at least as far as we can tell. If we are human, Spufford says, "that's where we live",[28] and it ranges way beyond the limits of bingeing on chocolate or purchasing exotic sex-toys, to affect the whole territory of human existence. A purely

---

[28] Francis Spufford, *Unapologetic* (London: Faber & Faber, 2012), p. 29.

"insider" view might, of course, acknowledge this, but leave scope for optimism about our natural capacity to handle it and eventually turn the ship around by our own efforts, or as a result of gradual human "progress". What the language of sin does is to appeal to a story or drama which we could not possibly tell ourselves, but have been told and shown, in which the HPtFtU is revealed to be far too deep rooted and pervasive for that. And it issues from something that is absolutely opposed in every fibre of its being to God and God's character, and infinitely subtle in its strategies of seduction, recruitment and conscription to its own ends of creatures like us. Whether we think of ourselves as perpetrators or victims of evil, therefore, (and scripture insists on picturing us as both at the same time, pointing us to yet another "tension" to be reckoned with—that between freedom and limit),[29] we are too far gone, too thoroughly in the thrall or the grip of sin and evil, ever to attempt or accomplish our own unilateral redirection towards the end for which God, we are promised, has created us. The reversal is necessarily radical and total, and its accomplishment, we are told, demands the decisive action of the creator in human nature, human history, and in our individual human lives—action that has been and is being undertaken by Christ and the Holy Spirit. But, even when we align ourselves or are aligned with this regenerative work of God in, and with, and through us, it demands our active participation rather than mere passivity. It begins and ends in God's hands alone, of course, and cannot proceed otherwise; but precisely because it is the sort of thing it is, it has at various levels to involve something done *by* us *with* God as well as something done *to* us *by* God. And it will and must involve the suffering of allowing sin to be put to death in us as we deliberately take up our cross and identify ourselves with Christ's suffering for us.

Does this not bring us to rather a dismal assessment of our humanity? Some have suggested that constant talk of sin in our day is somehow unfitting, baleful, an insult to God and humankind alike. One wonders which Bible such people are attending to and seeking to make sense of, or how they can possibly cope with the substance of Christian liturgy which consistently refers us to the fact that, whatever we make of it, it will hardly

---

[29]   See, for instance, Paul Fiddes, *Freedom and Limit: A Dialogue between Literature and Christian Doctrine* (London: Macmillan, 1991), Chapter 3.

permit us to suppose that the current human condition is one of dignity and basic goodness, needing only a bit of polish applied or some gentle nudging back on track and see it moving in the right direction. But, like the others treated in this chapter, the tension between the demands of good and evil upon us should not be seen simply as a zero-sum game. Of course, there is a sense in which, being fundamentally opposed to God, evil must indeed either hope eventually to displace or find itself unceremoniously displaced by God, there being no "place" for it to exist alongside God forever. If the imagery of a "final judgement" and the meting out of deserts at history's end means anything, it certainly means this. And yet, when it comes to estimating the gravity of human complicity in sin, the ratio between dignity and depravity is surely one of direct rather than inverse proportionality. In other words, it is precisely because of the greatness of the end for which God has created us, and towards which even now God is determined to direct and bring us, and because of the capacities and possibilities invested in us at our creation as creatures destined to be opened up completely to God, sharing fully in God's own life and glory, that the depth of our depravity and responsibility, and the direction of those same capacities and possibilities instead towards the ends of evil, must be gauged theologically. Only those who are created "little lower than the angels" can fall so far and so spectacularly, and cause so much damage in so doing. What the drama of our redemption in Christ reveals to us, though, is that our true end lies not in our restoration to some imagined former glory alone, but in the far greater glory of being the receptacles and reflectors of God's own uncreated glory on the earth. For, as the 1982 liturgy of the Scottish Episcopal Church reminds us daily, in Christ, God "made his home among us, that we might forever dwell in him".

Questions for discussion

1. What are the gains and losses of knowing ourselves to be embedded thoroughly in the material cosmos but participant too in a non-material realm of meanings, values, feelings, intentions, ideas and imaginings?
2. How does story aid our grasp of both our own humanity and that of others?
3. What do you make of the suggestion that the seriousness of our complicity in sin is a measure of the dignity of our true creaturely "end" and calling? How is what we are shown in Jesus relevant?

Further reading

Richard Bauckham, *The Bible and Ecology: Rediscovering the Community of Creation* (Waco, TX: Baylor University Press, 2010), Chapter 2.

Philip Edgcumbe Hughes, *The True Image: The Origin and Destiny of Man in Christ* (Grand Rapids, MI: Eerdmans, 1989).

C. S. Lewis, *Mere Christianity* (London: Fontana, 1955).

Jacques Maritain, *True Humanism* (London: Geoffrey Bles—The Centenary Press, 1938).

Marilyn Robinson, *Jack* (London: Virago, 2020).

CHAPTER 4

The end of the line? Life, death and the future of humanity

Robert Gillies

Introduction

We begin this chapter in a spirit of humility. A good friend from many years ago in seminary, the pastoral theologian Stephen Pattison, has written to me thus:

> [O]ne of the great limits of Christian theology is that it is so anthropocentric. The life of the planet has been there for millions of years before us, and evolutionary biologists tell us that whatever waves goodbye to the sun after fourteen billion years will not be like us because as a species we are quite recent and like the dinosaurs, we are quite likely to extinguish ourselves, quite soon perhaps. Theology behaves as if it knows the truth about eternity from eternity to all eternity, and yet our articulated theological record is only about five thousand years old, if that. So, it and the human species, seem to manifest delusions of grandeur, permanence and omniscience which really do not fit in with the history of God's world. It is not surprising that what we are interested in, and want to think most about theologically, is humanity whatever it is (and what a nasty destructive little species we often are). But it may be that in thinking about life, death and ends of life, we need to be a bit more modest and less anthropocentric so that the world may simply live. This

would then lead to a radical reframing of Christian theological
eschatology which might be all to the good.[1]

Trenchantly put, Pattison has set our course. With good healthcare largely
across much of the Western, developed world, even if disproportionately
favouring privileged and wealthier groups and societies, we now live
longer earthly lives than hitherto. Since the industrial revolution many
have enjoyed an increasing lifespan thereby accomplishing much that was
desired and more besides. Those of us so privileged are in a completely
different place from which to evaluate eternity than were our forebears
in previous centuries.

The downside to this, of course, is that some feel they inhabit a
meaningless eternity of infirm old age within which they feel exhausted.
As I write these words, I think of the quite remarkable person, now aged
ninety-three, who says to me each time I take Holy Communion to the
house, "I just want to die, but God won't let me."

There are also those who have to care for the increasing numbers
of the infirm in the affluent West. In so many cases, close relatives are
captive to situations of dementia, or muscle and nervous system wasting
diseases. A significant number of these conditions arise within longer
lifespans resulting from treatment successes brought about by antibiotics,
improving surgical techniques and remarkable treatments given to, for
example, cancer sufferers particularly at an early age. At a personal level I
know that, not many generations previously, I would have died at the age
of eleven from acute appendicitis, and even if not then, at age fourteen
from a footballing injury which developed gas gangrene, had it not been

---

[1]   Stephen Pattison, private correspondence, 25 November 2019, quoted with
permission. Ernst Troeltsch spoke of life on earth, "like breath on cold
window panes, which disappears the next moment". Though referring to
"entire organic life on this earth" his metaphor, if applied more specifically
to humankind, becomes all the more piercingly applicable. (cited from
Glaubenslehre, p. 64, translated and quoted by B. A. Gerrish (ed.) in "Ernst
Troeltsch and the Possibility of a Historical Theology", in John Powell Clayton
(ed.) *Ernst Troeltsch and the Future of Theology* (Cambridge: Cambridge
University Press, 1976), p. 117.

for the intervention of modern surgery and antibiotics together with quality nursing care.

As it is, I am still here, knowing not what health condition awaits me around life's next corner. So, in that personal vein I am led, accepting Pattison's lead, to write in a spirit of respectful obedience, humility and, let it not go unsaid, with personal gratitude for my own relative longevity. So much for the personal dimension. As this chapter opens outwards a wider horizon must now be viewed so as to map our course within broader and deeper coordinates.

Concentrations of carbon dioxide, methane and nitrous oxide are rising in the air around and above us. Most of this is due to human activity. Attempts to reduce these levels are given lip-service attention but to little practical international effect. Wastefulness is the global norm, despite good efforts in some quarters to reduce fossil-fuel reliance. Plastic recycling, for example, is ill-served if all that is done is to compress and package it, prior to loading on expensive ships and then to carry the stuff on a wasteful cruise to China or India, or wherever, for the new owner of it all to do with it what they will beyond our reach or control. How does all this fit in with the theological perspective which I aim to develop in the pages that end this chapter?

The human being

Doing theology was very different when humans were a minority species on earth with limited lifespans and many threats that cut short lives in their prime. Speaking in very general terms, our antecedents thought the world was quite recently created and humans were part of the whole thing from very near the beginning. In that context, it was perfectly reasonable for theology to support and laud the human endeavour, simultaneously consoling for whatever failure might occur or limitation be experienced. That worldview is now in the past, and though respectable given knowledge at the time, it cannot determine where we go next. Some of us in the West, and not least many who write the sort of theology book you are now reading, have long and well-resourced lives with relative biomedical security, at least for a time, so that our task must needs become much more questioning of anthropocentricity and not collude with its harmful effects on the world.

Following Psalm 139, we may indeed be fearfully and wonderfully made. If, however, we continue to put ourselves at the centre and minimize our now-recognized ephemeral connections to creation and nature, seeing ourselves as somehow outside and above it, God and other persons, and seeing each as instrumental to our own individual advance or preference, then we collude with the destruction of our environment and the extinction of our own species. And this may happen sooner than we might desire. In short, the human enterprise is truly successful—for that we should give thanks—but we have become so very dangerous to the world and to ourselves.

Against this backdrop the risk of being immobilized into inaction as we canter towards the cliff edge of Armageddon is great. Fear, leading to paralysis, is a real peril if no action is taken to reverse the damage humanity has already done to itself and its habitation. This, then, is the moment when humility must, paradoxically, assert itself. The issue is of not feeling so ashamed and ill-equipped that, on the one hand, we are morally disabled into non-action but on the other, we are not so cocky that we do not bother, even when faced with the inevitability of self-destruction, to do anything at all. Stephen Pattison again:

> I hope the theological tradition, which is one of our longest records of great and terrible ideas, of mistakes made for the best reasons, as well as a repository of insights and triumphs, may have wisdom to contribute here.[2]

Perhaps in this spirit we can see what ancient seams of wisdom may be mined, what new insights be developed and forgotten pathways reopened, thereby avoiding the accusation that we are doing little more than repeating the same old thoughts and doctrines so as to keep the wheels on the wagon for another mile or two.

---

[2]   Stephen Pattison, correspondence, 27 November 2019. I am indebted to Pattison for rich exchanges on this subject in connection with the early writing of this chapter.

Humility addressing creation

In his BBC Radio 4 *Today* Programme broadcast on 26 November 2019, Pádraig Ó Tuama, Leader of the Corrymeela Community in Northern Ireland, offered a thoughtful meditation on the place of trees in creation. He considered that whilst trees might be only part of the solution in reversing climate change and won't heal all the damage done by noxious gaseous emissions, they "will help slow things down".

What Ó Tuama said was not just based on a desire to put the climate right but arose from a deeper perspective from within the oriental religious tradition. He spoke of how, in the ancient Babylonian mythology, a community of gods fight and kill one of their group and from the body of this dead god grow two trees. This at the very least suggests what might survive when personal identity as we know it is extinguished. Ó Tuama, referring to the Hebrew Bible, the basis of the Christian Old Testament, said:

> The Garden of Eden was planted with trees that . . . had the knowledge of good and evil and contained life within them. Trees, the narrative implies, contain power and our relationship with them should be guarded in all senses of that word . . . Woodland contains and sustains life [through its photosynthetic activity, and] while looking to save nature, nature is also saving us . . . The poets who wrote mythologies were not making political points, they were making a deeper more intuitive point. They saw trees as the source of healing for the nations. They were right. And we should listen.

It will be worth our while to make an intuitive link from this meditation on trees to the Hebrew creation story, at the very least to see if any interesting new perspectives might arise as we do so.

Thoughts before tree fruits

I will restrict myself simply to the dialogue between the snake and the woman and man before the tree of the knowledge of good and evil as found in Genesis 3 and beginning at the very end of Genesis 2:

> And the man and his wife were both naked, and were not ashamed. Now the serpent was more crafty than any other wild animal that the Lord God had made. He said to the woman, "Did God say, 'You shall not eat from any tree in the garden'?" The woman said to the serpent, "We may eat of the fruit of the trees in the garden; but God said, 'You shall not eat of the fruit of the tree that is in the middle of the garden, nor shall you touch it, or you shall die.'" But the serpent said to the woman, "You will not die; for God knows that when you eat of it your eyes will be opened, and you will be like God, knowing good and evil." So when the woman saw that the tree was good for food and that it was a delight to the eyes, and that the tree was to be desired to make one wise, she took of its fruit and ate; and she also gave some to her husband, who was with her, and he ate. Then the eyes of both were opened and they knew that they were naked; and they sewed fig leaves together and made loincloths for themselves.[3]

At the heart of this well-known poetic scripture is language, or more precisely a conversation between a serpent, better known as the snake, and the first woman. The picturesque mythology in which this narrative is framed revolves around whether or not to eat from the tree at the centre of the garden, something God has forbidden. In conversation, the woman says one should not eat the fruit of the tree, on pain of death. Such is God's warning. Challenging this, the snake says there will be no such outcome.

So, reassured by the snake, the woman is emboldened to take fruit for herself and her husband from the tree at the centre of the garden. The outcome of doing so is that she and he have then come to know the difference between good and bad. To this we might also add the

---

[3]   Genesis 2:25–3:7.

difference between right and wrong. In other words, their disobedience has led to the acquisition of human knowledge and self-understanding. The snake was the literary foil that enabled the discourse which portrays what took place.

Inherent in what I intend as a fair and honest reading of this text is my view that both the woman and the man of this story *already had the capacity, and arguably the desire*, before conversing with the snake and eating the fruit, to acquire knowledge and self-understanding. As the product of God's creative work, they were thus endowed with this gift to pursue knowledge and thus gain insight and they saw to it, consequent upon the serpent's reassurance, that they put that gift to use.

By way of passing comment, it is important to recognize first, contrary to much popular understanding, that the snake did not lure, or seduce or trick either the woman or the man into eating from that tree. The snake simply reassured her that she would not die were she to do so. The Hebrew text, if taken literally reads—admittedly very clumsily in English—"She also gave *[the fruit]* to her husband with her."[4] Furthermore, and second, far from being a victim of what has often, and erroneously, been given as female enticement of the male, we see that he is a fully willing participant with her in taking and eating the fruit. Any reading of this passage that sees primary sin in the woman who then in turn caused the man's downfall by seduction is a serious emasculation of the biblical text. Nina Simone, in her 1961 alluringly melodic song "Forbidden Fruit", typifies this error:

> But Eve got tempted so she tried it and as all chicks do
> Teaser her man till he decided he'd just try some too.[5]

In verses that follow in Genesis, there is an exchange between God and the human couple. They are chastised for their disobedience. The man tries desperately to make excuses for his actions (nothing new there), and the woman in turn passes blame to the snake. Avoidance of culpability and transference of blame is generic across both women and men equally.

---

4   Sarna, p. 25 [parenthesis mine].

5   This quotation is from the song by Nina Simone, "Forbidden Fruit", words by Oscar Jr Brown ©Round Hill Carlin (cited exactly as per lyrics).

In these exchanges, language and conversation[6] are crucial as the woman and man's new-found human self-identities begin their formation. Language and its use were given by God to both the woman and the man in advance of their disobedience before, and of, God.

We can see therefore that, far from being a means of condemning humanity through raised awareness of their respective sexualities, this highly symbolic, poetic and mythological narrative acutely describes the human exercise of free choice. Where persons fail, it is through *disobedience* to God (and I would add failure to heed the demands of God's creation) not just through the *outcome* of what has been learned within God's creation. Failure to heed God's word, and to respond to the needs of God's creation, are inherent and pervasively destructive streaks in each person's ebb and flow of life. These stanzas from Milton's *Paradise Lost* demonstrate the point:

> . . . of this be sure—
> To do aught good will never be our task,
> But ever to do ill our sole delight,
> As being the contrary to his high will
> Whom we resist. If then this providence
> Out of our evil seek to bring forth good,
> Our labour must be to pervert that end,
> And out of good still to find means of evil . . . [7]

---

[6]   I recognize "speech" might in some contexts be a better term than "conversation", but I will deliberately stick with "conversation" as it denotes dialogical exchanges between two or more parties.

[7]   John Milton, *Paradise Lost*, Book 1, lines 158–65, in *Poetical Works*, ed., Douglas Bush (London: Oxford University Press, 1969), p. 216.

Language as gift from God

In the previous section, I sought to identify language and conversation as precursor and precondition given by God to women and men in the story of human disobedience before God and God's creation in the Garden of Eden story from the Old Testament. As such, language and conversation are taken as part of God's gift in creation to women and men. In themselves, language and conversation are not bad or wrong; it is when they lead to, and are put in the service of, disobedience before God and God's creation that human failure results.

In what follows I will take representative New Testament passages where language is underscored as a gift from God. The first comes from 1 Corinthians 12:4–11. Here "wise speech" and the facility to put "deep knowledge into words" are given as gifts from God. A second passage is from Romans 12:6–21. In this passage "inspired utterance, teaching and counsel" are similarly given as gifts of God's Holy Spirit.

1 Corinthians 12:4–11

Where wise speech is stressed in verse 8 of this passage it denotes a gift from God that enables speech and knowledge to issue in wisdom which in turn gives insight into what God is doing in the world. Unlike the Corinthian expectation that it is for those who are clever in matters of oratory to give voice to wisdom, here the origin and working of the gift comes from God. It is potentially available to all and not just the "clever".

It was accepted in the early church that one could pursue, and one would be expected to advance in, those gifts that were given by God. Such were not offered for the benefit of the particular individual who had been given that gift but were for the building up of the faithful Christian community. In this sense, the gifts of knowledge and of speech that outflow in wisdom are grounded in the gospel that Jesus taught and lived. Finny Philip in the *South Asia Bible Commentary* has written:

> [G]ifts are not "extras". They are [God's] way of getting his work done. They are the means he uses to fulfil his mission in the world through us, his people. They are intended to help us carry out God's work, reach out to those who might become members of

Christ's body, and strengthen the body of Christ by living lives
filled with joy, peace, effective work and worship. The Holy Spirit
both empowers us for various kinds of ministry and carries out
an inner transforming work by which he enables us to grow in
sanctification and obedience to God.[8]

At first sight, this may seem a long way from what we said above where
we noted that it was through the gift of speech and conversation that
Adam and Eve came to have insight into what was right and wrong,
good and bad and so on. But greater proximity is realized as we now see
how God-given gifts can be put to the service of the body of believers
that constitute the church through both mutual service and outreach. It
is insight such as this that enables even the most uneducated of persons
to see the ways of God in the world and by the most simple application
of speech then to share what this is.

I write these words on an afternoon when I have just returned from
a visit to close friends of a quite remarkable man who has recently died.
I heard stories of his very simple, but very secure faith. One such story
involved hearing a robin sing in the breaking dawn as this man and his
companion set out on their first morning to walk the *Camino* to Santiago
de Compostela. Upon hearing it, he had apparently said that this birdsong
was God's way of being with them on the journey and giving them his
protection. A robin's daybreak anthem accompanied them throughout
the pilgrimage. Whether it was the same, or a different, robin each day,
is immaterial. The man's "simple and secure" testimony highlighted
profound wisdom and arose from recognition of ordinary things that
tell of God's activity, and which are then shared with another through
God's ancient gift of insight.

Humans all too easily fail to honour the gift of insight that God has
given. Such happens through abuse of the natural world, failing to honour
others and by failing to listen and see God's hand in the world. In such,
wisdom, as might arise from this gift, is thwarted.

---

8   Finny Philip in Brian Wintle (ed.), *South Asia Bible Commentary* (Rajasthan:
     Open Door Publications, 2015), p. 1575.

Romans 12:6-21

All that we noted in the foregoing section applies here. Paul was consistent about this throughout his letters and not least by underscoring that where he mentions a gift from God its purpose is for others, for "building up". Arland J. Hultgren notes that, "Common to all is that they are gifts given according to the 'grace' (*charis*) bestowed."

Hultgren continues:

> The gifts may well be correlated with human abilities and temperaments that people have, based on creation ("natural endowments") . . . in all cases they are finally 'gifts' (*charismata*) of God's "grace" . . . as empowerment . . . for God's grace transforms those abilities considered to be natural and supplements them with new powers.[9]

Whilst I may not be entirely happy with the word "power", nonetheless if it is understood in the sense of "capacities", or in the sense of "making the gifts more fulfilled" or more "profound", then one can see a wealth of riches arising from the use of these gifts.

I have the privilege of having belonged, and still belonging, to church congregations where the Bible is mostly read in worship services by lay people. In some of these I have heard new things come from the most familiar of passages when read by folks in the most moving way imaginable that just seemed so natural to them. In ways that seem effortless, it was the case with each of these that God's word in the Bible was given new voice when that which was familiar was made to be heard in a way that was new and by God's grace, enriching. It was there for the building up of the body of the church.

And so in summary, we can see that God's gift of insight given in the first creation is now being harnessed to the ministry and mission of God's word made flesh through his church. Vulnerable and fragile as it is, and forever prone to personal and institutional corruption, we need to hear and recognize with humility what God places before us, and before it

---

9   Arland J. Hultgren, *Paul's Letter to the Romans: A Commentary* (Grand Rapids, MI: Eerdmans, 2011), p. 450.

kneel in humble reverence. Let us now, once more moving on intuitively, consider another facet of this study.

Moving on quickly to the fifteenth century

The relatively little known and appreciated Count Pico della Mirandola's *Oration on the Dignity of Man (De Hominis Dignitate)* (1486) represented a significant turn in the road from, on the one hand, Platonic form as the given nature of the human person and, on the other hand, the irretrievably lost and fallen nature derived literally and metaphorically from Adam and Eve. In the following, where God is given as addressing the first created person, Mirandola writes:

> We have given to thee, Adam, . . . that thou mayest feel as thine own, have as thine own, possess as thine own the seat, the form, the gifts which thou thyself may desire . . . In conformity with thy free judgment, in whose hands I have placed thee, thou art confined by no bounds; and thou wilt fix limits of nature for thyself. . . [that] thou mayest more conveniently look around and see whatsoever is in the world . . . Thou, like a judge appointed for being honorable, art the moulder and maker of thyself; thou mayest sculpt thyself into whatever shape thou dost prefer. Thou canst grow downward into the lower natures which are brutes. Thou canst again grow upward from thy soul's reason into the higher natures which are divine.[10]

Thus put, as Western civilization confidently glides into the Italian Renaissance, we find God's gift of free will to humanity well and truly in place deciding and enacting gloriously whatever direction is offered as opportunity and facility. Such was God's gift at the beginning of creation

---

[10]   Pico della Mirandola, *On the Dignity of Man*, translations by Charles Glenn Wallis, Paul J. W. Miller and Douglas Carmichael, (Indianapolis, IN: Hackett Publishing Company Inc, 1998), pp. 4–5.

to the human person and in Italy it flourished. The late Chief Rabbi, Lord Jonathan Sacks, succinctly develops this:

> By creating human beings "in His image", God gave us a similar freedom, thus creating the one being capable itself of being creative ... The human person alone has the possibility of self-transcendence. We may be a handful of dust, but we have immortal longings.[11]

He concludes that the Torah, the first five books of the Bible, are a "sustained exploration of human freedom, the greatest gift God gave man, as well as the most fateful, for freedom can be used or abused".[12] On this basis, we find our view reinforced that the gift of language truly is original in our creation by God. And with language comes the facility to communicate and to converse, one with another and, through our action upon it, with the wider created order. Whether that is for good or ill remains an open question.

With language we have the capacity to render things and the world around us differently from what we first encounter each to be. We can imagine a new created order, a new universe even. And with language comes the facility to shape things by collaborative effort with reference to a memory of what once was, and impelled towards establishing something that has yet to be. As we have already considered, the consequences of this happening in an untrammelled way might well be potentially self-destructive. To this we shall return but only after, first of all, what at first sight might seem a curious detour back in time to Saint Augustine. The reasons for this will become evident.

---

[11]   Jonathan Sacks, *Covenant and Conversation: Genesis, The Book of Beginnings* (New Milford, CT: Maggid Books and the Orthodox Union, 2009), p. 21.

[12]   Sacks, p. 22.

Augustine of Hippo (AD 354–430)

Augustine's personal struggle against his own all-too-human weaknesses is well attested, as is his earnest faith-seeking desire to overcome them. In Augustine's searching for a "resting place", in which his soul would be comfortable in knowledge of God as well as before God, he advanced through a sequence, or series, of reasonings which led him to recognize the hand of God in all things around him. In this intuition, in what might also be described as a mystical vision, he saw that God's "invisible things" are to be understood by what is visible. In other words, he saw God through the physical things around him. He writes in the *Confessions*, "And then I saw Thy invisible things understood by the things that are made."[13]

But even in this very moment of intuition Augustine falls short of that which he sought and needed. He continues:

> But I had no strength to fix my gaze upon them. In my weakness I recoiled and fell back into my old ways, carrying with me nothing but the memory of something that I loved and longed for, as though I had sensed the fragrance of the fare but was not yet able to eat it.[14]

It was that, which Augustine had glimpsed but by which he had not yet been grasped, which gives a clue as to where this present essay is progressing. In Chapter 18 of the *Confessions*, Book VII, he considers what it might mean to embrace, "that Mediator between God and men, Jesus Christ, who is a man, like them . . . calling to me, and saying, 'I am the way, the truth, and the life . . .'". And he continues despite much

---

[13]   Augustine, *Confessions,* Book VII, Chapter 17, tr. R. S. Pine-Coffin (Harmondsworth: Penguin, 1961), p. 151. The biblical allusion is Romans 1:20, "Ever since the creation of the world [God's] eternal power and divine nature, invisible though they are, have been understood and seen through the things he has made."

[14]   Ibid., p. 152.

earnest seeking, "I was not humble enough to conceive of the humble Jesus Christ as my God."[15]

What had moved Augustine, and which he was now famously about to commit to the written word, was the realization that that which is low in creation must fully submit to Christ in order thereby to be raised by Christ. In other words, by completely surrendering to Christ without reserve one is fully sanctified by Christ and thus brought to salvation. Augustine writes that by falling down before Christ and in complete subjection to Him, the submissive person is lifted, "over to Him . . . [thereby] fostering their love; to the end that they might go on no further in self-confidence, but rather should become weak, seeing before their feet the Divinity weak by taking our 'coats of skins'". Wearied of their own failed advancements and attempts to attain to the life of God, persons "might cast themselves upon It, and It rising, might lift them up".[16]

This is our direction. Crucially in Western Christianity have we lost the sense of the presence of God as a revered reality. I would add that we have also lost the vocabulary of salvation; we no longer know how to verbalize that which we need to put into words. What Augustine found in his search for God was the incontrovertible dictum that before one can find God one needs to acknowledge in humble submission that, paradoxically, one must accept that God has already found oneself. In the words of a modern, and now classic, prayer from the Anglican Communion services in both England and Scotland (and maybe elsewhere, as well), we find this, "Father of all, we give you thanks and praise that when we were still far off you met us in your Son and brought us home." "Being brought home" is a profound and deeply reverential, as well as biblically secure, restatement of what Augustine meant when he spoke of "being raised up".

This is a spirit of humility which demands that one fall down before God—and I would add before God's creation—and learn (from new if needs be) the language and the conversation of reverent response to all that is in front of one. By this I mean both before God who redeems and

---

[15]   Ibid.

[16]   *Confessions,* Book VIII. The "It" that is referred to probably relates to flesh that was there in the creation of humankind and which Christ Jesus took upon himself, raising it from that which is of the earth to that which is of heaven.

forgives and as before nature which, in turn, requires of us nothing less than responsible, reverent stewardship.

We have thus arrived at that point in our discussion where we must of necessity offer this reverent response before God and which, with humility, places us before God and his creation in obedient submission to all that God has created. In doing this, we have recognized that in creation God has gifted the human person with speech and conversation and has further divined that this gift might be directed towards its outflow with the gift of wisdom. In what we have said we have also recognized the human propensity to thwart and bring to naught all of what God and nature requires of us. Our response must therefore enter into the pattern of Jesus' life such that in falling (*pace* Augustine) before him we may be raised by him. Or, and equally, to follow the Communion Service prayer above, when we depart from God we must with reverent and submissive humility allow ourselves to be "brought home" by him.

From among the range of possible options, and there are many, that could be offered in response to what I have outlined above I want to single out "devotional prayer". And my starting point is Jesus facing the last hours of his earthly life. Though this particularly refers to the hours before his death we may view it metaphorically as the short period of time that is left before we humans self-destruct. "Devotional prayer", in the way I am suggesting here, is consonant with all that Jesus taught and lived, and when facing his mortal end it is consonant also with the life all Christians must live if they are to embody his life.

"Will you not watch with me . . . ?"

Imaginatively we place ourselves with Jesus in Gethsemane. It is a garden. Gethsemane is a name which means olive press. The easy way by which it is introduced in Matthew, Mark and Luke conjures the view that this was a familiar place to Jesus and his band of followers. Certainly we know from elsewhere in the scriptures that Jesus would go somewhere to be by himself, or to spend the night in prayer. Gethsemane, traditionally given to be on the lower and western side of the Mount of Olives, is barely any distance from the Temple Mount in Jerusalem, the place where

Jesus would have been taken once arrested. Indeed the Temple Mount overshadows "the garden" with only the shallow Kidron Brook in between them, and nowadays there is a fast and busy road as traffic hurtles past in both directions.

The event of Jesus going to Gethsemane with his followers is well attested in the Gospels. In common with other sections of scripture, differences in detail between the texts are not ironed out or resolved. The authenticity of the different narratives' reporting of the same event is preserved. For example, Luke speaks in general terms of Jesus being followed by his disciples to the Mount of Olives, while Mark and Matthew locate the place more precisely and specify three, "Peter and the two sons of Zebedee", named by Mark as "James and John". The writer of Hebrews also refers to it in 5:7–8. I will come back to that in just a moment.

A question arises. How does the scene in Gethsemane fit in with the earlier recorded teaching of Jesus and in particular with this chapter and the overall theme of the book you are now reading? In Luke, we find Jesus announcing: "I must proclaim the good news of the kingdom of God . . . for I was sent for this purpose."[17] Equally, and as his ministry in Galilee developed, Jesus ever more resolutely set his face "toward Jerusalem" not least because "the days [were drawing] near for him to be taken up [to heaven]".[18] Already we begin to see a link between what Jesus was doing in his teaching, healing and proclaiming work, and the coming end of his earthly life.

This, I hope, indicates that Jesus' direction was single and all that he did in every aspect of his life as recorded in the Gospels points to such. In other words, and to project forward to my conclusion, his time in prayer to the Father (whether alone or with others) cannot be separated from his teaching upon, let us say Mosaic law, his work of healing and his lived and voiced proclamation of God's kingdom all given within his own embodiment as God's Word made human.

I mentioned the Letter to the Hebrews a few moments ago. There are a couple of crucial verses in Chapter 5 which tell us something of what happened that evening in Gethsemane. "In the days of his flesh, Jesus

---

[17] Luke 4:43.

[18] Luke 9:51.

offered up prayers and supplications, with loud cries and tears, to the one who was able to save him from death, and he was heard because of his reverent submission. Although he was a Son, he learned obedience through what he suffered . . . "[19] This is an important text for it gives us an insight into why Jesus went into Gethsemane ("obedient submission"), and what happened there (he "offered up prayers and supplications, with loud cries and tears"), and he was heard as a consequence of this.

How did he pray? The text from Hebrews supports the Gospels' account whereby Jesus "threw himself on the ground and prayed". We might also conjecture that Augustine was echoing this. He had already described his mood as "[deeply . . .] grieved and agitated".[20] Not for Jesus on that occasion the kneeling posture,[21] nor yet standing,[22] or with uplifted hands.[23] To fall down in prayer is the humblest posture for prayer. It denotes, and for Jesus also signals, the attitude of self-abasing reverence to the familiar Father who, in an echo of the Lord's Prayer, accepts that it is the Father's will that must be done—not just for me, or for the Church, but that God's will must be done for the whole creation. For Jesus this was not a situation to avoid, though the temptation to do so would have been great. Grief, anguish, agitation, sorrow—all of these—seared deep into his soul.

Jesus' prayer in that special place was personal. Yes, he prayed for himself. But he also enjoined the sleeping disciples, slumbering and seemingly unaware (in every respect) of what was unfolding before them, that they be spared the test and the trial that was with increasing unavoidability pacing towards him at that very hour. Here again is something important for us to note. The disciples are asleep. Not even awake or watching. What is Jesus to do . . . Let them get their rest? Rouse them? First one, then the others? Upbraid them with words of urgency for what is about to unfold? We can read any of these responses in the scriptures. He voices his concern for them. And he returns to his

---

[19]   Hebrews 5:7–8.

[20]   Matthew 26:37.

[21]   Acts 21:5, Ephesians 3:14 (with the forehead to the ground).

[22]   Mark 11:15, Luke 18:11,13.

[23]   1 Timothy 2:8.

praying—three times as given in Matthew, twice in Mark, though not in Luke.

Here is a direct missionary motif for us. What do we do when Christians, particularly, are asleep on the job? Fail to watch for the coming of the Lord to them personally and uniquely? What range of options is available to us? Yes, to tell them to pray. Yes, to wake them up when they doze off, metaphorically speaking. Yes, to speak to them as they sleep. And yes, to pray for them as they sleep on. All of this is what Jesus did in Gethsemane. And the link between prayer and action is as equally available to us as we face down those who would seek our demise if not our downfall.

But there is also a sense of criticism here that cannot be easily avoided. Let me explain. The "sleep" *(hypnos)* that has overcome the disciples in the Gethsemane narratives has a definite negative connotation in that it signifies a failure to watch out either for danger on the one hand, or for opportunity on the other. Elsewhere in the New Testament *hypnos* and its cognates do mean simply "sleep". However, the negative consequences of failing Christ in our modern-day Gethsemane, of failing to recognize mortal threat and danger ahead, is a powerful analogy, metaphor and application of the biblical metaphor of his anguish in the Garden of Gethsemane; that is, "of going to sleep on the job". The point of this negative connotation is that we as disciples, *now,* have to answer the question "Can you not watch with me one hour?" The condemnation is that if we thus fail this then what else will we mess up?

Simply and devotionally waiting for and with Christ is the touchstone of all else, I propose. If one cannot do that then what use is one going to be in any number of Alpha course sessions? How can one be an activist if one cannot even spend a comparatively short space of time in quiet reflection in obedience to the will of God along the trajectory of obedience initially implored of the first disciples, and now of us?

Looking ahead

Textually, Mark's Gospel offers a wonderful continuum when the disciples are told to "stay awake" in Gethsemane.[24] This is a direct reprise of Jesus' teaching in the final parable cited by Mark in his Gospel, which comes at the end of Chapter 13: "Therefore, keep awake—for you do not know when the master of the house will come, in the evening, or at midnight, or at cockcrow, or at dawn, or else he may find you asleep when he comes suddenly. And what I say to you I say to all: Keep awake."[25]

To do the will of God is all-embracing. It is not restricted to what we might do on this day, or on that day. Nor is it restricted to bringing people to salvation, though of course it does mean that. It refers to the whole of life, in fact to the total orientation of life towards God and his creation both now and beyond. Devotional watching, waiting and staying with Christ has as its onward outflow, getting up and going. The two are inseparable. Devotional prayer, what many call the practice of contemplation, namely waiting on and with Christ, is amongst those requirements placed upon us in response to his presence as God's Word in person. Activism without devotional waiting and watching fails to recognize what is fundamental for persons called by God to nurture and tend the garden which God has provided for us.

Questions for discussion

1. Do you think theology is arrogant in its assertion that we are made in the image and likeness of God? If so, in what ways?
2. How important to you is the outside world in understanding God's creation? If you had to choose between these two, which means more to you: (a) a wonderful view; or (b) contact with other persons?
3. In what ways can we develop a simple rhythm of prayer that helps us understand our place in God's creation?

---

24   Mark 14:34.
25   Mark 13:35–37.

Further reading

George Mackay Brown, *Magnus* (Edinburgh: Polygon, 2008).

Vernon White, *Atonement and Incarnation* (Cambridge: Cambridge University Press, 1991).

Rowan Williams, *Being Human: Bodies, Minds, Persons* (London: SPCK, 2018).

Participation in God: Ecumenical insights into theological anthropology from Eastern Orthodoxy

John McLuckie

For some Anglican thinkers, the question of what it means to be a human being has been shaped by what might seem to be an unlikely source. A number of historical circumstances conspired to bring theologians of the English-speaking world into contact with some of Eastern Orthodoxy's most creative thinkers of the twentieth century. In particular, the emigration of a significant community of Russian intellectuals to Paris in the early decades of the century created a milieu in which such remarkable figures as Sergius Bulgakov, Vladimir Lossky, Paul Evdokimov, Georges Florovsky, Elisabeth Behr-Sigel, Alexander Schmemann and Mother Maria Skobtsova could bring Orthodox insights into dialogue with Western intellectual traditions. Many of these voices found a ready audience across the Channel, not least through the conferences and publications of the Fellowship of St Alban and St Sergius, an ecumenical grouping founded in 1928 to deepen understanding between Christians of East and West, with the Western tradition most significantly represented by Anglicans. Behind the scenes in the Fellowship, from the 1940s onwards, a scholarly and deeply pastoral "Monk of the Eastern Church",[1] Fr Lev Gillet, ensured through his role as chaplain to the Fellowship that its life was deeply rooted in prayer, spiritual counsel, scriptural reflection

---

[1] This was the pseudonym under which Gillet wrote many of his works of spirituality and theology.

and the liturgical life of the Church. This quiet role underlined a vital dimension of Orthodox theology, which is that it never exists separately from the life of prayer, is never a purely academic exercise and is always connected intimately with growth in the life of faith.

This engagement of Orthodox theologians with the English-speaking theological world was further energized later in the twentieth century by new generations of Orthodox, including converts from Anglican and Roman Catholic traditions like Kallistos Ware and John McGuckin, voices from European Orthodoxy like Dumitru Staniloae and John Zizioulas, and theologians working in North America such as John Behr. It was not, of course, a new phenomenon for churches with roots in the reformations of the sixteenth century to look east for insights into Christian life and faith that offered something different from the scholasticism of late medieval Catholicism, as the history of the Scottish Episcopal Church shows from time to time,[2] but it was the burgeoning ecumenical movement of the twentieth century that brought real engagement between the traditions. Between Anglicans and Orthodox, the international dialogue which began in 1973 has resulted in statements on such issues as ecclesiology, or the nature of the Church[3] and, most recently, ecology.[4] For our present consideration, however, it is the distinctive contribution of this dialogue in the area of theological anthropology that concerns us here. I do not intend to present an exhaustive account of theological anthropology in Eastern Orthodoxy, but will simply indicate some areas in which Orthodox thinking has offered distinctive insights to Anglicans and other Western Christians in the English-speaking world.

---

[2] See, for example, the work of Bishop Thomas Rattray (1684–1743) in seeking a model for the Eucharistic Liturgy in the Liturgy of St James.

[3] <https://www.anglicancommunion.org/media/103818/The-Church-of-the-Triune-God.pdf>, accessed 28 January 2021.

[4] <https://anglicancommunion.org/media/421995/icaotd_stewards-of-creation-hope-filled-ecology_nov2020.pdf>, accessed 28 January 2021.

The Buffalo Statement

The Buffalo Statement of 2015, *In the Image and Likeness of God: A Hope-Filled Anthropology*, is remarkable for showing an extraordinary level of agreement in an area which, in the dialogue's first statement of 1976, was previously seen as a point of division, or at least of a significant diversity of views.[5] That area is the key Orthodox doctrine of *theosis*, or divinization, which finds its most succinct formulation in the patristic maxim: "God was incarnate that we might be made god."[6] In 1976, the Moscow Agreed Statement noted that:

> To describe the fullness of man's sanctification and the way in which he shares in the life of God, the Orthodox Church uses the Patristic term *theosis kata charin* (divinization by grace). Once again such language is not normally used by Anglicans, some of whom regard it as misleading and dangerous. At the same time Anglicans recognize that, when Orthodox speak in this manner, they do so only with the most careful safeguards. Anglicans do not reject the underlying doctrine which this language seeks to express; indeed, such teaching is to be found in their own liturgies and hymnody.[7]

By contrast, the Buffalo Statement is happy to state, without caveat, that "God has become human not only that we may share in the divine life,

---

5   <https://anglicancommunion.org/media/208538/in-the-image-and-likeness-of-god-a-hope-filled-anthropology-2015.pdf>, accessed 29 January 2021. Also published by the Anglican Communion Office (2015). The Buffalo Statement is the fourth such document endorsed by the International Commission for Anglican-Orthodox Theological Dialogue (ICAOTD), which began its work in Oxford in 1973. Subsequent meetings were held in Moscow and Dublin.

6   Athanasius, *On the Incarnation*; tr. John Behr (New York, NY: SVS Press, 2011), p. 54.

7   Moscow Agreed Statement p. 3 <https://www.anglicancommunion.org/media/103815/the_moscow_statement.pdf>, accessed 29 January 2021.

but also that we may become fully human".[8] It is this dual movement "becoming" of the human person that we shall explore first in the context of the Buffalo Statement and then in the wider engagement of Anglicans with contemporary Orthodox thought. As we do so, we note the subtly different wording of our key question of what it means to be human. In this chapter, we explore more specifically the question of what it means to *become* human.

The Buffalo Statement offers a primarily positive view of the human person, though one that is also realistic about human frailty. For Anglicans who have inherited a view of human nature formed by the 39 Articles of Religion in the Book of Common Prayer, the human person is by nature inclined towards evil (Article 9) and has no natural capacity to turn towards God (Article 10). Buffalo, by contrast, offers a view of humanity in which "the divine image and likeness in the human person have been obscured through the Fall, but not obliterated".[9] It is worth listing in full the positive capacities of the human person outlined in the statement:

- God-awareness, prayer, worship, and adoration of the divine mystery;
- self-awareness, rationality, conscience, a sense of right and wrong; self-transcendence (*'ekstasis*), the ability to reach out beyond ourselves to God and others in love;
- self-sacrifice as voluntary self-giving and self-emptying (*kenosis*) for the sake of the other;
- freedom and responsiveness, self-restraint and growth;
- self-expression as creativity and inspired imagination;
- responsibility for creation.[10]

These capacities and characteristics are, in the anthropology of the agreed statement, a starting point for the human person who still bears the *image* of God. Through a "free cooperation with grace" the human person then

---

8   Buffalo Statement, p. 2.

9   Buffalo Statement, p. 14.

10   Ibid.

attains ever more fully the *likeness* of God, and it is this process of growth that is *theosis*, a transformation "from one degree of glory to another" (2 Corinthians 3:18). This growth is attained "through repentance and prayer, through the sacramental life, and through the life of service in obedience to the commandments of Christ".[11] It is this emphasis on growth and transformation that lies at the heart of a notion of the human person that is dynamically described as a matter of becoming as much as of being. This growth happens when we freely and joyfully embrace a Christlike life of selflessness, humility and love for God.[12] We shall return to this dynamic later.

The Buffalo Statement offers many other perspectives on the nature of the human person and one that stands out most significantly in the light of the most recent Anglican-Orthodox statement on ecology is the place of the human person in relation to the wider creation. Here, Buffalo describes the priestly character of that relationship in which "we offer the creation back to the Creator in joyful thanksgiving".[13] This dimension of the human role vis-à-vis the created world is preferred to notions of "stewardship", and where that term is used, it is used only to emphasize the truth that creation does not belong to humanity and that our responsibility towards creation is to render *service* for its healing and restoration. And if our relationship towards the rest of creation is indeed to be an interdependent relationship, it must be one drawn towards a "thou" rather than an "it". "Imbued with God's dynamic presence", creation is understood as "logical, dynamically structured, open, meaningful and alive".[14]

Buffalo also uses the language of "co-worker" in relation to human creativity as it participates in divine creativity, and it speaks very positively of our reasoning capacities (including spiritual understanding[15]) which

---

11 Buffalo Statement, p. 12.

12 Buffalo Statement, p. 22.

13 Buffalo Statement, p. 16, See also Adam, Chapter 10.

14 Buffalo Statement, p. 18.

15 Orthodox thinking traditionally describes the *nous* as a higher form of reasoning, spiritual understanding which refers to "the capacity of an intelligent creature for the transcendent encounter with God, in prayer". It

are exercised through science, the arts and technology and directed towards the wellbeing of all creation. Human artistry has the potential to lead us, through beauty, to a "deeper life of praise and wonder before the Creator".[16]

Another area where Buffalo offers some positive insights is in the vexed question of how human freedom relates to divine initiative in the life of faith. The statement affirms the fundamental freedom of the human person as "an essential aspect of the divine image in humankind".[17] This is the freedom to choose between one course of action and another which "is innate to every human being and, while it can be reduced or distorted, it can never be totally destroyed, for it pertains to the *image*".[18] Using again this distinction between image and likeness, Buffalo then goes on to describe another kind of freedom which pertains to the latter, and this is "the freedom to cooperate in obedience with God's love" as a liberation from sin. This is a freedom that may only be attained by the grace of God, and here the statement acknowledges a difference of language in the two traditions, with Orthodoxy preferring to talk of the presence of the Spirit and of the divine energies rather than employing the language of justification by grace through faith which prevails in Western theology.

There are other themes in the Buffalo Statement which I do not intend to elaborate here, such as an emphasis on the fundamentally relational character of the human person, but it is worth noting that it did not address divisive issues relating to gender, sexual identity and sexual relationships to any significant extent.[19] My interest in presenting this brief overview of the document is in highlighting some key areas in which Anglican Christians can draw on insights from Orthodoxy in order to draw out aspects of theological anthropology that might otherwise

---

is related to but distinct from the rational powers of the human being. See John McGuckin, *Standing in God's Holy Fire* (London: Darton, Longman and Todd, 2001), p. 171.

[16]   Buffalo Statement, p. 19. The text does, however, recognize the contingent nature of our creative and reasoning capacities and their potential misuse.

[17]   Buffalo Statement, p. 31.

[18]   Ibid.

[19]   See also, Alison Jasper, Chapter 12.

remain in the background. In summary, the first aspect is *theosis* and transformation, the second is an affirmation of the innate human capacity to reach out towards God, and the third is the priestly calling of humanity in relation to creation.

Theosis

The key Orthodox doctrine of *theosis* is well summarized as the aim of the Christian life in Lev Gillet's book *Orthodox Spirituality*:

> This participation [in the divine nature] takes [human beings] within the life of the three Divine Persons themselves, in the incessant circulation and overflowing of love which courses between the Father, the Son and the Holy Spirit, and which expresses the very nature of God. Here is the true and eternal bliss of [humanity]. Union with God is the perfect fulfilment of the "kingdom" announced by the Gospel, and of the charity or love which sums up all the law and the prophets. Only in union with the life of the Three Persons [are human beings] enabled to love God with [their] whole heart, soul and mind, and [their] neighbours as [themselves].[20]

Having noted a significant movement in Anglican willingness to embrace the language of *theosis* between the Moscow and Buffalo statements, it is worth mentioning one Anglican proponent of this doctrine, A. M. Allchin, whose short work on this theme sought to uncover its presence in Anglican thought. *Participation in God*[21] is subtitled, "A Forgotten

---

[20]   Lev Gillet, *Orthodox Spirituality* (London: Fellowship of St Alban and St Sergius, 1945), p. 22.

[21]   London: Darton, Longman and Todd, 1988. Allchin explores the writings of Richard Hooker and Lancelot Andrewes, as well as Charles Wesley, Williams Pantycelyn and E. B. Pusey. It is also possible to find strong traces of the doctrine of *theosis* in Anglican liturgical texts. In the Scottish Liturgy of 1982: "In Christ your Son, our life and yours are brought together in a wonderful

Strand in Anglican Tradition", and although its content is indeed mostly focused on Anglican thinkers, its impetus clearly comes from Allchin's own sustained engagement with Orthodoxy. He summarizes his understanding of *theosis* in this way:

> To become fully human, to realize our human potential, we need to enter into communion with our Creator. We can become ourselves only by transcending ourselves. He that will find his life must lose it. There is nothing static about this communion. It is the beginning of a process that will lead us through death into life, life in this world and life in the world beyond this one, "an eternal progress into the inexhaustible riches of the divine life".[22]

Allchin does not consider *theosis* to be an abstract theological notion and is clear that it is, for him, an understanding that makes a decisive difference to the way we live our lives in this world. With his friend, the Romanian theologian Dumitru Staniloae, he affirms that nothing contributes so much to our deification as compassion shown to those in need. In reaching out to those in need, we are participating with the divine energies which are active in this world:

> By our action in service of others we make these energies our own, and thus the whole of the human family is bound together by the action of God energizing in the action of man, the suffering of God at work in the suffering of man, the love of God in the love of man.[23]

---

exchange. He made his home among us that we might forever dwell in you." From the Scottish Book of Common Prayer, 1929: "that we, receiving the benefits of his passion, and being quickened by his resurrection, might be made partakers of the divine nature" (preface for Maundy Thursday).

[22] Ibid., p. 6. The quotation at the end of the paragraph is from John Meyendorff, *Byzantine Theology* (New York, NY: Fordham University Press, 1974), pp. 225–6.

[23] Ibid., p. 72.

Allchin insists that, as well as drawing us closer to God, this active participation in God's work in the midst of creation also draws human beings closer to one another: "the whole history of the human race is, in a hidden way, recapitulated in the life of each one of us".[24] There is a circular dynamic at work here, which reflects the joy-filled flow of love between the persons of the Holy Trinity. Healed and transformed as we are drawn into the life of God, we, in turn, extend that healing work to those around us. Seeking the wellbeing of those around us, we find ourselves drawn more fully into the life of God.

The dynamic character of *theosis* is explored in a more recent work on theological anthropology from an Orthodox perspective. John Behr's *Becoming Human* builds on and distils his earlier work on Irenaeus and Clement, offering a meditative reflection on the theme.[25] Noting how the language of Genesis 1 differs when it comes to the creation of human beings, Behr suggests that the "let us make" in the place of "let there be" indicates an incompleteness in the creation of the human being. One only becomes a human person through a process of growth, transformation and dying to self, only by supplying for oneself the "fiat" that was absent at our creation. Our growing into humanity is accomplished fully only through the second Adam, who is revealed to be the fully human being at his Passion. The words on Pilate's lips—"behold the *anthropos*" (John 19:5)—are confirmed at Jesus' final words from the cross; "it is accomplished" (John 19:30). What is accomplished is the creation of the true human being, and it is achieved through the voluntary self-giving of the incarnate Word. Likewise, argues Behr, Christians who are baptized into the death of Christ also "use" their death to instruct them in the way to live as a fully human being: "In and through Christ, we now have the possibility of freely using the givenness of our mortality to be reborn, by choice, so coming to be in a life without end."[26] The character of this life is that we "no longer live for [ourselves] in an ego-centric mode of

---

[24]   Ibid., p. 76.

[25]   New York, NY: St Vladimir's Seminary Press, 2013, see also *Asceticism and Anthropology in Irenaeus and Clement* (Oxford: Oxford University Press, 2000).

[26]   Behr, *Becoming Human*, p. 53.

life, but rather live ecstatically, beyond [ourselves], for [our] neighbours and for God".[27] Once again, we see an approach to *theosis* that can never be individualistic, that always entails a deepening of our communion with others just as our communion with God is deepened. As Stavros Yangazoglou puts it, we are immortal when we are "open to communion with others and with the eminent Other".[28]

Perhaps one of the most attractive aspects of the doctrine of *theosis* in a contemporary context which values experiential knowledge is that it affirms the possibility of a genuine, deep, transformative and direct experience of God in this life.

Human capacity for God

We noted the Buffalo Statement's positive view of the capacities that are innate within human persons to reach beyond themselves towards God and others, a stance which seems considerably more optimistic than the language of the Thirty-nine Articles of Religion, which were shaped by a view of the completeness of humanity's fall from God. Orthodox approaches to ascetical effort should be seen in the light of this more positive evaluation of our innate capabilities. It is variously seen as a kind of "training" in the spiritual life and as a therapeutic exercise in which we are freed from the grip of harmful compulsions. One of the key ways in which this ascetical effort is practised in Orthodoxy is through fasting, a practice which has largely fallen from use in Western Christianity. Perhaps, rescued from any kind of notion of "taming evil flesh", fasting might be recovered by Western Christians as a fruit of the ecumenical encounter with Orthodoxy in this area of anthropology. Fasting also offers a particular view of the human relationship with the created order which restrains excessive consumption, expresses a reverence for all life and acts as a preparation for feasting which may then be embraced

---

27   Ibid., p. 56.

28   "Current Understandings of Human Being and Orthodox Anthropology", in Pantelis Kalaitzidis et al. (eds), *The Orthodox Handbook on Ecumenism* (Oxford: Regnum Books, 2013), p. 707.

more freely as an expression of joy in created goodness. In his influential overview of Orthodox theology, history and practice, John McGuckin describes fasting as an "ascesis[29] of love" which is "a peaceful way of cleansing the mind as well as the body" and "makes the person more alert, energized and peaceful".[30]

Although it has benefits in and of itself, fasting, in Orthodox practice, is usually seen as an act of preparation for a feast—either the reception of Holy Communion or the celebration of a major feast like Pascha, the Nativity or the Dormition. As such, Schmemann described it as something "to help us recover the vision and taste of *new life*"[31]—a refining of our spiritual as well as physical taste buds so that they are better able to savour the joy of a life that has been, and is being, healed and restored in Christ. John Chryssavgis picks up this theme in his work on ecological theology, *Creation as Sacrament*, where he describes ascesis, including fasting, as "refinement and restoration" rather than "detachment and destruction":

> We are called to relearn how to notice and feel, how to hear and smell, as well as how to taste and touch. In order to perceive this world in the light of the next, we need to acquire new sense, spiritual senses, becoming entirely new people.[32]

Chryssavgis goes on to discuss the role of such ascetical practice in the overcoming of the greed that lies at the heart of overconsumption and poses such a threat to the wellbeing of the planet itself. In that light, we turn now to a third insight from Orthodoxy's approach to theological anthropology—the priestly calling of the human person in relation to the creation.

---

[29] "Ascesis" is the practice of self-discipline.

[30] John Anthony McGuckin, *The Orthodox Church* (Chichester: Wiley-Blackwell, 2011), p. 354.

[31] Alexander Schmemann, *Great Lent* (New York, NY: SVS Press, 1990), p. 13, emphasis in the original.

[32] John Chryssavgis, *Creation as Sacrament* (London: T&T Clark, 2019), p. 124.

Priests of creation

We have noted Buffalo's use of priestly language to describe the human role vis-à-vis the rest of creation. It is also used by Chryssavgis in his important work on ecological spirituality. As advisor to the Ecumenical Patriarch on environmental concerns, his insights are of particular weight and relevance. Buffalo spoke of the human priestly vocation of "offering" creation back to God and of a sacramental encounter with God through a renewed relationship with creation. Chryssavgis echoes this language but also speaks of the Paschal mystery at the heart of creation's restoration, noting how the whole creation is transformed through the self-offering of Christ on the cross.[33] The priestly role of the human person with respect to creation is intimately bound up with the Paschal mystery, not only as a model for the kind of self-denying ascesis we mentioned above, but also in relation to creation's present and ultimate restoration and healing. Like Buffalo, Chryssavgis also sees the priestly role of the human being as the best way to interpret the ambivalent language of stewardship; we are careful and humble custodians of something sacred, those who lovingly tend a living shrine to a loving God. Finally, Chryssavgis invokes the language of "icon" to describe creation as "a visible and tangible revelation (apocalypse) of the presence (*parousia*) of the Word of God".[34] Human beings, then, in their priestly calling, venerate the icon of creation as a window on the divine.

Conclusion

The Buffalo Statement of 2015 succinctly offers theological insights on the nature of the human person which have not been in the foreground of Western theological discourse. We have briefly explored three of these insights: the fundamental calling of the human person to *theosis*,

---

[33] He cites, for example, a liturgical text for the Feast of the Exaltation of the Cross which proclaims that "every tree of the forest can rejoice, for their nature has been sanctified by Christ, who planted them at the beginning and now hangs stretched out on the tree". Ibid., p. 123.

[34] Ibid., p. 199.

participation in the life of the Holy Trinity; a positive assessment of the innate capacities of the human person which resets our relationship with the created world, including our own bodies; and a sense of the high calling of the human race to be priests of creation, lovingly tending that which God created good, and offering it back to God in a sacrifice of praise.

Questions for discussion

1. How do you respond to the language of divinization? Does it challenge language of God as "wholly other"?
2. How can Christian theology offer a balanced view of the human person that recognizes brokenness while affirming innate goodness?
3. How important is it to recover a sense of humanity's priestly role towards the creation?

Further reading

In the Image and Likeness of God: A Hope-Filled Anthropology—*The Buffalo Statement* (London: Anglican Consultative Council, 2015), at <https://anglicancommunion.org/media/208538/in-the-image-and-likeness-of-god-a-hope-filled-anthropology-2015.pdf>, accessed 29 January 2021.

A. M. Allchin, *Participation in God* (London: Darton, Longman and Todd, 1988).

John Behr, *Being Human* (New York, NY: St Vladimir's Seminary Press, 2013).

John Chryssavgis, *Creation as Sacrament* (London: T & T Clark, London, 2019).

CHAPTER 6

Compassion, human and divine

Harriet Harris

This chapter seeks to show the following: that we have the biological constituents required to cultivate compassion, and, if willing to receive it, the theological grace to ignite and sustain that cultivation; that compassion is healing, and holds in harmony rather than in tension the love for ourselves, others and our world; that compassion is significantly different from empathy, and that we are more able to practise and sustain compassion when we are not overwhelmed by empathy; and that herein lies a way of understanding why Christian tradition for so long upheld a view that the God of compassion does not suffer.

Compassion and human nature

The study of compassion has been developing since the 1980s, across the life sciences and social sciences.[1] A key question has been whether compassion, and related conditions of sympathy and empathy, are part of the evolutionary process, enabling the level of care-giving necessary to nurture complex life forms, and the levels of cooperation necessary to their survival.[2] A contrary view is that compassionate tendencies are

---

[1] See also Reid, Chapter 9.

[2] See Jennifer L. Goetz, Dacher Keltner, and Emiliana Simon-Thomas, "Compassion: An Evolutionary Analysis and Empirical Review", *Psychological Bulletin* 136:3 (2010), pp. 351–74; Paul Gilbert, "The Evolution and Social Dynamics of Compassion", *Social and Personality Psychology Compass*

not conducive to the survival of the fittest. Research is leaning more in the direction to which Darwin himself leant: that sympathy is conducive to flourishing.

> In however complex a manner this feeling may have originated, as it is one of high importance to all those animals which aid and defend one another, it will have been increased through natural selection; for those communities, which included the greatest number of the most sympathetic members, would flourish best, and rear the greatest number of offspring.[3]

It had long been debated by philosophers how "sympathy" played out in human nature and society, and whether human nature is fundamentally self-serving. In the centuries preceding Darwin, Machiavelli and Hobbes, La Rouchefoucauld and Mandeville saw self-interest as the organizing principle of human behaviour. By contrast, Bishop Butler, Rousseau and Hume (the last two taking the most empirical approach) noted qualities of human sympathy towards others, Hume writing that even to "the most careless observer there appear to be such dispositions as benevolence and generosity; such affections as love, friendship, compassion, gratitude . . . plainly distinguished from those of the selfish passions".[4]

With the development of the biological sciences, empirical sense could be made of the capacities animals develop for raising their young, and defending members of their group.[5] It is not that the biological sciences instruct us to value compassion, or any other quality, but rather that they

---

(2015), pp. 1–16, 10.1111/spc3.12176; P. A. Spikins, H. E. Rutherford, and A. P. Needham, "From Hominity to Humanity: Compassion from the earliest archaic to modern humans", *Time and Mind* 3:3 (2010).

3   Charles Darwin, *The Descent of Man, and Selection in Relation to Sex* [1871], eds J. Moore and A. Desmond (New York, NY: Penguin, 2004), p. 130.

4   David Hume, *An Enquiry Concerning the Principles of Morals*, Appendix p. 2. For wider historical discussion see C. Daniel Batson (ed.), *The Altruism Question* (Abingdon: Taylor and Francis, 1991).

5   Paul Gilbert and Choden, *Mindful Compassion* (London: Robinson, 2013), pp. 103–13, and see footnote 1.

can indicate where there is directional change towards compassion (or other qualities that we wish to understand). We can with some confidence say that evolution provides the requisite elements for compassion. We might even say that evolution leads us to compassion, but we cannot say that it does so inevitably. We have great capacity for compassion and also for its opposites: indifference, and zero-sum competitiveness. If we wish to be compassionate persons, we need to develop our compassionate capacity through practice.

Compassion research not only looks for the evolutionary factors requisite for compassion, but tests the notion that we are most healthy as human beings, socially, physically, mentally, when we live compassionately.[6] This research is multi-disciplinary, holding that the practice of compassion leads to a healthy mind;[7] that compassion in healthcare improves patient recovery rates and outcomes, and reduces lawsuits;[8] that compassion in organizations increases effectiveness and decreases sickness and sick leave;[9] that compassion in communities heals loneliness.[10]

---

[6] Emma M. Seppälä, Emiliana Simon-Thomas, Stephanie L. Brown, Monica C. Worline, C. Daryl Cameron, and James R. Doty, *The Oxford Handbook of Compassion Science* (Oxford: Oxford University Press, 2017).

[7] <https://greatergood.berkeley.edu/video/item/teach_compassion_dan_siegel>, accessed 29 January 2021.

[8] Stephen Trzekiak and Anthony Mazzarelli, *Compassionomics: The Revolutionary Scientific Evidence that Caring Makes a Difference* (Pensacola, FL: The Studer Group, 2019); John Ballatt, Penelope Campling, Chris Maloney, *Intelligent Kindness: Rehabilitating the Welfare State* (Cambridge: Cambridge University Press, 2011, 2020); Margaret Hannah, *Humanising Healthcare: Patterns of Hope for a System under Strain* (Bridport: Triarchy Press, 2014).

[9] Monica C. Worline and Jane E. Dutton, *Awakening Compassion at Work: The Quiet Power that Elevates People and Organisations* (Oakland, CA, Berrett-Koehler Publishers, 2017).

[10] Julian Abel and Lindsay Clarke, *The Compassion Project: A Case for Hope and Human Kindness from a Town that Beat Loneliness* (London: Aster 2020).

There is something of a compassion industry related to our pursuit of happiness—promoting compassion on the grounds that it makes us happy,[11] and potentially thereby undermining the value of compassion as an intrinsic good. Yet, to make empirical claims that can be tested need not be inconsistent with a view that compassion is a good in its own right regardless of measures as to its effects.

Nor need we succumb to egoistic vs altruistic, individual vs collective, individualist vs communitarian binaries. We can adopt what Rowan Williams terms a personalist approach, where we see ourselves not as atomistic individuals, wholly free to set our own agenda and to be out of cooperation with others, but rather as persons who are spoken to, attended to and loved into being.[12]

Compassion as an answer to the question "How are we to live?"

It was perhaps a by-product of the Renaissance, when the study of human nature took centre stage, that the ambiguity between self-interest and sympathy for others came to seem oppositional. The question arose: are human beings primarily self-interested or altruistic by nature? This issue need not arise when the leading question is: how are we to live a good life? (as the Greeks asked) or, how are we to live according to God's will? (as was asked in the Abrahamic religions).

Plato and Aristotle explored friendship as the area where self-interest and care for another might come together, though both seemed to come

---

[11]   See, for example, Emma Seppälä, *The Happiness Track: How to Apply the Science of Happiness to Accelerate your Success* (San Francisco, CA: HarperOne, 2016), whose final chapter is on "why compassion serves you better than self-interest", pp. 141–64. Cf NHS "5 steps to mental wellbeing", which include connecting with and doing things for others <https://www.nhs.uk/conditions/stress-anxiety-depression/improve-mental-wellbeing/>, accessed 29 January 2021.

[12]   Rowan Williams, *Being Human: Bodies, Minds, Persons* (London: SPCK, 2018), pp. 41–5.

down on the side of our friendships being ultimately for the sake of our own selves. Aquinas, in his work of bringing together Christian and Aristotelian thought, seemed untroubled about the mixed motives of a person grieving for a "friend's hurt as though he were hurt himself", and grieving because realizing that "the same may happen to themselves".[13] Both are ways in which God arranges that mercy, pity, charity are enacted.

Harmony of love for God, self and other

This absence of strain between self-love and love of others is important for achieving a wholeness in the living out of compassion. Compassion needs to be directed towards oneself as well as others, especially if we are to be able to sustain the qualities required for extending compassion to others over time, and in hardship. The teaching of self-compassion is gaining significance particularly within the caring professions, though it is often met with resistance due to the feeling that self-compassion must be selfish. Hopefully, the discussion below of Paul Gilbert's Compassion Focused Therapy will help put such qualms to rest.

The Judaeo-Christian teaching to love God with all our heart, soul, strength and mind and to love our neighbours as ourselves conveys a harmony between these three loves, and perhaps an order to them too. Aquinas thought so, arguing that we ought to love God more than ourselves, and love ourselves more than our neighbour.[14] Quoting the commandment, he argued: "It seems to follow that man's love for himself is the model of his love for another. But the model exceeds the copy. Therefore, out of charity, a man ought to love himself more than his neighbour."[15]

C. S. Lewis gives voice to this same ordering of love:

> To love you as I should, I must worship God as Creator. When
> I have learnt to love God better than my earthly dearest, I shall

---

[13] *Summa Theologica* (*ST*) II-II, 30, 2.

[14] *ST* II-II, 26, 3–4.

[15] *ST* 11–11, 26, 4.

> love my earthly dearest better than I do now. In so far as I learn
> to love my earthly dearest at the expense of God and instead of
> God, I shall be moving towards the state in which I shall not love
> my earthly dearest at all. When first things are put first, second
> things are not suppressed but increased.[16]

Jesus taught that we are to love not only our neighbours, but strangers too, and enemies (Luke 6:35). Aquinas, using the term *caritas* (charity) for love, explains that our love for our enemies comes from our prior love for God: "Charity is the friendship of man for God . . . The friendship of charity extends even to our enemies, whom we love out of charity in relation to God, to Whom the friendship of charity is chiefly directed".[17]

In theological terms, the seeds of compassion are the love with which God first loved us (1 John 4:19), and the love that we give back to God, and to ourselves and one another for the love of God.

Compassion in scripture[18]

The model of this love is the God of compassion and mercy (several Hebrew and Greek words are translated into English variously as compassion, mercy, pity and gentleness). In the Hebrew Bible, compassion is a divine quality, though one which human beings are increasingly instructed to emulate: to do justice, love mercy, and walk humbly with your God (Micah 6:8). The God of the Hebrew Bible is conveyed with much pathos, having faithful love (*hesed*) and compassion for Israel (see Exodus 34:6–7; Isaiah 63:7–9), delivering them many times, grieving over their sins, leading them "with cords of human kindness, with bands of love" (Hosea 11:1–4), becoming wrathful and repenting of his anger: "my heart recoils within me; my compassion grows warm and tender. I will not execute my fierce anger; I will not again destroy Ephraim; for I am

---

[16] *Letters of C. S. Lewis*, ed. W. H. Lewis and Walter Hooper (London: HarperCollins, 1988), p. 498.

[17] *ST* 11–11, 23, 1.

[18] See also Taylor, Chapter 1.

God and not mortal; the Holy One in your midst and I will not come in wrath" (Hosea 11:8–9; cf. Exodus 32:11–14; 1 Samuel 15:11).

By New Testament times, compassion is a characteristic or teaching that distinguishes Jews and Christians in the Graeco-Roman world.[19] Compassion is seen to motivate Jesus in his healing miracles and his feeding of the masses. Jesus is said to be "moved" by the suffering, hunger, or plight of those in his midst. Nicholas Taylor writes: *splagchnizomai* connotes an involuntary movement of the internal organs, *splagchma*, provoking a physical and emotional reaction of compassion to the circumstances confronted by Jesus, to which his acts and words of healing are the response; Matthew 9:36; 14:14; 15:32; 18:27; 20:34; Mark 1:41; 6:34; 8:2; 9:22; Luke 7:13; 10:33; 15:20. The Evangelists vary in which miracles they attribute to this reaction.[20]

The Authorized Version of the Bible refers to the "bowels" in order to convey the deep movements of pathos within, as the following examples show: "Then spake the woman whose the living child was unto the king, for her bowels yearned upon her son" (1 Kings 3:26, KJV); "Is Ephraim my dear son? . . . for since I spake against him, I do earnestly remember him still: therefore my bowels are troubled for him; I will surely have mercy upon him, saith the LORD" (Jeremiah 31:20); "Mine eyes do fail with tears, my bowels are troubled, my liver is poured upon the earth, for the destruction of the daughter of my people; because the children and the sucklings swoon in the streets of the city" (Lamentations 2:11); "Put on therefore, as the elect of God, holy and beloved, bowels of mercies, kindness, humbleness of mind, meekness, longsuffering" (Colossians 3:12); "But whoso hath this world's good, and seeth his brother have need, and shutteth up his bowels of compassion from him, how dwelleth the love of God in him?" (1 John 3:17).[21]

---

[19] Cf. Bruce W. Longenecker, *Remember the Poor: Paul, Poverty, and the Greco-Roman World* (Grand Rapids, MI: Eerdmans, 2010), pp. 19–131.

[20] For this and several points in the discussion of compassion and scripture I am grateful for Nicholas Taylor's "Compassion in Scripture", a paper written for the Doctrine Committee of the Scottish Episcopal Church, 2017.

[21] For discussion of links between organs and emotions in scripture, see Cardinal Ravasi, "Towards a Biblical Theory of Emotions", in D. Evers, M.

If we see others in need, and close up our "bowels of compassion" against them, the love of God does not dwell in us.

Defining compassion, sympathy and empathy

From the biblical tradition we get a strong, visceral sense of what it is to be moved by compassion. It is important that a definition of compassion include this quality of being moved deep within the body, for it is perhaps this deep sensation that most effectively provokes us to respond to suffering.

Compassion is defined variously by compassion researchers, usually as containing three elements:

1. noticing suffering (in others, in oneself, in the world and environment);
2. being attuned to or moved by the suffering;
3. responding to relieve the suffering.

The quality of being moved is pivotal and is sometimes conveyed by the terms "sympathy" and "empathy".

David Hume spoke of "sympathy" to convey the sharing of the feelings of others. Hume's friend Adam Smith believed that pity or compassion are based on sympathy, which, following Hume, he defined as "our fellow-feeling with any passion whatever".[22] Today, the term "sympathy" is sometimes regarded unfavourably as implying a patronizing disposition or aloofness, in contrast to "empathy" whereby we take in the feelings of the other and get alongside them.[23]

The word "empathy" came into English usage at the turn of the twentieth century. Ironically, the author Vernon Lee used "empathy" so

---

Fuller, A. Runehov and K.-W. Saether (eds), *Do Emotions Shape the World?* (London: Springer, 2016), pp. 159–76.

[22] Adam Smith, *The Theory of Moral Sentiments*, I. i. 1. 5.

[23] As in this video by Brenee Brown <https://www.thersa.org/video/shorts/2013/12/brene-brown-on-empathy>, accessed 29 January 2021.

as to better explain "sympathy": that sympathy is exercised only when our feelings enter, and are absorbed into, the form we perceive.[24] "Empathy" literally means "in pathos", "in passion" or "in suffering". It is often used to mean taking in the feelings of another and might thereby be thought to be almost the same as "compassion", which literally means "to suffer with".

Compassion is not empathy

However, distinctions between "empathy" and "compassion" are important to uphold philosophically and in the teaching of compassion science and practice for at least four reasons.

First, empathy is an amoral concept. It denotes feeling, but not a moral direction of response to the feelings aroused. Effective torturers are likely to be empathetic, in the sense of being well attuned to the feelings they can raise and manipulate in their victims.[25] This is how they know which emotional buttons to press. We would not, however, regard them as compassionate.

Second, empathy can cause us to be biased, if we are swept up in the feelings of a particular situation, person or group.[26]

Third, empathy denotes feeling but not action or response, whereas responding to suffering is an integral part of compassion.

Fourth, we may be overwhelmed by the feelings that empathy induces in us and begin to feel the same helplessness as those with whom we empathize: we have climbed into the pit with them, and none of us are able to emerge.

This fourth concern is one to which we will return: the danger of being overwhelmed by the suffering of others, and therefore of withdrawing from them.

---

[24] Lauren Wispé, "History of the Concept of Empathy", in Nancy Eisenberg (ed.), *Empathy and Its Development: Cambridge Studies in Social and Emotional Development* (Cambridge: Cambridge University Press, 1990), p. 17.

[25] Paul Bloom, *Against Empathy: The Case for Rational Compassion* (New York, NY: Ecco, 2016).

[26] Bloom, *Against Empathy*.

Compassion in healing ourselves and our world

For insights into how compassion ministers healing or wholeness, we might look at the work of clinical psychologist Paul Gilbert, founder of the Compassionate Mind Foundation.[27] Gilbert, like Rowan Williams and like the sociologist Richard Sennett,[28] is seeking and proposing remedies to the uncooperative, competitive, angst-making individualism that pervades Western culture.

Gilbert developed Compassion Focused Therapy out of his practice as a cognitive behavioural therapist. He observed that for some patients, addressing their beliefs was not adequate therapy without also addressing the emotions by which they were processing the supposedly more positive beliefs that a therapist might encourage them to adopt. If they were carrying an underlying sense of shame, guilt, failure or punishment, new beliefs may not be healing for them. Gilbert speaks of this in a conversation recently held at the Compassion Salon, where he describes how he tried to convince a lady suffering from a deep sense of unworthiness that she was loved by a wonderful husband and children. When he asked her how she heard those words, she heard them as shouting and criticism: "Don't you know that you are loved by a wonderful husband and children, what's the matter with you?"[29]

In his therapeutic work, Gilbert brings a compassionate understanding to our self-criticism, anger, shame, fear, depression and anxiety. Most pertinent here, and as able to speak to Williams' and Sennett's critique of competitive individualism, Gilbert has developed a theory of emotional systems.[30] He identifies three different emotion-regulation systems at work in us:

[27]   <https://www.compassionatemind.co.uk/>, accessed 29 January 2021.

[28]   Williams, *Being Human*; Richard Sennett, *Together: The Rituals, Pleasures and Politics of Co-operation* (London: Allen Lane, 2012).

[29]   Paul Gilbert in conversation with Julian Abel, at The Compassion Salon, 22 Oct 2020, <http://www.compassionsalon.co.uk/?page_id=460>, accessed 29 January 2021.

[30]   Paul Gilbert, *The Compassionate Mind* (London: Little, Brown Book Group 2013), pp. 23–30.

1. threat and self-protection system;
2. incentive and resource-seeking system;
3. soothing and contentment system.

The threat and self-protection system functions to enable us to respond quickly to threats so as to protect ourselves. This system triggers what we have come to know as the fight, freeze or flight response. It is a source of painful and uncomfortable feelings, such as fear, anxiety, anger and disgust. We may feel more able to have compassion for these feelings when we realize that they have evolved as part of a protection system and do an important job. If the threat and self-protection system is overworked and not soothed, we can become stuck in a stress-response, with the stress hormone cortisol coursing through us as though we were perpetually under threat.

The incentive and resource-seeking system functions to give us positive feelings that guide, motivate and encourage us to seek the resources needed for our survival and prospering. We experience excitement or pleasure when we achieve, complete, accomplish or win at things. Dopamine is the most significant chemical here. Like the threat system, the incentive system is necessary for survival and flourishing, and like the threat system it can also become over-stimulated as we seek more dopamine hits. We may experience as "threat" whatever seemingly blocks our wants or goals, and then the threat system is activated.

The soothing and contentment system helps to restore our balance and bring us to the state of rest as when "animals aren't defending themselves against threats and problems and don't need to achieve or do anything because they have enough of everything, [and] they can be content".[31] The relevant chemicals here are endorphins and the hormone oxytocin. They give us feelings of wellbeing, calm and safety. Affection and kindness are related to this third system; they have soothing effects upon us, as when a crying infant is soothed, and they stimulate the production of oxytocin.

The three emotion-regulation systems help us to understand how our emotions relate to the evolution of our species. They also help us to see how we become stressed and distressed when our threat and incentive

---

[31] Gilbert, *Compassionate Mind*, p. 26.

systems come out of balance with our soothing system. Gilbert argues that much in modern society overstimulates both the threat and incentive systems: we feel we need to do more, and we feel that we want more, and we may feel a need to achieve at the cost of others, or win such that others lose. Now we are close to describing the sort of uncooperative selves that Sennett describes—looking to control their world, and increasingly indifferent to others, losing a sense of belonging with others and of being responsible for others—and the toxic environment of winners and losers that Michael Sandel captures in *The Tyranny of Merit*.[32]

In the realm of education, which Sandel is partly addressing, the tyranny of merit is very apparent in the rise of perfectionism, imposter syndrome, severe fear of failure, and most tragically, the link between a fear of being at the bottom of the pile and suicidality. These dis-eases are among the most prevalent that compassion-focused therapists are addressing.

The practice of compassion is relevant not only in providing the soothing attentiveness and kindness that are part of the third emotional system, but also in receiving with compassionate understanding the stress and drive emotions that are necessary to systems 1 and 2. Compassionate understanding involves a) noticing the uncomfortable emotions, b) acknowledging rather than ignoring them, c) accepting rather than chastising them—for our emotions have jobs to do related to our survival and flourishing—and then d) responding in ways that relieve the suffering. Compassionate responses may include soothing. They may also include developing a mindful detachment from the emotions and accompanying thoughts, such that we do not become lost in them or define ourselves by them. For example, instead of coming to see ourselves as angry, resentful or guilty, we can see the emotions and thoughts for what they are: entities that come and go. Often we can let them go, let them pass on without getting stuck in them. But also often they invite further understanding and work, and so compassionate responses also

---

[32]   Sennett, *Together*; Michael Sandel, *The Tyranny of Merit: What's Become of the Common Good?* (London: Penguin Random House, 2020).

include the courage to work with the painful emotions, and the courage to address situations that are causing pain.[33]

The sociologist Sennett and the clinical psychologist Gilbert both agree that what has been harmed can be remade. Cooperation in human development admits of repair,[34] and our neural pathways are able to wire and rewire according to new associations that we introduce and embed.[35] Gilbert first aims to show that compassion can help us in our lives; that it can soothe our anger and anxiety and give us courage to face and work skilfully with these difficult emotions. He then aims to train people actively, so as to cultivate compassionate selves:

> In contrast to our compassionate selves that are linked to the soothing/affiliation system, the "selves" that arise from the threat or drive systems will pop up very easily without much effort on our part. There is the angry self that thinks: "Don't mess with me!"; the ambitious self that thinks: "I want to be rich and famous"; and of course the selves from the drive system: "I must get this or that done today; so much to do." Anger and anxiety are easy to activate and we don't . . . think . . . : "I need to practise being angry or having panic attacks!" . . . But . . . we do need to actively train in compassion because although the seeds exist within us they tend to be buried in the mud of the evolved mind, covered over by all the hustle and bustle of life with all its frustration, tragedies and stresses.[36]

It is possible to sign up to courses that teach self-compassion. Kirstin Neff is the pioneer of this work, and she teaches three important steps:

- Kindness to oneself, which includes learning to parent and soothe oneself, and changing how we talk to ourselves (moving away from chastising self-criticism);

---

33 Gilbert, *Compassionate Mind,* pp. 413–17, 444–74.

34 Sennett, *Together,* p. 219 (cited in Williams, *Being Human,* p. 44).

35 Gilbert, *Compassionate Mind,* p. 34.

36 Gilbert and Choden, *Mindful Compassion,* p. 354.

- Recognizing our shared humanity, and therefore that what we suffer is true for all or most other people too—this connects us with other people and their suffering, so that we are not turned in only on ourselves, and helps us not to feel alone;
- Mindfulness: seeing clearly and accepting non-judgmentally what is happening in the present moment.[37]

Tara Brach has developed a form of mindful meditation called the RAIN meditation, which conveys one way in which mindfulness is drawn upon within the teaching of compassion.[38] RAIN stands for:

- **Recognize** suffering, pain, difficult emotions;
- **Allow** (rather than ignore or judge) the suffering, pain, or emotions;
- **Investigate** them with interest and care;
- **Nurture** them with compassion.

Neurologically and socially, we can perhaps begin to see how introducing mindful and compassionate patterns of behaviour change the neural pathways within us, and the relational patterns outwith us, to calm our frightened and driven selves. It is a tenet of compassion-teaching that compassion is a win-win dynamic: the givers and receivers of compassion all benefit, and nobody loses, unlike the zero-sum dynamics played out in the competitive arenas in which we often live and work.

Neff and Brach are both influenced by Buddhist approaches, and teach a humanist-Buddhist-inspired compassion ethic. When we bring theological insights to bear on our understanding of compassion, we are returned to the theological source of compassion: the love of God for us, and the love we return to God and thereby show to ourselves and to others (and to our world).

In the Judaeo-Christian tradition, compassion is understood first and foremost as a divine attribute, the practice of which we are invited, by

---

37   Kirstin Neff, *Self-Compassion* (London: Hodder and Stoughton, 2011), pp. 39–106.

38   Tara Brach, *Radical Compassion: Learning to Love yourself and Your World with the Practice of RAIN* (London: Penguin Random House, 2019).

grace, to share. We receive and live out the love of God. John Swinton describes practices that cultivate compassion, or any other aspect of Christian life, as resulting "from participating in and receiving grace, and as such . . . find[ing] their dynamism not in the human will, but in the vitalizing power of the Holy Spirit".[39] To practise and live out compassion is to participate in the life of God, to be participants in the divine activity that heals us and our world.[40]

Compassion is a quality and practice that brings healing to us and to our world. Is it a part of human nature? Biologically, we have evolved with capacities that can make for compassion, but we need to cultivate it. Theologically, we are created and sustained in love by God, and are commanded to love as God loves us: if willing to receive, we are given the grace to do so. The practice of compassion, understood theologically, is a practice within the love and life of God.

"Compassion fatigue"?

There is one final question I would like to consider, and it is a question that arises from objections to compassion that I encounter, especially within the caring and teaching professions: won't compassion lead me to burn out?[41]

---

[39] John Swinton, *Raging with Compassion: Pastoral Responses to the Problem of Evil* (Grand Rapids, MI: Eerdmans, 2007), p. 82.

[40] Herein lies a theological question for another time, as to whether compassion is purely a gift of grace, such that we are incapable of compassion without the power of the Holy Spirit to vitalize it; whether we have the *capacity* for compassion, but are unable to realize it of ourselves; or whether, as would be a more humanist approach, we possess the capacity and potential for compassion within ourselves *and* the choice to cultivate it can be made regardless of grace.

[41] For other frequent objections to compassion see Marti Balaam and Harriet Harris, "Burnout, Mistreatment and Stress", in John Dent, Ronald Harden and Dan Hunt (eds), *A Practical Guide for Medical Teachers 6e* (Amsterdam: Elsevier 2021), pp. 369–76.

In responding to this question, a distinction between compassion and empathy comes to the fore. Compassion, we have said, involves these three elements:

1. noticing suffering (in others or in oneself);
2. being attuned to or moved by the suffering;
3. responding to relieve the suffering.

Empathy is a great educator at stages 1) and 2), in helping us to acknowledge the suffering in others, or indeed in our own selves, and to wish to respond, rather than to ignore or push the suffering away. However, if we do not learn to move in and out of empathy in order to respond effectively to suffering, we can become overwhelmed by the feelings, unable to respond, and can even become non pro-social as we start to lose compassion for those who have caused us to feel helpless.

In other words, empathy of itself can lead us to switch off from the feelings of others; a hardening of our hearts towards them. This process is often called "compassion fatigue", although "empathy fatigue" would be a more accurate phrase. Tania Singer and research colleagues have conducted a range of experiments that show how empathy can lead practitioners down the path of exhaustion, whereas compassion tends to energize and bring a sense of hope to its practitioners.[42] It is therefore critically important, and sometimes life-giving or life-saving, to distinguish compassion from empathy.

Singer and Klimecki write: "In contrast to empathy, compassion does not mean sharing the suffering of the other: rather, it is characterized by feelings of warmth, concern and care for the other, as well as a strong motivation to improve the other's wellbeing. Compassion is feeling *for* and not feeling *with* the other." Empathy can lead to what they call "empathic distress", which is "a strong aversive and self-oriented response to the suffering of others, accompanied by the desire to withdraw from a situation in order to protect oneself from excessive negative feelings".

---

[42]   Tania Singer and Mathias Bolz (eds), *Compassion: Bridging Practice and Science*, (EBook, Max Planck Society, 2013), <http://www.compassion-training.org/>, pp. 462–88.

Compassion, on the other hand, "is conceived as a feeling of concern for another person's suffering which is accompanied by the motivation to help. By consequence, it is associated with approach and prosocial motivation".[43]

Singer and Klimecki draw on research by Daniel Batson and Nancy Eisenberg in the fields of social and developmental psychology, confirming that people who feel compassion in a given situation help more often than people who suffer from empathic distress. They propose that people can be trained in compassion by meditative techniques that involve holding others in mind with kindness. Indeed, people can also be trained in empathy using meditative techniques, but studies show that those who are trained in empathy experience the pain of others as though it were their own first-hand pain (as the pain centres show up in the brain) and are more likely to respond with negative feelings and to withdraw. By contrast, those who are trained in compassion respond to the distress of others not by replicating the pain sensation in themselves, but by activating positive, pro-social emotions and behaviours.

In running compassion workshops for educators and health professionals, I explore with them whether it is possible to feel empathy but also to pull away from it in order to respond with compassionate actions and choices. This question arose for me after attending a masterclass on Complicated Grief Therapy.[44] Dr Kathy Shear, creator of this therapy, has designed interventions to help people who are stuck in their grief due to complicating factors. One intervention is to have the client hold an imaginary conversation with the person who has died, and to do so in front of the therapist. We were shown training videos of one such conversation, in which a grieving mother held a conversation with her fifteen-year-old boy who had died of cancer. She talked through with her son how traumatized she felt that he had had an operation before he died, which caused him to live his remaining few months bedridden. It was a very tearful conversation, which took several sessions for the client

---

[43]   Tania Singer and Olga M. Klimecki, "Empathy and compassion", *Current Biology* 24:18 (2014), R877–R878.

[44]   Edinburgh 2018, run by Dr Kathy Shear, Director of the Center for Complicated Grief in New York.

to complete. She eventually reached the point where she could "hear" her son say to her, "I love you Mom, you were a great Mom, and we made the right decision." It was clearly a healing process. One of the counsellors on the workshop asked Kathy Shear how she had managed to keep the mother at the process of holding this painful conversation. "Wasn't your empathy screaming at you to let her stop?" "Oh no," Shear replied, "that is no place for empathy. You have to pull right back on your empathy there or you would never get her through it. But once she has got to the end, you can bring the empathy back in and say 'That was really tough, wasn't it?'" Empathy teaches us how things feel, but it can hinder us from taking or leading on a compassionate action that would bring about healing.

Some of the ways that I explore with teachers and healthcare professionals moving in and out of empathy are to use our posture and angle of the head; to ground ourselves, being aware of the floor beneath our feet, and the seat supporting us; to practise non-attachment to the feelings that arise; to consider the longer-term benefits of an intervention, such as chemotherapy, or interruption of studies, even though the pain of them is initially hard to bear; and to avoid what in Buddhist parlance is known as "idiot compassion".[45] Idiot compassion may lead you to take or evade actions for the sake of relieving your own distress at the suffering of others (e.g. allowing a student to continue with their studies against your better judgement, because of their distress at the thought of interrupting). Idiot compassion reveals too much attachment and partiality, and an inability to sit with one's own discomfort. It enables or perpetuates the conditions of suffering. Rowan Williams' account of "educated passion" seems to be the opposite of idiot compassion. Educated passion is not self-protective or acquisitive, but is "a proper use of passion, sometimes to undercut other sorts of passion".[46]

Although Singer and Klimecki promote compassion over and against empathy, I find it helpful to explore whether we can move in and out of

---

[45] "Idiot compassion" is a term used by Buddhist teacher Trungpa Rinpoche and elaborated by Pema Chödrön in *The Places that Scare You: A Guide to Fearlessness* (London: Harper, 2004), pp. 116, 118.

[46] Williams, *Being Human*, pp. 73–7. Cf. Rowan Williams, *Being Disciples: Essentials of Christian Life* (London: SPCK, 2016), pp. 77–8.

empathy for the sake of compassion. I want to make sense of the biblical witness to the depth at which we can be moved by the condition of others, whilst also allowing that the biblical passages do not suggest that feeling moved in the depth of our being, our "bowels", causes distress, feelings of helplessness and withdrawal. Rather, when harnessed to the prospect of compassionate response, being deeply moved can provoke kind action towards those who suffer.

Compassion and divine nature

In making sense of the need sometimes to pull back from empathy in order to practise compassion, I wonder if help may be found in the Orthodox tradition that God is both compassionate and impassible: that God has compassion but does not suffer. The notion of the non-suffering God has received revision in the past century, in the wake of World War I, and even more so of the Holocaust. In the face of human suffering, it is urged in much contemporary theology that God must be said to suffer; that God cannot be passive, unmoved, unchanged. Moreover, such biblical content as has been rehearsed in this chapter is said to point to a God who suffers.[47]

Yet, the tradition of the impassibility of God was developed, albeit in relation to Greek ideas that that which is perfect does not change, in order to make the point that God loves perfectly: "God is impassible in that he does not undergo change of emotional states as do humans, but he is nonetheless utterly passionate in his love, mercy and goodness because, as the eternal and self-existing God, he is all perfect and unchanging in

---

[47]   There are many texts in defence of a God who suffers, including B. R. Brasnett, *The Suffering of the Impassible God* (London: SPCK, 1928); J. K. Mozley, *The Impassibility of God: A Survey of Christian Thought* (Cambridge: Cambridge University Press, 1926); Jürgen Moltmann, *The Crucified God* (London: SCM Press, 1974); Richard Bauckham, "'Only the Suffering God can Help': Divine Passibility in Modern Theology", *Themelios* 9: 3 (1984), pp. 6–12.

these attributes."[48] Irenaeus, for example, sees God as "total sympathy, and total love", precisely, Thomas Weinandy argues, because God's mercy and love are not predicated on a changeable being: "For God to be impassible and immutable is not to deny love and compassion of him, but to establish in his unchangeable perfect being a love that is absolutely and utterly passionate."[49] In a rather unfashionable move, but one that resonates with what we are discovering about the human capacity to sustain compassion, Weinandy defends the notion of a God who is passionate but who does not suffer, and who is therefore best able to sustain loving, passionate care:

> while the divine attribute of impassibility primarily tells us what God is not, it does so for entirely positive reasons. God is impassible in that he does not undergo successive and fluctuating emotional states; nor can the created order alter him in such a way so as to cause him to suffer any modification or loss. Nor is God the victim of negative and sinful passions as are human beings, such as fear, anxiety, and dread ⋯

God is perfectly compassionate not because God suffers with those who suffer, but because God's love, undiminished by changeable passion, wholly embraces them.[50]

Jesus, being fully human, does suffer, and exemplifies what it is humanly to live out the compassion of God. He identifies wholly, compassionately, with us, and with the most wretched among us through his excruciating death on the cross. He does so with an astonishing detachment, necessary to render his self-giving entirely free and purely loving: "Father, forgive them, for they know not what they do" (Luke 23:34).

48   Thomas G. Weinandy, *Does God Suffer?* (Edinburgh: T&T Clark, 2000), p. 79.

49   Weinandy, *Does God Suffer?*, p. 94.

50   Weinandy, *Does God Suffer?*, p. 164.

Concluding remarks

Drawing upon compassion science alongside scripture and tradition, this chapter offers a beginning of a suggestion: that as we grow in our understanding of the human capacity for sustained compassion, we might appreciate in new ways traditional teaching on divine impassibility. This suggestion requires further empirical research on the effects of empathy and compassion, and further theological exploration of the relation between divine and human compassion, and indeed of the role of divine grace in human compassion. Suffice to say here that notions of compassion, within the burgeoning industry of compassion science and teaching, must be nuanced regarding the benefits or otherwise of feeling as others feel.

Questions for discussion

1. When have you noticed the presence or absence of compassion in a situation? What difference do you think the presence or absence of compassion made to what happened, and to how you felt?
2. When do you experience compassion being stirred in you, and when a hardening of heart? What can you do to stoke the compassion?

Further reading

Paul Gilbert, *The Compassionate Mind* (London: Little, Brown Book Group, 2013).

Tania Singer and Mathias Bolz (eds), *Compassion: Bridging Practice and Science* (EBook, Max Planck Society, 2013) <http://www.compassion-training.org/>, accessed 29 January 2021.

John Swinton, *Raging with Compassion: Pastoral Responses to the Problem of Evil* (Grand Rapids, MI: Eerdmans, 2007).

Rowan Williams, *Being Human: Bodies, Minds, Persons* (London: SPCK, 2018).

CHAPTER 7

Being human in the European tradition and the Post-Enlightenment response

David Jasper

[In the Middle Ages] individual and social life, in all their manifestations, are imbued with the conceptions of faith. There is not an object nor an action, however trivial, that is not constantly correlated with Christ or salvation. All thinking tends to religious interpretation of individual things.
J. Huizinga, The Waning of the Middle Ages *(1924)*

The melancholy, long, withdrawing roar
Matthew Arnold, "Dover Beach"

At the heart of my thesis in this chapter is a profoundly melancholy reflection: that our understanding of what it is to be human, and to know the good in Western cultures, has been rooted in an essentially metaphysical concept of God, and that the progressive loss of such a concept has lain at the heart of the tragedy of the European sense of human flourishing in a post-Christian world. This is not to suggest that such an understanding of the human is necessarily the only possibility, but that such has been the case in the West.[1]

Part of my argument is drawn from a reading of Charles Taylor's book *Sources of the Self* (1989), which begins with the assertion that

---

[1] China, for example, would suggest an ancient and wholly different, largely non-metaphysical understanding of religious tradition.

"selfhood and the good, or in another way selfhood and morality, turn out to be inextricably intertwined themes".[2] As religious commitment has declined in modern consciousness, so has the exercise of moral discretion, illustrating once again what Martha Nussbaum once called the fragility of goodness.[3] Nussbaum later illustrated this fragility in moral philosophy from the flaws explored in the late fiction of Henry James, above all *The Golden Bowl* (1904).[4] One of this novel's central characters, Maggie Verver, is a young woman who aspires to moral perfection, even after her marriage wishing "to remain, intensely, the same passionate little daughter she had always been".[5] But nothing stays the same—the wife cannot remain, perfectly, the father's daughter. As another of James' flawed characters, Kate Croy in *The Wings of the Dove* (1902), concludes, "We shall never be again as we were!"[6]

And we, and perhaps our Christian theology, have never quite accepted that conclusion, and the consequence, it may be, is a melancholy one. Furthermore, we have never quite accepted that it is, finally, impossible, after Matthew Arnold, to do theology on Dover Beach,[7] or at least the theology of the ancient Christian tradition. Iris Murdoch, who as a post-Christian thinker, readily admits that the decline of religion poses acute

---

[2] Charles Taylor, *Sources of the Self: The Making of the Modern Identity* (Cambridge, MA: Harvard University Press, 1989), p. 3.

[3] Martha Nussbaum, *The Fragility of Goodness: Luck and Ethics in Greek Tragedy and Philosophy* (Cambridge: Cambridge University Press, 1986).

[4] James' title is taken from Ecclesiastes 12:6: "... and the golden bowl is broken, and the pitcher is broken at the fountain, and the wheel broken at the cistern, and the dust returns to the earth as it was".

[5] Henry James, *The Golden Bowl*, quoted in Martha Nussbaum, *Love's Knowledge: Essays on Philosophy and Literature* (Oxford: Oxford University Press, 1990), p. 126.

[6] Henry James, *The Wings of the Dove* (Harmondsworth: Penguin, 1971), p. 457.

[7] See, Nicholas Lash, *Theology on Dover Beach* (London: Darton, Longman and Todd, 1979), after the poem by Matthew Arnold, "Dover Beach" (1867). The title of Don Cupitt's book and television series *The Sea of Faith* is also taken from this poem which epitomizes the experience of Victorian religious doubt.

ethical issues and seems to suggest in *The Sovereignty of Good* (1970) that, if God is now indeed "dead", then we need to suppose something very like God if we are to retain our moral sense and our sense of being human:

> I shall suggest that God was (or is) a *single perfect transcendent non-representable and necessarily real object of attention*; and I shall go on to suggest that moral philosophy should attempt to retain a central concept which has all these characteristics.[8]

What, then, holds us in our humanity? Does the fading of metaphysics and, it may be, the Divine Being from our culture mean also the fading of our humanity, our identity as human beings? And has our struggle to preserve the Church and its theology as far as possible unchanged finally reached its probably inevitable end? Or is there a possibility of a future for humanity that involves a sense of divine presence that, as yet, we have barely begun to discover means of articulating?

From the medieval to the modern mind

What it was like to be a human being in Europe in the Middle Ages is now almost inconceivable to us. True, we are all inheritors of the two forms of consciousness that lie at the heart of Christianity and European culture: the Hebraic and the Hellenic. The first is entirely theocentric and communal. The second is philosophical and individualistic. Their very languages, Hebrew and Greek, reflect these differences. But to be human in medieval Christendom was first to be entirely focused in every aspect of life upon the reality of God, and to be a part of a community and social structure that set aside the individual within a rigid and hierarchical society. Theologians like Anselm of Canterbury (1033–1109) concerned themselves with ontological arguments for the existence of God, while

---

[8]   Iris Murdoch, "On 'God' and 'Good'", in *The Sovereignty of Good* (London: Routledge & Kegan Paul, 1970) p. 55 (emphases in the original). Also Murdoch, *Metaphysics as a Guide to Morals* (Harmondsworth: Penguin, 1992).

the Church took upon itself the task of thinking for the individual in almost every aspect of life.

Only gradually, with the waning of the Middle Ages, did things begin to change. The "new science" began to take hold of the European mind and the individual genius of the philosophical mind started to assert itself in the face of the Church's authority. It could be said of a Dominican friar, Giordano Bruno (1548–1600), in the words of one modern commentator, that he "was not a Christian theologian . . . He accommodated aspects of Platonism, pagan and Christian, on sufferance".[9] An admirer of Copernicus, Bruno (like Spinoza after him) subsumed God pantheistically into the workings of nature—but Europe was not ready for such thinking, and he was burnt at the stake for heresy in 1600. But the tide in the affairs of men had turned long before this. Martin Luther (1483–1546) brought about a crack in the authority of the medieval Church which finally left the individual standing alone before God, struggling with his own solitary spiritual autobiography. Luther was, in fact, for all his piety, the herald of what Owen Chadwick was later to describe as the secularization of the European mind, the first in a long line of theologians and philosophers that concludes with Immanuel Kant and his proclamation of that Enlightenment that is "man's [sic] emergence from his self-incurred immaturity".[10] Kant, it might be said, was the first truly secular Protestant—a Luther without the idea of God who is constitutively at the centre of all things.

In many respects the medieval mind was innocent of doubt. It was also deeply poetic, while between the sixteenth and the eighteenth centuries, the mind becomes increasingly mathematical and scientific and questions of ethics and moral philosophy became more urgent in a world that was felt to be less innocent and was increasingly afflicted by doubts. It

---

[9]   Dilwyn Knox, "Wonder and the Philosopher's Perfection: Giordano Bruno", in Francesca Bugliani Knox and Jennifer Reek (eds), *Poetry, Philosophy and Theology in Conversation: Thresholds of Wonder*. The Power of the Word IV (London: Routledge, 2020), p. 41.

[10]   Immanuel Kant, "An Answer to the Question: 'What is Enlightenment?'", in Kant, *Political Writings*, ed. Hans Reiss (Cambridge: Cambridge University Press, 1991), p. 54.

was, perhaps, no accident that by the end of the eighteenth century the medieval world was increasingly idealized, for example in the stories and poetry of Sir Walter Scott, and later in the ecclesiology and architecture of Augustus Pugin, the art of the pre-Raphaelites, and many Anglican high-church people.

At the heart of Descartes' (1596–1650) *Discourse on Method* is a fascination with mathematics that is the foundation for his radical assertion of the nature of human being, "*cogito ergo sum*" ("I am thinking, therefore I exist"). Henceforth the world is no longer theocentric but anthropocentric, and although Descartes offers his own proof of the existence of God, he finds God entirely from within himself. It is a far cry from Anselm's *Proslogion*, and by now the Western mind has shifted from a fascination with ontology, the origins, nature and character of being, to a concern for epistemology—the theory of knowledge, and how the human being comes to know and think. Humankind is self-obsessed. There is, of course, gain, but also loss, not least in the dualism of mind and body which is bequeathed to us by Descartes, with all our existential anxieties in a world that is felt to be desacralized, and in which the profane is embraced even while there remains a lingering and persistent nostalgia for the sacred.[11] That nostalgia is never entirely to go away, for we can never quite believe that things will never be the same as they were.

Existentialism, of course, did not truly come upon us until Søren Kierkegaard in the nineteenth century. But it cast its shadow back upon the eighteenth century also, and indeed much earlier than that. Modernity and its obsession with power is anticipated by Thomas Hobbes (1588–1679) in *Leviathan*, a book, said Samuel Pepys, "the Bishops will not let be printed again", and in which Hobbes affirmed that the "life of man" was, under the conditions of war, "solitary, poore, nasty, brutish, and short".[12] In such a world, suspicion was replacing faith as the primary characteristic of the Western mind, and reason demanded that evidence be provided for all things. This was a key element even in the natural

---

[11]   Marshall McLuhan, *The Gutenberg Galaxy* (Toronto: University of Toronto Press, 1962), following the thought of Mircea Eliade.

[12]   Thomas Hobbes, *Leviathan* (1651), Part 1, Chapter 13, ed. C. B. MacPherson (Harmondsworth: Penguin, 1968), p. 186.

theology of one bishop, Joseph Butler (1692–1752) of Durham, in his influential work *The Analogy of Religion* (1736). Philosophers, on the other hand, from John Locke to David Hume, were concerned with addressing the problems of how human knowledge is possible, and the very nature of human being. Indeed, asked Hume, can it even be said that "I" really exist? For Locke, the mind begins merely as a *tabula rasa* upon which life prints impressions as experience develops. In short, our mind is at the outset and essentially a blank sheet.[13] But in the eighteenth century we see also the rise of that wearisome trope of irony, the greatest of the tropes of classical rhetoric, in the master hand of Voltaire (1694–1778) as we seek to find ourselves in this "best of all possible worlds".[14] Is it irony—or rather its more recent cousin, weary cynicism—that, forgetful of the good, anticipates only the present nihilism of the French social theorist Jean Baudrillard and others?

But it is Immanuel Kant (1724–1804) who, like Luther in his time, provides the philosophical key to the modern and later postmodern world. Abandoning ontological arguments and the noumenal (except in terms of regulative principles), Kant does not deny the power of intuition in reasonable reflection (*Anschauung*), but finally holds all thought within strict limits, and within these limits we "must have the courage to use our *own* understanding"![15] There is no God, finally, to help and guide us. In Kant's *Religion within the Limits of Reason Alone* (1793), Christianity is interpreted solely in ethical terms, its religious profundities addressed in the weariness of the opening sentence of the work:

> That "the world lieth in evil" is a plaint as old as history, old even as the older art, poetry indeed, as old as the oldest of all fictions, the religion of priest-craft.[16]

---

[13] It might be noted that neuroscience today would think very differently from this.

[14] Voltaire, *Candide* [1759], tr. John Butt (Harmondsworth: Penguin, 1968), p. 144.

[15] *Political Writings*, p. 54.

[16] Immanuel Kant, *Religion within the Limits of Reason Alone* [1793], tr. Theodore M. Greene and Hoyt H. Hudson (New York, NY: Harper & Row,

But although Kant sets the anxious tone of all modern thought and culture, there is something missing, even in the more obscure reaches of the major work of his old age, *The Critique of Judgement* (1790), with its concern for aesthetics and teleology, which gave rise to the anxious and complex European movement known as Romanticism and, more philosophically, in Germany to the idealism of Fichte, Schelling and Hegel.

From Romanticism to Nietzsche

At the heart of European Romanticism lies the struggle between the Christianity of the old world and its metaphysics, and the human ego of the new, more bourgeois world of European culture. For Kant, ideas that have their philosophical beginnings in Plato and the pre-Socratics were merely *regulative*, while for the English poet and Christian thinker Samuel Taylor Coleridge (1772–1834) they remained firmly, if problematically, *constitutive*. For God was now an uncomfortable problem to be solved. In the words of Elinor Shaffer:

> Coleridge's two main interests, Christian theology under the penetrating probes of Enlightenment criticism, and a new poetry of the supernatural, met in the need for a modern mythology. For Herder, Eichhorn and Coleridge, the two interests were inseparable.[17]

It was Coleridge also who rather casually remarked in 1830 that there are only two kinds of people—Aristotelians and Platonists.[18] If this is

---

    1960), p. 15.

[17] E. S. Shaffer, *"Kubla Khan" and The Fall of Jerusalem* (Cambridge: Cambridge University Press, 1975), p. 32.

[18] "Every man is born an Aristotelian or a Platonist . . . They are the two classes of men beside which it is next to impossible to conceive a third." S. T. Coleridge, *Table Talk* Volume 1, ed. Carl Woodring, *The Collected Works* (Princeton: Princeton University Press, 1990), pp. 172–3. See further, David Newsome,

indeed the case, then the medieval age of Christendom was resolutely Aristotelian, while the philosophical heritage of Plato and its aftermath haunts the last 200 years of our history with the comforts (and sometimes threats) offered by institutional religion under continuous and relentless fire.

I have already briefly alluded to Owen Chadwick's book *The Secularization of the European Mind in the Nineteenth Century* (1975), which has its origins in the Gifford Lectures delivered in the University of Edinburgh in 1973–4. Chadwick suggests that the word *secularization* began as a rather emotive term suggesting something like *anti-clericalism*.[19] "Emotive" indeed, but nevertheless emotion in serious thinking can be powerful and there has been a fatal and growing tendency within churches and institutional religion to ignore their intellectual life and traditions, and the crucial importance of these, in a suicidal attempt to bury heads in the sand and in a refusal to take anyone outside ecclesiastical boundaries with much respect. And yet Owen Chadwick writes:

> Sometimes [secularization] meant a freeing of the sciences, of learning, of the arts, from their theological origins or theological bias. Sometimes it meant the declining influence of churches, or of religion, in modern society. Then the sociologists, heirs of Comte, aided by certain historians and anthropologists, did a service by showing how deep-seated religion is in humanity and in the consensus which makes up society. They therefore made the word unemotional.[20]

Religion, as contemporary China is discovering, is extremely hard to eradicate from human society, though it is increasingly difficult to say exactly what we mean by the term religion. Certainly for Charles Taylor,

---

Two Classes of Men: Platonism and English Romantic Thought (London: John Murray, 1974).

[19] The first instance of the word in the *Oxford English Dictionary* is 1706.

[20] Owen Chadwick, *The Secularization of the European Mind in the Nineteenth Century* (Cambridge: Cambridge University Press, 1975), p. 264.

in *The Secular Age* (2007), the age of social and institutional religion has now been replaced by something far more individualistic and intangible, though religion continues to adopt some extremely toxic as well as benign forms. Undoubtedly one of the greatest religious thinkers of the nineteenth century was Karl Marx, though he fully embraced and addressed (unlike more or less everyone else) the Western crisis of metaphysics. Most of us have ignored that crisis as something too remote or difficult for thought, but we need only consider the tragedy of the USSR and Eastern Europe in the early twentieth century to recognize its dire consequences. In the words of Yuval Noah Harari in his deeply prosaic but occasionally perceptive work *Sapiens* (2011):

> [Communism] had theologians [though of a profoundly ungodly variety] adept at Marxist dialectics, and every unit in the Soviet army had a chaplain, called a commissar, who monitored the piety of soldiers and officers. Communism had martyrs, holy wars, heresies, such as Trotskyism. Soviet Communism was a fanatical and missionary religion. A devout Communist could not be a Christian or a Buddhist, and was expected to spread the gospel of Marx and Lenin even at the price of his or her own life.[21]

Nothing like this had been seen in religion since the authoritarianism of medieval Christendom.

Such serious Christian theology as there was in the nineteenth century attempted to be, after thinkers like Coleridge, deeply synthetic, and the only philosopher who gave a profound lead to this was Georg Wilhelm Friedrich Hegel (1770–1831). It is no accident that one of the relatively few responsibly serious Christian leaders after him, Archbishop William Temple, offered the Church of England a neo-Hegelian theology that has been almost entirely ignored and is now forgotten. That is a great pity. In his brief book *Christianity in Thought and Practice* (1936) Temple writes:

---

[21]   Yuval Noah Harari, *Sapiens: A Brief History of Humankind* (London: Vintage, 2011), pp. 254–5.

> My mind always tends to work to some extent along the lines
> of the Hegelian *triad* of *thesis, antithesis,* and *synthesis,* always
> remembering that each *synthesis* which is reached becomes
> in its turn a *thesis* to which a new *antithesis* will arise; so that
> the process never reaches an ultimate conclusion, but is always
> moving on. And I regard the whole habit and system of thought
> which was characteristic of the Middle Ages as, from this point of
> view, a *thesis* to which the history of philosophy from Descartes
> until the present day has presented an *antithesis.*[22]

One wonders how far since Temple's time Anglican theology, by and
large, has kept in tune with modern and postmodern thought.

Meanwhile, and in profound contrast, one of the most influential
thinkers in late-nineteenth-century Europe, Friedrich Nietzsche (1844–
1900) made his mark on almost every serious writer in the early twentieth
century and opened the door, among other things, for National Socialism
in Germany, more commonly known as Nazism—with all its ghastly
consequences. In 1863, in *The Gay Science*, Nietzsche proclaimed the
death of God. He was not the first to do so (Hegel had used the expression
much more subtly), but he was by far the most influential. Nor was he
the first to employ the voice of a madman to proclaim his most profound
insight, for St Anselm had done so centuries earlier in proposing an
argument for the existence of God. Nietzsche writes:

> The madman jumped into their midst and pierced them with
> his eyes. "Where is God?" he cried; "I'll tell you! *We have killed
> him*—you and I! We are all his murderers . . . What then are those
> churches now if not the tombs and sepulchres of God?"[23]

Typically, of course, few within the Church have been prepared to read this
modern parable in context let alone take it seriously. In his final works,

---

[22]   William Temple, *Christianity in Thought and Practice* (London: SCM Press,
       1936), pp. 39–40.

[23]   Friedrich Nietzsche, *The Gay Science* [1863], tr. Josephine Nauckhoff
       (Cambridge: Cambridge University Press, 2001), pp. 119–20.

written when he has been driven mad by his own thinking, *Twilight of the Idols* (1889) and *The Anti-Christ* (1895), Nietzsche makes his final assault on institutional Christianity and its self-deceptions. And in perhaps his most profound work, *The Genealogy of Morals* (1887), Nietzsche, like a few other serious thinkers in the nineteenth century, addressed the matter of the human will—a subject which haunts all Western thinking since the beginning of the sixteenth century. For Christianity the will, exercised within the grace of God, has always been a problem in the matter of salvation. In his essay on Blaise Pascal, T. S. Eliot puts this very clearly:

> It is recognized in Christian theology ... that free-will of the natural effort and ability of the individual man and also supernatural *grace*, a gift accorded we know not quite how, are both required in co-operation, for salvation. Though numerous theologians have set their wits at the problem, it ends in a mystery which we can perceive but not finally decipher.[24]

Nietzsche, however, is far more precise and less apologetic on the question of the will.

> It signifies, let us have the courage to face it, a will to nothingness, a revulsion from life, a rebellion against the principal conditions of living. And yet, despite everything, it is and remains a *will*. Let me repeat, now that I have reached the end, what I said at the beginning: man would sooner have the void for his purpose than be void of purpose.[25]

---

[24] T. S. Eliot, *Selected Essays*, third edition (London: Faber and Faber, 1951), p. 413. It may be noted that William Temple devotes one of his Gifford Lectures (delivered at the University of Glasgow, 1932–4) to the question of "freedom and determinism". The exercise of free will and of determinism are carefully balanced in Temple's understanding of human freedom. See, *Nature, Man and God* (London: Macmillan, 1964), pp. 223–45.

[25] Friedrich Nietzsche, *The Genealogy of Morals* [1887], tr. Francis Golffing (New York, NY: Doubleday, 1956), p. 299.

It has to be acknowledged that the twentieth century in the history of the West reflects far more precisely the vision of Nietzsche than that of Pascal and the Jansenist Christian theologians of whom Eliot was writing. Even before the outbreak of war in 1914, the Swiss linguist Ferdinand de Saussure (1857–1913) had effectively demolished the tool of language as something stable and to be relied on. Language, like science, thus embraced theories of relativity which the common culture or religion and society could not or would not seriously embrace. There was too much to lose. Not least, Christian theology remained chained to ancient metaphysical structures and principles. Kant and Schleiermacher remained obsessed with an address to "religious experience", though actually without any serious metaphysic (Nietzsche was right, it seems— God had died at the hand of the theologians), and thus theology managed to absolve itself from the crucial task of theological *thinking* in a modern context.[26] Theology was, essentially, made irrelevant by its own hand, though still suffering from delusions of relevance. But the scar or trace of God remains—and to this I shall return at the end of this essay in a discussion of the thought of Paul Ricœur. For now, the problem is well expressed by Stanley Cavell in his book *The Claim of Reason*, describing the thought of the Christian mind:

> As long as God exists, I am not alone. And couldn't the other suffer the fate of God? It strikes me that it was out of the terror of this possibility that Luther promoted the individual human voice in the religious life. I wish to understand how the other now bears the weight of God, shows me that I am not alone in the universe. This requires understanding the philosophical problem of the other as the trace or scar of the departure of God.[27]

---

[26]   See Carl Raschke, *Theological Thinking: An Inquiry* (Atlanta, GA: Scholars Press, 1988).

[27]   Stanley Cavell, *The Claim of Reason: Wittgenstein, Skepticism, Morality and Tragedy* (Oxford: Oxford University Press, 1979), p. 470.

The twentieth century

As history and the march of time gave every evidence of this crisis in our humanity, a few philosophical voices outside theology and the Church were uttered but largely ignored. Above all Wittgenstein and then Heidegger called attention to theological questions and addressed the matter of thinking in the twentieth century. They worked in a time when, as we were reminded by the psychoanalyst Carl Jung, "modern man" was in search of a soul in a condition of utter solitariness. Jung wrote:

> The spiritual problem of modern man is one of those questions which belongs so intimately to the present in which we are living that we cannot judge of them fully. The modern man is a newly formed human being; a modern problem is a question which has just arisen and whose answer lies in the future.[28]

Jung repeatedly makes it clear that this "modern man" and "medieval man" would have barely comprehended each other and "the modern man has lost all the metaphysical certainties of his medieval brother". It is precisely the loss of such certainties that lies at the heart of Heidegger's philosophical quest, though he was always very clear about the difference between his own thought and the Christian understanding of the "religious" or theological.[29]

There is a clear lineage to be discerned. Heidegger's teacher was Edmund Husserl (1859–1938), and Husserl begins and centres his work upon the thought of Descartes.[30] We can easily trace the root of the problem. The issue of metaphysics in the thought of Nietzsche

---

[28] Carl Jung, *Modern Man in Search of a Soul* [1933], tr. W. S. Dell and Cary F. Baynes (London: Routledge, 1973), p. 226.

[29] See George Pattison, *The Later Heidegger* (London: Routledge, 2000), p. 204.

[30] It may be noted in passing that one of the most influential French phenomenological thinkers today is Jean-Luc Marion, who also began his studies as a student of Descartes' philosophy. See *Jean-Luc Marion: The Essential Writings*, ed. Kevin Hart (New York, NY: Fordham University Press, 2013), III, "Reading Descartes", pp. 199–249.

and Heidegger is well summarized by Gayatri Chakravorty Spivak, the translator of one of the major European thinkers at the end of the twentieth century, Jacques Derrida (1930–2004). She writes:

> The clôture [enclosure] of metaphysics found the origin and end of its study in presence. The questioners of that enclosure—among them Nietzsche, Freud, Heidegger—moved toward an articulation of the need for the strategy of "sous rature" [under erasure]. Nietzsche puts "knowing" under erasure; Freud "the psyche," and Heidegger, explicitly, "Being." As I have argued, the name of this gesture effacing the presence of a thing and yet keeping it legible, in Derrida's lexicon, is "writing,"—the gesture that both frees us from and guards us within, the metaphysical enclosure.[31]

An important, indeed crucial, point is being made here. The shift from medieval to modern culture in Europe was a movement from a largely illiterate and visual culture to a literary and verbal one. From the early sixteenth century, Protestantism focuses relentlessly upon the *word* of God *written* in scripture, but it is only at the end of the last century, and long after the linguistic crisis that was so clearly demonstrated by Saussure (though its seeds lie in Aristotle), that the ambivalences of *écriture* [writing] as the guardian of metaphysics were finally revealed.

Less fashionable now than he was some thirty or forty years ago, the French Jewish thinker Jacques Derrida cannot easily be dismissed as an icon of our time, identified by the move from modernity to postmodernity, and the dissolution of what he named the *logocentricity* of the Western, and largely Christian, tradition. "In the beginning was the Word" we are accustomed to affirm in our Christmas Gospel—or is this actually so? Here is Derrida's solemn warning, that

---

[31]   Gayatri Chakravorty Spivak, Translator's Preface to Jacques Derrida, *Of Grammatology* (Baltimore, MD: The Johns Hopkins University Press, 1976), p. xli.

in spite of itself, . . . a historico-metaphysical epoch *must* finally determine as language the totality of its problematic horizon. It must do so not only because all that desire had wished to wrest from the play of language finds itself recaptured within that play but also because, for the same reason, language itself is menaced in its very life, helpless, adrift in the threat of limitlessness, brought back to its own finitude at the very moment when its limits seem to disappear, when it ceases to be self-assured, contained, and *guaranteed* by the infinite signified which seemed to exceed it.[32]

This assertion must be taken with the utmost seriousness. It is for many, perhaps, another expression of the death of God in the loss of the "infinite signified"—and thus, in effect, the death of self. The roots of such "postmodernity", or perhaps better its seeds, lie in the meditations on language within Romantic thought, and it harks back also to the prophetic voice of Nietzsche, that God, the infinite signified, is indeed dead. The words we speak and by which we define things and ourselves, and articulate thought and create meaning—are themselves disintegrating in a sea of relativity and lack the guarantee of that "infinite signified"—God, perhaps—that once gave meaning to all human life and culture. Of course, there is much more to Derrida and postmodernity than this, but it seems now that society moved on too quickly from the warnings then being given at the end of the twentieth century, heading post-haste into our culture of decreasing attention span and the decay of the intellect as constructive of the self.

At the heart of our very humanity is the human capacity to reflect, to think, and to think critically, creatively and, it may be, metaphysically. Perhaps at no period in the history of Western culture has this capacity been more ignored than in our own time. Even when the vast majority of people in Europe were illiterate (and this was the case until not so many hundreds of years ago), European thought, first in the Church and then in science and the arts, was a delicate and highly cultivated instrument, grounded in history and metaphysical structures. But it was only in the earlier part of the twentieth century, and after the first great

---

[32]   Jacques Derrida, *Of Grammatology*, p. 6.

mechanized slaughter of millions in human history in the Great War of 1914–18, that the French essayist Julien Benda published his searing and now largely forgotten classic *La Trahison des clercs* (*The Treason of the Intellectuals*, 1927)—lamenting the intellectual corruption of the age. At the heart of this lament is the recognition that when the hatred of culture becomes a part of culture, then the life of the mind loses all meaning. Its consequences in that departed century are all too clear.

We live increasingly in what Marshall McLuhan once famously called a Global Village.[33] In our overcrowded and overused planet we stand like rabbits in the headlights, constantly distracted and seemingly incapable of the profound thought that is needed to rediscover who we are, why we are here and what our future is. Religion, as has already been asserted, is clearly dying in the West in its traditional institutional forms and those left to lament its departure are decreasing in number every year. But religion, too, like most dying animals, can be dangerous and toxic, especially when oversimplified—and yet there may still be time to rethink fundamental values and ideas, though they cannot simply be endlessly reintroduced in ancient and largely unusable forms. The development of the history of ideas in the West since the end of the Middle Ages, as I have briefly alluded to it, will not allow that. But any signs of rethinking that may be discerned in our time are too often dismissed as either overdifficult for the lazy mind, or else demanding of different categories of thought that we are unwilling to adjust to. It was not so long ago that a bishop dismissed as nonsense my reference to the careful and fragile assessment of Christian theology as necessarily "weak" and the nature of Christianity's place in contemporary Europe as suggested by the Italian Roman Catholic philosopher Gianni Vattimo. Perhaps the paradox seemed too great, though the idea of a kenotic, self-emptying theology is hardly new.[34] Vattimo was also one of the architects of the

---

[33] Marshall McLuhan, *The Gutenberg Galaxy* (1962), and *Understanding Media* (1964).

[34] Philippians 2:6–11.

European constitution at the Convention on the Future of Europe led by Giscard d'Estaing.[35] Of him it has been written by Santiago Zabala that

> Vattimo thought that it would be a mistake to add the specific words "Christian values" to the constitution because it is precisely in order to uphold these same Christian values that Europe is secular: the force of the Gospels and of Jesus' teaching provides the foundation of the secularity of any democratic state today.[36]

The radical rethinking of a "weak" philosophy and a paradoxical Christian theology (though there are other attempts to do so besides those of Vattimo by such figures as the American theologian John Caputo) seems to be beyond us, by and large. Books such as Bradley Onishi's *The Sacrality of the Secular* (2018) do appear, seeking to unravel and reconstitute the categories that have defined our sense of what it is to be human since the Enlightenment and perhaps before it. But they barely touch our consciousness in the Church.

Conclusion

There has possibly never been a time when we have thought so little about what it means to be truly human or what constitutes true human flourishing either with or without God. Not least is this true of theology and the theologians.[37] I make that bold statement as an act of defiance and in the faint hope that others will prove me to be utterly wrong. The former Archbishop of Canterbury, Rowan Williams, has recently published a

---

[35] It is painfully sad to reflect on this achievement in the context of post-Brexit Britain.

[36] Santiago Zabala, "Introduction: Gianni Vattimo and Weak Philosophy", in *Weakening Philosophy: Essays in Honour of Gianni Vattimo* (Montreal: McGill-Queen's University Press, 2007), p. 28.

[37] David Klemm and William Schweiker in their book *Religion and the Human Future* (Oxford: Wiley-Blackwell, 2008), pp. 38–9, write perceptively of the "plight of theology" and the "marginalization of the theologians in culture".

small volume of essays entitled *Being Human* (2018) addressing, initially, the nature of consciousness and concluding with the matter of humanity transfigured. Dr Williams writes:

> It is, first of all, good news about humanity itself—the humanity that we all know to be stained, wounded, imprisoned in various ways. This humanity—yours and mine—is still capable of being embraced by God, shot through with God's glory, received and welcomed in the burning heart of reality itself.[38]

This is good for sermons, spoken to the dwindling numbers who still choose to attend church and listen to them. But sadly, such language no longer persuades me of anything and gives me little hope for the future of what Charles Taylor calls our selfhood and the good.

During the last six hundred years Europe has moved from a society at the heart of which is an unconditional belief in God, to one in which humankind is the centre and driver of all things, and possibly we have even moved further into the age of the post-human.[39] But let us stay for a moment longer with Descartes—*cogito ergo sum*. For we have failed to take even that familiar tag with genuine seriousness. I think—that is what is at the heart of all things. It is how we think, how far we are prepared to take thought, how far we refuse to think and become victims of a simple and devastatingly, indeed brutally effective rhetoric that has no dealings with the difficult question of truth, that really matters. One or two more serious European thinkers in the twentieth century, people like Emanuel Levinas and Paul Ricœur,[40] did continue to recognize that the essence of our existential and moral being lies not in ourselves but in the acknowledgement of our relationship with the other, or with others. And perhaps let us not go too far as yet and imagine that this "other" is indeed

---

[38] Rowan Williams, *Being Human: Bodies, Minds, Persons* (London: SPCK, 2018), p. 106.

[39] See also Fuller, Chapter 8 and Stoddart, Chapter 11.

[40] Emmanuel Levinas, *Totality and Infinity*, tr. Alphonso Lingis (The Hague: Martinus Nijhoff, 1979). Paul Ricœur, *Oneself as Another*, tr. Kathleen Blamey (Chicago, IL: University of Chicago Press, 1992).

God. The sense of the other is one of those simple yet profoundly difficult lessons that has been known in various forms but never truly learnt or, perhaps, believed in. Augustine taught us this in the early centuries of the Christian Church when he indeed wrote of human being and God:

> The thought of you stirs him so deeply that he cannot be content
> unless he praises you, because you made us for yourself and our
> hearts find no peace until they rest in you.[41]

Paul Ricœur suggested something similar, though in a quite different tone, in his Edinburgh Gifford Lectures of 1986 as he addressed the question of selfhood: oneself *as* another—*soi-même comme un autre*. As a theologian I have to recognize and learn from Ricœur, that in the question of what it means to be human, we are now too far gone in unreflective self-absorption to be worthy, at least in the first instance, of further genuine theological reflective thought. We are not grown-up enough for serious theology and so we have to begin at a much earlier stage. Rowan Williams begins too far down the line to be any longer heard or understood except by very few people. Theology quickly descends to mere piety, and that is hard to share. If there is to be any hope in recovering a sense of what it is to be human, we must first address with all philosophical seriousness the consequences of the drift in sensibility away from God and metaphysics since at least Descartes. It will not be an easy task, and perhaps it is now almost impossible as the basic and pressing questions of physical survival press so immediately upon us. What lessons have we learned from the recent pandemic—or do we simply hope that everything will go back to what it was? This will not be so. But Ricœur's words are legitimate for all that. He writes at the outset of *Oneself as Another* (1992):

> It will be observed that this asceticism of the argument . . . leads
> to a type of philosophy from which the actual mention of God
> is absent and in which the question of God, as a philosophical

---

[41]   St Augustine, *Confessions*, tr. R. S. Pine-Coffin (Harmondsworth: Penguin, 1961), p. 21.

question, itself remains in a suspension that could be called agnostic.[42]

We can, indeed, never be again as we were. The golden bowl is cracked even though we may not see or wish to see the fault line in it. And now we are no longer worthy of more than a cautious agnosticism—until we regain the intelligence and the moral integrity to articulate anything like the actual mention of God. As we reflect upon the crucial question as to what it means to be human in our current post-Enlightenment culture in Europe and the West, Ricœur's wise and cautious words need to be heeded. All too often we call upon the name of God to step in when the initial responsibility lies with ourselves in the matter of freedom in our responsible social and moral selves. As children of the Enlightenment, we need to heed Kant's words afresh, but in our own time and far more radically than, I think, he intended—that we must strive, both within the Church and beyond, to emerge from our self-incurred immaturity and learn again to think for ourselves.

Questions for discussion

1. Matthew Arnold concludes his poem "Dover Beach" with these lines:

> And we are here as on a darkling plain
> Swept with confused alarms of struggle and flight,
> Where ignorant armies clash by night.

Could this still describe the human condition today? In what sense has humanity progressed in the last 200 years?

2. If belief in God might now be described as "optional", how should theology respond to this?

---

42 Paul Ricœur, *Oneself as Another*, tr. Kathleen Blamey (Chicago, IL: University of Chicago Press, 1992), p. 24.

3. I began by describing the heart of my chapter as a "profoundly melancholy reflection". With what tools should Christianity be responding to this?

Further reading

David F. Ford, *The Future of Christian Theology* (Chichester: Wiley-Blackwell, 2011).

David E. Klemm and William Schweiker, *Religion and the Human Future* (Oxford: Blackwell, 2008).

Charles Taylor, *Sources of the Self: The Making of Modern Identity* (Cambridge, MA: Harvard University Press, 1989).

Rowan Williams, *Being Human: Bodies, Minds, Persons* (London: SPCK, 2018).

CHAPTER 8

Unique? Scientific constraints around theological anthropology

Michael Fuller

Introduction

Human beings have many wonderful attributes: we can think, imagine, dream, invent, and develop deep and sustaining relationships with those around us. We have built phenomenal societal structures enabling us to extend our life expectancy through mutual care and through treatment of illness and injury. Christians have also generally assumed that humans have a unique capacity to relate to God; that is to say, that in addition to all those other things that characterize humanity in terms of what we are and what we do, there is a theological aspect which should bear upon our understanding of ourselves, since that understanding is incomplete without it. Moreover, that tradition also considers the capacity of human beings to relate to God as making us somehow special—perhaps, even, unique—in the created order. This understanding is often framed in terms of the *imago Dei*, the image of God, which is referred to in the first creation narrative in the biblical book of Genesis, where it is stated that "God created humankind in his image, in the image of God he created them; male and female he created them" (Genesis 1:27).

Our modern, Western, scientific understanding of ourselves and of our universe, however, places a number of constraints around such an understanding. We now know our planet, which is part of a planetary system orbiting an unremarkable star, to be one of many: a remarkable set of conditions obtain on it, which has allowed organic life to evolve here, but it is perfectly possible that such conditions might obtain on other planets, too. Within our biosphere, we are now aware of the biological building-blocks which we share with all other life on our planet, and indeed of our close biological kinship with other species who share our planet with us. So, to what extent does it still make sense to think of ourselves as special, or even unique? This chapter sets out some of the ways in which the notion of the *imago Dei* has traditionally been understood, and then looks at various ways in which modern scientific understandings of the universe allow us to set parameters around those understandings—firstly concerning our place in the universe, and then concerning our place on planet earth.

The *imago Dei*

In what sense might humans bear the "image of God"? Clearly, rather more is intended by this description than any idea that human beings resemble God in a physical sense.[1] Of course, many of the poetic evocations of God found in scripture and in the Christian tradition speak of God in anthropological terms, as parent, king, shepherd and so on, and God is said to possess human bodily attributes: such allusions have encouraged artists to present God in human form, but it has always been acknowledged that such representations are not to be understood literally, and indeed there have been movements within the history of Christianity which have violently rejected them (the iconoclastic movement, for example, and the Western Reformation). Broadly, there have been three ways in which the *imago Dei* has been understood.

1. *Substantive understandings.* These maintain that there is a particular characteristic of human beings which is unique to them, and which is bestowed upon them by God. For example, some have held that it is our faculty of reason which is unique:[2] this faculty is the endowment of God which makes us different from

---

[1]   See also Taylor, Chapter 1.

[2]   See also Jasper, Chapter 7.

all other creatures in God's creation. Others have suggested that it is spiritual awareness that marks out human beings as distinct.

2. *Relational understandings.* These understand humans being made in the image of God to mean that we, uniquely, are able to relate to God. This is the kind of view being expressed by Augustine, when he wrote: "You have made us for yourself, and our heart is restless until it rests in you."[3] There is something about the way in which we are constituted which means that we, uniquely amongst living creatures, yearn for God, and we are able to fulfil that yearning thanks to God's image within us. It is also suggested that the human capacity to love and to form relationships reflects the *imago Dei*, since the triune God embodies relationships within Godself.

3. *Functional understandings.* These reckon that there is something which humans, and only humans, can do from a theological point of view. The quotation above from the book of Genesis continues: "God blessed them, and God said to them, 'be fruitful and multiply, and fill the earth and subdue it; and have dominion over the fish of the sea and over the birds of the air and over every living thing that moves upon the earth'" (Genesis 1:28). It has been suggested that the notion of dominion expressed in these verses means that Christianity bears "a huge burden of guilt" for the ecological crisis which we currently face;[4] the debates around this issue will not concern us here, but there has been a widespread understanding among Christians in recent decades that human beings are to be thought of as stewards of God's creation, entrusted with a particular role within it, and required to fulfil that role in order to ensure the flourishing of the natural order as a whole (and of human beings specifically). We are, as it were, charged by God

---

[3]   St Augustine of Hippo, *Confessions*, tr. H. Chadwick (Oxford: Oxford University Press 1992), p. 3.

[4]   Lynn White Jr, quoted in Paul D. Murray and David Wilkinson, "The Theology of Creation within the Christian Tradition", in Christopher Southgate (ed.), *God, Humanity and the Cosmos*, third edition (London: T&T Clark International, 2011), p. 51.

with responsibilities that no other creature can discharge. This view might urge that we are the priests of creation, representing God to God's creation, and God's creation to God. This, it has been maintained, is a function which humans uniquely can perform.

There are a number of ways in which the modern scientific worldview poses interesting questions for each of these understandings of human uniqueness, which have consequences for our understanding of the idea of the *imago Dei*. The following sections explore various such questions.

Are we alone in the universe?

Extraterrestrial Intelligence (ETI)

Does our uniqueness lie in our planet being the only one which has life existing on it? Or is there life on other planets too? These are questions which have excited people for centuries and which of course forms the basis of much science fiction. They provide the impetus for contemporary projects such as the Search for Extraterrestrial Intelligence (SETI)— basically, scanning the skies systematically looking for modulated electromagnetic waves, which might indicate the presence of other beings which are technologically advanced enough to communicate in this way—and also the search for exoplanets, planets orbiting stars which can be detected either through their gravitational influence or by the intermittent lessening of light from a star as a planet passes in front of it. Several thousand such planets have now been detected. When such a planet is reckoned (a) to be rocky rather than gaseous, and (b) to lie within the so-called "Goldilocks zone", which permits water to be liquid on its surface, there is immediate speculation about whether it might be habitable for organic life.

Now, there is of course a huge difference between "organic life" and a species like *homo sapiens*. Some of the more excitable commentators in this field give the impression that the presence of water—and perhaps methane and ammonia—virtually guarantees that this will lead to single-celled organisms, which in turn virtually guarantees that eventually multicellular, intelligent life forms will evolve. However, even if it is acknowledged that the odds against life as we know it originating and evolving by chance are astronomically small, if there are an astronomically large number of places where it might happen, that makes it statistically more likely. Does it make it likely that it has happened more than once?

An attempt to quantify the likelihood of finding ETI has been quantified in the Drake Equation:

$$N = R_. \cdot f_\mathrm{p} \cdot n_\mathrm{e} \cdot f_\mathrm{l} \cdot f_\mathrm{i} \cdot f_\mathrm{c} \cdot L$$

Where N is the number of technically advanced civilizations in our galaxy, and $R_.$ is the mean rate of star formation in our galaxy, f_p is the fraction of stars with planetary systems, n_e is the number of planets in such systems that are ecologically suitable for the origin of life, f_l is the fraction of such planets on which life in fact develops, f_i is the fraction of such planets on which life evolves to an intelligent form, f_c is the fraction of such worlds in which the intelligent life form invents high technology capable at least of interstellar radio communication, and L is the average lifetime of such advanced civilizations.[5] Many of these figures can of course only be crude estimates, but they are being gradually refined with the discoveries of more exoplanets. As this happens, the question posed back in the 1950s by Enrico Fermi becomes more and more pressing: "Where is everybody?"[6] (The fact that the increasing likelihood of our discovering ETI is accompanied by a deafening silence is sometimes referred to as the Fermi paradox.)

The religious consequences of the discovery of ETI

If organic life of any kind were to be discovered on another planet then its evolution into complex intelligent life forms like us would presumably at least be possible, so the idea that human life is unique would become unsustainable. What might be the religious consequences of this?

---

[5]   *Encyclopedia Britannica*, <https://www.britannica.com/science/Drake-equation>, accessed 13 December 2020.

[6]   Cf. A. Kracher, "Are we special? Humanity and extraterrestrial life", in M. Fuller, D. Evers, A. Runehov and K.-W. Sæther (eds), *Issues in Science and Theology: Are We Special?* (Cham: Springer, 2017), p. 33.

It is sometimes assumed that the discovery of ETI would be deeply problematic for those of a religious disposition. One of the classic instances of conflict between science and religion, which was cited as such from the nineteenth century onwards, is the case of Giordano Bruno (1548–1600), who was tried and executed for heresy; and one of the things in which he believed was the existence of the possibility of there being many inhabited worlds in our universe.[7] But is this necessarily a problem for religious believers? Not according to a survey carried out by Ted Peters and Julie Froehlig, which analysed over 1300 responses and concluded:

> This survey has sought to provide data relevant to confirming or disconfirming the following hypothesis: *upon confirmation of contact between earth and an extraterrestrial civilization of intelligent beings, the long-established religious traditions of earth would confront a crisis of belief and perhaps even collapse.* Responses from persons self-identifying with one of seven major religious traditions report that they do not fear an impending collapse in their own religious belief system.[8]

Indeed, one of the interesting results of this survey is that the understanding that the discovery of ETI would be problematic for religious people was held primarily by those who identified as non-religious!

Of course, there are issues for Christians, in particular, that would accompany the discovery of ETI. One of the most obvious would relate to soteriology: how would those extraterrestrials be brought into a relationship with God? Put crudely, did Jesus die for aliens from the planet Zog, or did God reveal Godself to such aliens in some other way? The former answer would suggest a mission imperative; the latter would suggest that Jesus is not the only way by which intelligent beings might come to God. Either way, some hard theological thinking would

---

[7]   See also Jasper, Chapter 7.

[8]   T. Peters and J. Froehlig, "The Peters ETI Religious Crisis Survey", <https://counterbalance.org/etsurv/PetersETISurveyRep.pdf>, accessed 13 December 2020.

need to be done. The terms "astrotheology"[9] and "astrochristology"[10] have recently been coined to refer to the frameworks within which such thinking might be carried out. But all this begs the question: why should there be a problem in reconciling Christian faith with the discovery of ETI? If God has created so bountiful a universe, why should it not contain intelligent life elsewhere within it? (This has been referred to as the "Principle of Plenitude".[11])

What might non-terrestrial life be like?

Another issue may be considered here. In the event of there being life "out there", what is the likelihood of it being exactly like life on earth, from a biochemical point of view? Is the "tree of life", which relates us and all the other creatures on our planet to each other, itself unique, or might other such "trees" be possible? Elisabeth Loos has described how recent work in the field of synthetic biology has involved such processes as:

> the integration of unnatural amino acids [into proteins] . . . the alteration of DNA and with that the creation of so-called XNA . . . and the implementation of a quadruplet nucleotide code instead of the natural triplet code. The relatively new biotechnological possibility of turning theoretical considerations into actual biological parts (and, the hope is, eventually into synthetic xenobiological organisms) enables researchers to examine if and how "xeno-life" can work—here on Earth, but also in the broader universe.[12]

---

[9] Cf. A. Losch, "Astrotheology: On exoplanets, Christian concerns and human hopes", *Zygon* 51:2 (2016), pp. 405–13.

[10] Cf. T. Peters, "Astrobiology and Astrochristology", *Zygon* 51:2 (2016), pp. 480–96.

[11] E. Loos, "Is Life Unique? Perspectives from Astrobiology and Synthetic Xenobiology", in M. Fuller, D. Evers, A. Runehov and K.-W. Sæther (eds), *Issues in Science and Theology: Are We Special?* (Cham: Springer, 2017), p. 19.

[12] Ibid., p. 22.

This field of synthetic biology has also opened up some fascinating possibilities for exploring how life might have developed in conditions unlike those which obtain on earth—in environments with much greater temperatures, for example, or greater gravity or atmospheric pressure. Such explorations are of great theoretical interest, and they may help us to engage with ETI should we discover that it has developed along a different tree of life to that on earth.

Do xenobiology and synthetic biology raise any theological issues around human uniqueness in addition to those that would be raised by the existence of ETI itself? Probably not. Creatures with fundamentally different biologies from our own may perhaps be more difficult for us to communicate with, but their existence is surely no more problematic than would be that of extraterrestrials who shared our biological building-blocks.

Are we unique amongst terrestrial creatures?

Let us now consider how (if at all) human beings might be considered unique amongst life on earth. The following observations might be made the basis of claims for human uniqueness:

1. Humans are substantially different from all other creatures—there is something different about our physical make-up, or our mental capacities (e.g. the capacity to make and use tools, or to communicate with one another).
2. Humans alone are capable of that range of experiences which we call "spiritual".

These relate respectively to the "substantive" and "relational" understandings of the *imago Dei* that were discussed above.

Let's look at these claims in turn.

DNA
It is commonplace today to think about the relationships between animals and between plants in terms of the amount of DNA which they share, and

an often-quoted fact is that humans share 97.5 per cent of our DNA with chimpanzees.[13] It is thereby implied that we are not so very different from our primate cousins. It is also the case that we share about 60 per cent of our DNA with fruit flies.[14] How exactly this is worked out, and what (if any) significance such observations have in terms of genetics given that "quantity of DNA" does not map straightforwardly onto "active genes" is a complex issue which we will not go into now,[15] but the fact that we might share a lot of DNA with other creatures implies a degree of kinship only at one level. Even if we do share a great deal of our DNA with chimps, it does not appear unreasonable to suppose that small changes at the level of DNA can produce very large changes at the level of the organism.

We might also at this point consider our relationships with extinct hominins. It is reckoned that we share 99.5 per cent of our DNA with Neanderthals, for example;[16] and these are just the best known of our evolutionary cousins. There are also Denisovans (regarding which some DNA information is available), and *Homo floresiensis* and *Homo naledi* (for which, so far, it is not). If the *imago Dei* is to be linked to humankind on the basis of our genetic distinctiveness, then the obvious question is: at what stage did we become genetically distinct enough for this label to apply to us? Did Neanderthals possess the *imago Dei*? Did other early hominins? This leads in turn to the question: is the *imago Dei* still reflected (albeit perhaps in a limited way) in creatures like chimpanzees?

Human capabilities

In terms of what humans can uniquely do, and the physical and mental capacities that might distinguish us from other species, we are of course aware that other animals—and not just primates—are capable

[13] A. Peacocke, *Theology for a Scientific Age*, enlarged edition (London: SCM Press, 1993), p. 220.

[14] Robin McKie, "Six Nobel Prizes—What's the Fascination with the Fruit Fly?", <https://www.theguardian.com/science/2017/oct/07/fruit-fly-fascination-nobel-prizes-genetics>, accessed 14 December 2020.

[15] On human genetics, see also Reid, Chapter 9.

[16] J. P. Noonan et al., "Sequencing and Analysis of Neanderthal Genomic DNA", *Science* 314 (2006), pp. 1113–18.

of communication, through sound and through visual means, and that other animals also use tools. Such capabilities were, so far as we can tell, possessed also by extinct hominins like Neanderthals. There have been interesting experiments carried out with the aim of enabling inter-species communication, either verbally or through the use of symbols, but these have to date been largely unsuccessful.[17] Similarly, it has been observed that other creatures, including primates and some birds, are capable of using tools in order to achieve particular ends. Although we can communicate vastly more complex ideas through spoken language than any other non-human creature, and although our tool-making and tool-using capabilities are likewise different by orders of magnitude, clearly the difference is one of scale, not of capability per se.

Spirituality

So far, we have been thinking about substantive understandings of the *imago Dei*, relating it to our physiological essence and our physical capabilities, and such understandings appear to be misguided. What about more relational understanding of the *imago Dei*? Are humans unique in their capacity for spiritual experiences: for understanding the transcendent, and entering into relationships with God?

Let us go back to extinct hominins. As is well known, Neanderthals seem to have buried their dead (although the evidence that they did so with accompanying floral tributes has been contested). It is conjectured that *H. naledi* also buried their dead in a formal way.[18] This may indicate some kind of ritual practice, which may in turn indicate some kind of spiritual or transcendental awareness on the part of these early hominins.

---

[17] M. Weker, "Animal in Human, Human in Animal: On Similarities and Differences in Human and Animal Behaviour", in M. Fuller, D. Evers, A. Runehov and K.-W. Sæther (eds), *Studies in Science and Theology* Vol. 16. (Halle: Martin-Luther-University Halle-Wittenberg, 2018), pp. 57–69.

[18] R. Herce, "Is *Homo naledi* Going to Challenge Our Presuppositions on Human Uniqueness?", in M. Fuller, D. Evers, A. Runehov and K.-W. Sæther (eds), *Issues in Science and Theology: Are We Special?* (Cham: Springer, 2017), p. 103.

This might suggest that humans are not unique in possessing such "spiritual" awareness.

Interestingly, this relational understanding of the *imago Dei* has also been brought into question through observations which suggest that modern-day primates also display behaviour which may be interpreted as "religious". The primatologist Jane Goodall has written of "primate spirituality", interpreting particular behaviours of chimpanzees as indicative of a religious awareness—in particular, certain behaviours in front of waterfalls, and what she describes as a "rain dance".[19] James Harrod goes further, arguing that

> a comprehensive review of primatology reports reveals that chimpanzees do perform ritualized patterns of behavior in response to birth, death, consortship, and elemental natural phenomena.... In the course of these performances, chimpanzees decontextualize and convert everyday communicative signals to express non-ordinary emotions of wonder and awe. The patterning of chimpanzee ritual behaviors evidences all the components of a prototypical trans-species definition of religion.[20]

Animal ceremonies of various kinds have also been reported. Maria Weker describes these in the following terms: "When applied to the animal world, the term 'ceremony' is used to describe a sequence of actions aimed at exerting influence on another animal. Most ceremonies in animals are genetically programmed, hereditary, unlearned sequences of poses, movements and vocalizations."[21] This suggests that, insofar as ceremony and ritual behaviour is considered to be characteristically "religious", then animals are capable of displaying "religious" behaviour.

---

[19] Cf. L. Oviedo and J. R. Feierman, "Does Religious Behavior Render Humans Special?", in M. Fuller, D. Evers, A. Runehov and K.-W. Sæther (eds), *Issues in Science and Theology: Are We Special?* (Cham: Springer, 2017), p. 109.

[20] J. B. Harrod, "The Case for Chimpanzee Religion", *Journal for the Study of Religion, Nature and Culture* 8:1 (2014), p. 8.

[21] Weker, op. cit., p. 62.

All this is necessarily speculative: we can only understand imperfectly (if at all) what chimpanzees and other non-human animals are thinking when they display what appears to us to be religious behaviour (and, of course, this will also depend very much on how such behaviour is defined). However, it is perhaps not going too far to suggest that, in the same way that some human traits like speech are present in vestigial ways in other creatures, so human capacities such as the ability to experience and relate to God and a transcendent reality may likewise be present in other creatures. How this capacity originated is another area of great interest. Some researchers within the cognitive science of religion have suggested that there may be an evolutionary basis for such beliefs in human beings, but this is beyond the scope of the present chapter.[22]

Sin[23]

Another interesting line of thought on human uniqueness which has been developed from comparisons of ourselves with other primates has been to ask the question in more negative terms. We have been thinking about all those amazing things that humans can do, and how that might distinguish us. But are there darker ways of conceiving human uniqueness? We know that humans are capable of grotesque savagery in our behaviour towards others, although similar behaviour to this has been noted in the animal world—for example, cats playing with mice, or killer whales with seals, before killing them. But can this be taken to another level of description? The theologian Ernst Conradie has asked the question: can only humans sin? He notes that many commentators have answered that question with a definite affirmative: animals have no moral sense and therefore cannot meaningfully be said to sin. However, drawing on the work of the animal ethologist Frans de Waal, Conradie notes that some primates appear to

---

[22] See M. Ruse, "Biologically Evolutionary Explanations of Religious Belief", in F. Watts and L. Turner (eds), *Evolution, Religion and Cognitive Science* (Oxford: Oxford University Press, 2014) for an account of the background to such a view; and J. Barrett, *Cognitive Science, Religion and Theology* (West Conshohocken, PA: Templeton Press, 2011) for an outworking of it.

[23] See also Taylor, Chapter 1, and Hart, Chapter 3.

have a kind of proto-morality: this leads him to question whether humans are unique in possessing a moral sensibility. Conradie concludes:

> [de Waal] questions the ways in which the Judaeo-Christian tradition has emphasized the discontinuity between humans and other animals by placing humans on a pedestal as the only species with a soul, created in the image of God. He describes the evolutionary continuity not only in terms of genetic (biological) features of human existence but also in terms of noble human characteristics such as empathy, reciprocity and fairness. Conversely . . . [s]uch uniqueness may also be found in forms of torture, cruelty, deception, exploitation, indoctrination and environmental destruction.[24]

Perhaps, again, we are talking about issues of scale here: humans and primates may both be conscious of issues which we would call moral issues, and hence of behaviour which both we and they know (emotionally, if not rationally) to be "wrong", but we are able to go much further in terms of conscious wrongdoing than other creatures are able to do. This, indeed, may be an important point that is made by the traditional story of the Fall.[25]

Artificial intelligence

A further set of issues around human uniqueness arises when we consider not only other intelligent creatures in the natural world, but also the potential development of artificial intelligence.[26] Where would that leave us when thinking about the *imago Dei*? Sara Lumbreras puts it thus:

> The last decades have witnessed an unprecedented development of Information and Communication Technologies (ICTs) and

---

[24] E. Conradie, "Do Only Humans Sin? In conversation with Frans de Waal", in M. Fuller, D. Evers, A. Runehov and K.-W. Sæther (eds), *Issues in Science and Theology: Are We Special?* (Cham: Springer, 2017), p. 132.

[25] See further, Taylor, Chapter 1.

[26] See also Stoddart, Chapter 11.

Artificial Intelligence (AI), which have modified the way that interpersonal relationships are established and could also modify the way that human specificity is understood, even challenging the concept of human specialness. These technological advances have led some authors to anticipate that soon there will be machines built in our own image and to which we will relate as equals.[27]

This leads Lumbreras herself to argue that there is an irreducible *authenticity* which is expressed in the way in which we respond to subjective states and subjective stimuli, and that it would not be possible for artificial intelligences to make such responses.

It is probably safe to say that the jury is out regarding what will and will not be possible for future artificial intelligences. Some enthusiasts point to an imminent "singularity"—a point in time after which there will be exponential growth in computer capability, at which point machine intelligence will outstrip our own, with incalculable consequences for society.[28] Others, like Lumbreras, maintain that there will always be some irreducible aspect of humanity that it will not be possible to simulate artificially. The issue, of course, is that if we are at some point able to produce machines which are more intelligent than ourselves (however such "intelligence" might be assessed), then what does this say about intelligence as a marker of human distinctiveness? If the *imago Dei* is conceived in relational terms, then could a machine created *imago hominis* be said to bear the *imago Dei* also—by reflection, as it were,

---

27   S. Lumbreras, "Strong Artificial Intelligence and *imago hominis*: The risks of a reductionist definition of human nature", in M. Fuller, D. Evers, A. Runehov and K.-W. Sæther (eds), *Issues in Science and Theology: Are We Special?* (Cham: Springer, 2017), p. 157.

28   See D. Brin, D. Broderick, N. Bostrom, A. Chislenko, R. Hanson, M. More, M. Nielson and A. Sandberg, "A Critical Discussion of Vinge's Singularity Concept", in M. More and N. Vita-More (eds), *The Transhumanist Reader* (Chichester: Wiley-Blackwell, 2013), pp. 395–417 for a discussion of this concept.

or even as a "second generation" image? Noreen Herzfeld sounds a cautionary note here:

> An intelligent computer may act, in some ways, in a human-like manner. . . . We may even find ourselves acting in a relational way toward such a machine. Yet, just as we live as imperfect images of our creator, striving to grow in God's image and likeness yet always falling short of the mark, so our creation in AI will fall short of the human.[29]

Given the extraordinary rapidity of developments in the field of computing, it is difficult to foresee exactly what the future might hold in terms of artificial intelligence; but as Lumbreras and Herzfeld indicate, there are clearly issues with assuming that it is intelligence that marks out human beings as unique, if comparable intelligence can be expressed in artificial devices which yet fall short of humanity.

Posthumanism

In addition to the possibility of our constructing intelligences greater than our own, there are also the possibilities of using technological enhancement to improve ourselves, whether this is done through prostheses, neural-machine interfaces, or advanced forms of genetic engineering. This is the project sometimes referred to as transhumanism, or posthumanism.[30] These are terms which have been variously understood. Max More elucidates them as follows.

> Transhumanists want to apply technology to overcome limitations imposed by our biological and genetic heritage. Transhumanists regard human nature not as an end in itself, nor as perfect, and not as having any claim on our allegiance. Rather, it is just one point along an evolutionary pathway and we can learn to reshape our own nature in ways we deem desirable and valuable.

---

[29] N. Herzfeld, *In Our Image: Artificial Intelligence and the Human Spirit* (Minneapolis, MN: Fortress Press, 2002), p. 94.

[30] See also Stoddart, Chapter 11.

... Becoming posthuman means exceeding the limitations that define the less desirable aspects of the 'human condition.' Posthuman beings would no longer suffer from disease, aging and inevitable death (but they are likely to face other challenges).[31]

However these terms are understood, it might be urged that they introduce a fluidity to the concept of "humanity", and they suggest that any uniqueness we possess now is transient as we ourselves are developing through our use of technology—making us, perhaps, even more unique.

Conclusion

Where does all this leave us in our search for something that makes human beings special, or unique? What aspects of our scientific worldview need to be taken into account when considering human uniqueness? To summarize, it would appear that:

- Although, as far as we are aware, our earth is the only planet in the universe on which intelligent life has evolved, and although the distances involved and the difficulties in communication over those distances mean that even if there is life "out there" the chances of our ever interacting with it are low, it is by no means beyond the realm of the possible that such life exists. We are not therefore necessarily unique in terms of our being the only life form to have evolved an advanced intelligence. However, it has been urged that this is not a theological problem, in that such life might simply be seen as witnessing to the wonderful fecundity of the universe as God's creation.
- In terms of the biochemistry on which life as we know it is based, we may again not be unique in that it is conceivable that other living systems might in theory come about, having a different biochemical base (so-called xenobiology). Were

---

[31] M. More, "The Philosophy of Transhumanism", in M. More and N. Vita-More (eds), *The Transhumanist Reader* (Chichester: Wiley-Blackwell, 2013), p. 4.

such xenobiochemical systems to give rise to conscious life, the difficulties this would present to us theologically would be no different from those posed by other alien life forms.

- We share significant percentages of our DNA with other living organisms on our planet (the vast majority of it in the cases of the present-day higher apes) and with our hominin ancestors. This physiological/biochemical criterion would therefore not appear to be a good one on which to base any claims for human uniqueness. Clearly, much of our genetic inheritance is shared with other creatures. It might, however, be urged that the higher functionalities possessed by humans do not map in any linear way onto what is unique in human DNA, so that the quantitative approach that comments on how much DNA we share with other creatures is unhelpful in thinking about qualitative differences.

- Related to this, there are interesting questions to be posed around human uniqueness when we think about extinct hominins. How similar to us might they have been in terms of what we perceive to be our "higher" capacities? If there is evidence to suggest that they were similar to us—even, in the case of Neanderthals, being capable of interbreeding with human ancestors—then to what extent might it make sense to think of Neanderthals possessing the "image of God"?

- There are many similarities between animal and human behaviours, to the extent that it has even been suggested that some animals display proto-religious behaviour. Such activities in animals would suggest, once again, that this is not a fruitful area in which to look for that which makes humans unique. Interpreting animal behaviour in this way can only be speculative, and since we cannot know what is going on in the mind of a creature like a chimpanzee it is problematic to base too much on such interpretations. However, if it were somehow to be demonstrated that animals other than humans are capable of experiencing some sense of transcendence, even some intimation of the reality of God, this would surely not be problematic. The idea of nature as a whole responding to God is found in the Bible (e.g. Psalm 98:7–8: "Let the sea roar, and all that fills it; the world and those who live in it. Let the floods clap their hands; let the hills sing together for joy at the presence of the Lord"). If God is immanent in nature, then why should not any creature capable of any apprehension of that fact respond to it?

- In the same way that humans appear to possess particular capabilities for good to an extent not matched by other creatures, so too they possess greater capabilities for evil. Moral awareness may not be something unique to humans, but our capacity for acting immorally, and for seeing that behaviour through a theological lens as "sinful", may conceivably be something that differentiates us from other creatures.

- Artificial intelligence may, in due course, lead to our generating computer-based systems which we deem to be more intelligent than humans. These would be systems which may learn faster and perform complex tasks faster than humans, and they may even possibly prove capable of doing things which humans, in virtue of our limited intelligence, are incapable of doing. What would such developments tell us about human uniqueness? If such an intelligence is considered to bear the image of humankind, being related in this way to its originator, might it be thought of as itself bearing the image of God as well, reflected or refracted through humanity?

- Finally, we noted that "humanity" is itself a contested concept. With the possibility of technological enhancement we are changing what is possible for our species. This suggests perhaps that the *imago Dei* is best not understood as a static concept, but rather one which grows and develops as we ourselves grow and develop.

Here, then, are some of the ways in which human uniqueness has been discussed, and some of the ways in which traditional arguments used regarding human uniqueness have been either expanded or found wanting in the light of contemporary science. Any theological anthropology for the twenty-first century must be cognizant of the constraints which such discussions place around its construction.

Questions for discussion

1. How (if at all) would the discovery of life on other planets make you feel about your faith?
2. "Risen apes, not fallen angels". How does this description of humankind bear on traditional Christian thinking?
3. How do you feel about the suggestions in this chapter for the development of thinking machines, and of post-humans? Were such developments to occur, how would they make you think about human uniqueness, and about humans' relationship to God?

Further reading

N. Herzfeld, *In Our Image: Artificial Intelligence and the Human Spirit* (Minneapolis, MN: Fortress Press, 2002).

M. More and N. Vita-More (eds), *The Transhumanist Reader* (Chichester: Wiley-Blackwell, 2013).

K. Ward, *The Big Questions in Science and Religion* (West Conshohocken, PA: Templeton Press, 2008).

D. Wilkinson, *Science, Religion and the Search for Extra-terrestrial Intelligence* (Oxford: Oxford University Press, 2017).

CHAPTER 9

The biochemistry of being human

Delyth M. Reid

Introduction

Any account of what human beings are must acknowledge that we are physical creatures. Our bodies are extraordinarily complex, and scientific investigation is leading us to a greater and greater understanding of them and of how they operate, right down to the molecular level. A key aspect of our humanity which we must consider in the context of any discussion of what it means to be human is therefore the biochemistry which underpins the formation and activities of our bodies. This is the subject of the present chapter.

The biochemistry of life must take place in water, the fluid medium in which the precursors of bioactive molecules first appeared in the primordial rock pools 3.5 billion years ago. This is why scientists get so excited when they find evidence for liquid water on other planets. Thinking on how the early biochemical reactions culminated in the creation of ourselves and the almost infinite complexity of living things, we cannot fail to experience awe and wonder. Even flies are masterpieces of biological engineering. Furthermore, they have life, which is something that we all share but has confounded us in understanding its meaning ever since we began contemplating it. As the popular saying puts it, "the whole is greater than the sum of its parts": this is actually what we see when looking at any living organism or even a cell growing in a culture dish. I can extract the white cells from my own blood, grow them in a dish and watch them move and divide independently from any instruction from my mind. But these cells are not me. They only relate to me in that they contain my unique genetic code. Furthermore, we can grow heart muscle cells in a dish until they form a thin layer of heart tissue and produce synchronized contractions. But this is not a heart.

When considering what makes us human, or any organism the way it is, it is important to remember the interplay of genes with the environment. This was recognized many years ago, but we now know that this varies for any particular gene, depending on how influenced it is by external factors including nutrition, and mental and physical demands. For humans, identical versus fraternal twins and separated-at-birth twin studies have given much credence to this notion. More recently still, genes are thought to be more important than the 10,000 hours practice rule for mastery of sports, music and other skills.[1]

Humans are related to all life on earth

Within all eukaryotic (non-bacterial) cells are the same subcellular organelles including the nuclei, containing the DNA coiled in chromosomes, the energy-generating mitochondria and the protein-assembling endoplasmic reticulum[2] and Golgi bodies.[3] Chlorophyll-containing chloroplasts are, of course, unique to photosynthetic plants. The biochemistry of life is played out within and on the surfaces of all these subcellular organelles and within the cell cytoplasm. The milieu of hundreds of biochemical reactions is aided by such compartmentalization. Many of these reactions are common to all life and the genes controlling them have remained virtually unchanged during the divergence of species: they would have been the same in the long-extinct dinosaurs and ancient amber-locked insects.

---

[1] Bret Stetka, "What Do Great Musicians Have in Common? DNA" , <https://www.scientificamerican.com/article/what-do-great-musicians-have-in-common-dna/>, accessed 13 April 2021.

[2] Endoplasmic reticulum: a cell organelle necessary for the synthesis of large protein molecules.

[3] Golgi body: a cell organelle required for the modification and packaging and export of proteins.

Highly conserved genes often control metabolism and other essential life processes and are known as "housekeeping genes".

Thus, we are connected to all of life on earth, even to the unwelcome flies in our homes, whose reaction times we can scarcely match. Because their housekeeping genes are largely the same as ours, researchers have been able to use fruit flies to investigate gene control and regulation, which has yielded ground-breaking information, without needing to use mammals such as mice.

Genes other than the housekeeping genes are responsible for producing the diversity of life. As one would expect, the more phenotypically similar species appear, the more their genotypes[4] have in common. DNA holds the instructions for making functional proteins, some of which are structural, enzymatic, cell membrane ion channels or pumps, or cell membrane receptors for neurotransmitters and hormones. Widely known proteins in ourselves include insulin, antibodies, haemoglobin, digestive enzymes and transporter proteins for cholesterol. When the gene for a common ion channel residing in a cell membrane is sequenced for several species, it can be seen that it is quite rare for the sequences to remain identical over millions of years of evolutionary separation. Mutations in DNA occur randomly and are often corrected by the cell. But a few are useful and allow the fine tuning of protein function to serve the organism in a new environment. Any mutation that increases the survival of the species, even if it offers only a small advantage, will be selected over time. Some parts of the protein remain identical despite this passage of time, suggesting that these conserved regions are essential to the function of that protein and any mutations in these regions would have been incompatible with life. In mammals, for example, offspring with lethal mutations are not usually able to progress to term and will be reabsorbed or spontaneously aborted.

Small molecular differences on several levels, as coded by the DNA, are enough to create all the life on earth that has gone before us and is still to come. The overall body shape of vertebrates is determined by skeletons

---

4   Genotypes are the sets of genes that an organism carries whereas phenotypes are the physical expression of these (e.g. height) and may be influenced by the environment (e.g. food availability).

that originated from a winning design about 500 million years ago, in the sea. Subsequently some vertebrates left the water and branched out into terrestrial habitats where natural selection over generations created animals perfectly adapted to a vast array of lifestyles. I have been asked, how could an elephant have evolved from an ancestral mouselike creature? There are mechanisms that determine the dimensions and shapes of bones and the same genes operate in several regions of the body during embryonic development and beyond. Evolutionary changes require time and environmental pressure, but it takes fewer gene alterations to change the shape and size of an animal than was first thought. On a short timescale, dog breeding produced size variations from teacup dogs to Saint Bernards. Dogs were domesticated from grey wolves thousands of years ago and very few genes are responsible for the wide choice available to buyers today. It is unlikely that any of the traits selected by humans are beneficial to the canine species.

Taking on the human form

Evolutionary biology seeks to understand the genetic basis of adaptations. Commonly, fish are used as models for adaptation in vertebrates. Geneticists have compared the genomes between and within species in order to identify specific regulatory genetic alterations which control skeletal evolution and, for us, the appearance of bipedalism in our ancestors. Most people have heard that we share about 99 per cent of our DNA with chimpanzees. This fact is expected to amaze us, but within that 1 per cent is an enormous potential to turn into a human. Further analysis has extended this to be 4 per cent and there are many layers of complexity when translating the genotype of a human or chimpanzee to a phenotype.[5]

Gene-sequencing technology has undergone a revolution in what it can achieve. Excitingly, a wealth of genetic data is emerging from

---

[5] A. Vary, D. H. Geschwind, E. E. Richler, "Explaining human uniqueness: genome interactions with environment, behaviour and culture", *Nature Reviews Genetics* 9 (2008), pp. 749–63.

primates, extinct hominins and modern human populations, enabling us to understand more fully what makes us uniquely human from a genetic perspective. Changes in the regulation of certain pre-existing genes, including those that regulate the growth and differentiation of tissues, were pertinent to becoming human.

All cells in the body contain the same DNA and in order to become a body, rather than a grey mushy heap of identical cells, cell differentiation into tissues and organs must take place. This is achieved through the regulation of genes. To become a fully differentiated cell residing in, say, the liver, it must switch off all unnecessary genes, in this case those for producing hair or muscle, whereas genes pertaining to producing enzymes for the degradation of foreign chemicals, such as paracetamol and alcohol, must be switched on. The turning on and off, or regulating, of genes requires further genes that code for enhancer and repressor proteins which bind to the gene needing regulation.

Consider how our feet are so different from those of a chimpanzee, whereas the skeletal make-up of our hands is not so diverged. Research has uncovered a family of regulatory proteins known as Bone Morphogenic Proteins (BMP), which control bone growth and shape. A protein named Growth/Differentiation Factor 6 (GDF6) belongs to this family. GDF6 has been studied in many species ranging from stickleback fish to humans and is required for bone and joint formation including those of the skull and digits. Thus, changes in the activity of the gene in these areas facilitated the diversity of vertebrate bodies we see today and in the fossil record. During human evolution, the enhancer gene that controls expression of GDF6 in the feet was deleted, enabling the shorter toes necessary for our transition to bipedalism.

Natural selection has influenced our genome at different times during our evolutionary past resulting in gene deletions, duplications, modifications, gain and loss of regulatory enhancers and the introduction of new layers of control of their expression. Many such changes took place to create the modern human.[6]

---

[6]   W. Fu, J. M. Akey, "Selection and adaptation in the human genome", *Annu. Rev. Genomics Hum. Genet.* 14 (2013), pp. 467–89.

Modern humans

The term "species" is used to refer to a group of organisms which are so similar that they regularly interbreed to produce fertile offspring. Speciation happens during evolution, when populations split and become physically isolated from one another until, eventually, over many generations, they have changed so much that they can no longer breed together to produce fertile offspring. Neanderthals are generally thought of as a distinct species from modern *Homo sapiens*, based on differences in cranial and pelvic shapes. However, genetic evidence points to interbreeding, which has led some to suggest that they were a subspecies and should be named *Homo sapiens neanderthalensis*. Modern gene-sequencing technology has permitted the extraction of early hominid DNA from their remains, allowing comparisons with modern humans. The results of these analyses have shown that we are virtually 100 per cent identical to *neanderthalensis*, as opposed to 94–99 per cent with chimpanzees, and many of us carry specific Neanderthal alleles of the same genes found in humans.

Modern humans arose around 100 to 200 thousand years ago, when the evolution of the brain appears to have stabilized following a slackening of evolutionary pressure. Of course, our "minds" continued to develop with the handing on of accumulating knowledge and the expansion of our thinking and communication. Stone tools may have been quickly perfected, but humans did not stop there. We continued to look for ways in which to improve our lot. Human societies rapidly progressed in the last 10,000 years, since we were hunter-gatherers, much too fast for our brain structures to evolve to cope with the stresses and strains of modern life. It is, therefore, unsurprising that our brains now struggle to keep up and that stress-related illnesses arise when we spend too much time in the "fight or flight" mode induced by adrenalin and cortisol (stress hormones). We are not born knowing how to deal with the stresses of the modern human environment and must make an effort to adapt to its pressures and demands as we meet them.

The human brain and the seat of the soul

Mammals retain the primitive parts of the brain, the hippocampus and amygdala, where emotions are generated. Further sensations arrive via the vagus nerve. These structures evolved long before the profound development of the cerebral cortex. The modern human cerebral cortex, which houses our consciousness, struggles to interpret the primal messages and strives to construct a narrative for them. The primitive brain structures are not a source of reliable information and yet the strength of feelings they convey can cause us to overlook any rationalization we have for what is truly happening in the real world.

There is much scope for different understandings of soul and mind, and their interactions with the brain. At one time, it was believed that the pineal gland was the seat of the soul. This is a small organ at the base of the brain, which is sometimes referred to as the third eye because it contains elements similar to those of the retina. Mostly its functions pertain to circadian rhythms like sleep. As to what the soul is, or if it exists at all, this is not a question that modern science even wants to address. But that does not mean that it does not exist. The closest science comes to addressing the soul is the attempt to understand consciousness.

We might imagine that our personalities are determined by our souls. Science has shown that personality is heritable and relates to neuroneal structures in different parts of the brain, and that brain injury can alter personality. Since the domestication of animals, we have been selectively breeding dogs for personality in addition to those physical traits that suit our purposes. The importance of the environment in personality development for human babies, and similarly for our pets, is of significant importance. We must be nurtured with love and kindness without which the behavioural consequences in adulthood can be catastrophic.

Some of us can feel our souls filling our bodies and imagine our emotions and creativity emerging from here. We commonly believe that the arts and music nurture our minds and souls, and some use them to praise and give thanks to God. We may feel our emotions viscerally, in our chests, hearts and guts. They can be triggered through our senses, but the brain is the control centre for all these sensations. Neuroscience points to physical structures of the brain that are responsible for the emotions and the many hormones and neurotransmitters that are involved with their induction and intensity. Creativity involves many parts of the brain, including the reward system. Traces of our ancestors' creativity have been left behind in the forms of cave art and carvings, although these may have had more to do with hope for successful hunts than for pleasure.

Philosophers and psychologists are possibly no more qualified to speculate on what the mind is than are the rest of us. Perhaps the mind is more tangible than the soul and consists of the collected memories, experiences, interpretations of accumulated knowledge, thoughts and ideas. All this is stored, deeply interconnected and played out within the physical structures of the brain. Compared with the workings of other parts of the body and despite scientific advancements, we remain very ignorant of the human brain, mind and consciousness. Yet, it is where we live and is the source of all our behaviours, thoughts, beliefs and emotions.

Hormones holding us together

Without hormones floating along in our blood, humans would fall apart. Most of the cells in our bodies express specific receptors on their membranes to engage the variety of hormones necessary to direct, synchronize and coordinate essential physiological and biochemical functions, including regulating fuel metabolism, growth and development. They also have wide-ranging effects upon the brain and behaviour. They were the first family of signalling molecules to be discovered and are synthesized within endocrine glands including the pituitary, gonads (sex hormones), adrenals (adrenalin), pancreas (insulin), thyroid (thyroxin) and hypothalamus (see later). They are controlled through complex feedback systems often involving other hormones. Diseases, including genetic mutations involving hormones or their receptors, produce adverse effects but some of these, including diabetes, dwarfism, and hypo- and hyperthyroidism, can be controlled by hormone replacement therapies.

There are many studies of sex hormones in relation to behaviour, mental health and psychiatric conditions, further to their more obvious roles in reproduction. Their effects on brain function, connectivity and cognitive

functioning are broad and diverse.[7] They are known to affect the degree
to which the right and left cerebral cortexes functionally specialize. It has
been known for decades that men are generally more hemispherically
lateralized than women. This is because women have a thicker corpus
callosum, which is the bundle of neurones connecting the hemispheres.
Brain specialization begins during foetal development where the sex
hormones have organizational effects on the brain and continues again
during puberty where they facilitate further brain gender dimorphism.

In adult life, the sex hormones are likely to be responsible for observed
gender differences in prevalence, onset, symptom profiles and disease
outcome in mental and physical illness. Mental health examples include
schizophrenia, where women tend to exhibit less impairment than men, and
post-traumatic stress disorder where women are more affected than men.[8]

It is worth spending further time on the biochemical effects of the
sex hormones, because we are all saturated with them to varying degrees
throughout our lives. Women have been the butt of jokes regarding
perceived behavioural changes and moodiness, put down to premenstrual
tension/syndrome/dysphoric disorder (PMT/PMS/PMDD) and
menopause. Regarding men, there is a common misconception that
testosterone causes aggression and that this is heightened in people with
raised testosterone. But testosterone is not the root of all evil.

Women's battle with hormones

The influences of progesterone and oestrogen on the female brain changes
over a woman's lifetime and fluctuates with the ovarian cycle. These
hormones have the ability to modulate the activity of neurotransmitters
and endorphins (see below) in the cortex and amygdala, affecting

---

[7] Markus Haussmann, "Why sex hormones matter for neuroscience: A very
     short review on sex, sex hormones, and functional brain asymmetries",
     Journal of Neuroscience Research 96 (2017), pp 40–9.

[8] A. Gogol, et al., "Sex differences in schizophrenia, bipolar disorder, and post-
     traumatic stress disorder: Are gonadal hormones the link?", *British Journal
     of Pharmacology* 175 (2019), pp. 4119–35.

cognition and emotion. There have been surprisingly few investigations into the effects of oral contraception on the normal delicate balance of sex hormone neurotransmission modulation. Further to this, there is a lack of data on the effects of high dose sex hormones in transgender people. Functional Magnetic Resonance Imaging (fMRI) studies are emerging to look at the contribution of oestrogen in brain responses to emotional and cognitive stimuli, usually in the form of facial expressions. Generally women showed different brain activation patterns between the follicular and luteal menstrual phases, and oral contraceptives and hormone therapy likely substantially determine functional changes in neural activity. However, it is difficult to compare published data due to broad differences in the complex methodologies employed.[9]

Pregnancy, birth and lactation all involve significant hormonal changes in women's bodies, which affect neurotransmission in functional ways to promote care of the baby. Oxytocin instigates birth, lactation, bonding and the feeling of love. However, the interaction of the environmental situation, individual genetics and experiences with the overall dramatic hormonal changes can cause severe depression in one out of ten women. This is beyond the normal postpartum "baby blues" tearfulness. Perinatal depression (PND) refers to episodes of depression that occur during pregnancy or up to a year following the birth. As well as distress to the mother, the development of the baby can be affected, furthering the mother's anxiety. The stress hormone, cortisol, increases during pregnancy up to 60 to 700 times higher than pre-pregnancy. The control and feedback systems for cortisol are complex and in pregnancy involve the placenta, which itself further increases maternal cortisol. Normally, the overall result is intended to reduce maternal sensitivity to external stressors but where the control systems are not working properly, the cortisol induces depression.[10] Several studies are pointing to cortisol

[9] Simone Toffoletto, Rupert Lanzenberger, Malin Gingnell, Inger Sundström-Poromaa, Erika Comasco, "Emotional and cognitive functional imaging of estrogen and progesterone effects in the female human brain: A systematic review", *Psychoneuroendocrinology* 50 (2014), pp. 28–52.

[10] S. Seth, Andrew J. Lewis, M. Galbally, "Perinatal maternal depression and cortisol function in pregnancy and the postpartum period: a systematic

and hormonal disregulation in the causes of PMDD. Fortunately, it is likely that current and future investigations will more clearly expose the effects of these on mental health, including PND. Then, with new specific treatments, women will be able to take further control of their biochemistry for their own wellbeing.

Testosterone

The biological effects of the testes were known over two thousand years ago, most obviously by the practice of creating eunuchs for a variety of social and cultural purposes. From the effects of castration, Aristotle formulated his hypothesis on fertilization which is one of the first scientific observations in reproductive biology.[11]

Testosterone has been the most studied androgen (male hormone) to date. It was Ernest Laqueur, in 1935, who isolated it from bull testes and named it,[12] and in the same year Adolf Butenandt[13] in Göttingen and Leopold Ruzicka[14] in Basel independently synthesized it. This improved its therapeutic use over the hitherto unpleasant consumption in crude form, where it was effectively destroyed by digestive enzymes in any case. In the 1950s and 1960s, scientists modified testosterone in order to enhance its anabolic (molecule-building and hence body-building and

---

literature review", *BMC Pregnancy and childbirth* 16:124 (2016) Open Access.

[11] Aristotle, *Historia Animalium* (History of Animals), tr. D'Arcy Wentworth Thompson (Oxford: Clarendon Press, 1910).

[12] K. David, E. Dingemanse, J. Freud, E. Laqueur, "Über kristallinisches männliches Hormon aus Hoden (Testosteron), wirksamer als aus Harn oder Cholesterin bereitetes Androsteron", *Hoppe-Seylers Zeitschrift für Physiologische Chemie* 233 (1935), pp. 281–2.

[13] A. Butenandt, Hanisch G., "Über Testosteron. Umwandlung des Dehydro-Androsterons in Androstendiol und Testosteron; ein Weg zur Darstellung des Testosterons aus Cholesterin", *Hoppe-Seylers Zeitschrift für Physiologische Chemie* 237 (1935), pp. 89–92.

[14] L. Ruzicka and A. Wettstein, "Synthetische Darstellung des Testikelhormons Testosteron", *Helvetica Chimica Acta 18* (1935), p. 986.

energy-storing) effects. Today we mostly hear about anabolic steroids through their illegal use in athlete doping.

Early studies with animals and men suggested that there was a correlation with testosterone and aggression, but recent studies employing new techniques have revealed the human situation to be much more complex. Early studies were often limited by small numbers of subjects and the choosing of violent criminals without sufficient recognition of the effects of prison life on testosterone levels. Furthermore, multiple samples are required over a period of time because it is now known that testosterone levels fluctuate diurnally, with blood and saliva levels dropping in the evening.[15] The human response to testosterone is dependent upon personality, psychological state at the time of test, and the influences of the prefrontal cortex where emotions are perceived and controlled, these emotions being further influenced by cultural expectations of self-control. The neuroneal cell membranes in the amygdala, hippocampus and prefrontal cortex express receptors for interacting with testosterone, and these neurones contain the enzymes required for its synthesis. Thus, testosterone can be produced locally at these sites within the brain, allowing a finer and more immediate response to aggressive stimuli than can the distally produced testicular testosterone. Neuro-imaging studies have shown that testosterone activates the amygdala and reduces its sensitivity to the prefrontal cortex's restraining efforts. Threatening environmental stimuli, such as viewing an aggressive face, also enhance activity in the amygdala and hypothalamus promoting aggressive emotions.

Carre and co-workers conducted a double-blind study in 121 healthy adult men who received either testosterone or a placebo and subsequently engaged in a well-validated decision-making game that measures aggressive behaviour in response to social provocation.[16] They showed

---

[15] M. L. Batrinos, "Testosterone and Aggressive Behavior in Man", *International Journal of Endocrinology and Metabolism* 10, pp. 563–8, published online 30 June 2012.

[16] J. M. Carre et al., "Exogenous Testosterone Rapidly Increases Aggressive Behavior in Dominant and Impulsive Men", *Biological Psychiatry* 82 (2017), pp. 249–56.

for the first time that the administered testosterone (within sixty minutes) could increase aggression in men but only in those scoring relatively high in dominance and impulsivity. Defreyne and co-investigators appeared to confirm this finding, showing that testosterone therapy was not associated with an increase in aggression in transgender men nor a decrease in aggressive behaviour in transgender women on anti-androgen and oestrogen therapy.[17] Unsurprisingly, however, some individuals reported increased aggression simply due to anxiety experienced during transitioning. Furthermore, Geniole and co-workers proved a genetic component to testosterone-enhanced aggression in men with different personality profiles.[18] A genetic polymorphism (variation) in an androgen receptor gene, which increases its activity, is thought to enhance the subjective pleasure derived from aggression, through the dopamine reward system (see below).

MAOA, the so-called warrior gene

In the 1990s, the media took great interest in a rage-associated gene. The gene codes for the enzyme monoamine oxidase A (MAOA) and it is an example of how one gene product (protein) can fulfil multiple essential roles. Despite its nickname, MAOA does not promote aggression, but rather it keeps it under control.

MAOA is located on the membranes of mitochondria (the sub-cellular energy houses). Here it engages in the oxidation of monoamines (part of a recycling process), which includes the neurotransmitters serotonin, epinephrine, norepinephrine and dopamine. This means that changes to the MAOA gene would have implications for mental health and psychiatric disorders. Furthermore, it is essential for normal foetal tissue

---

[17]   J. Defreyne, G. T'Sjoen, W. P. Bouman, et al., "Prospective Evaluation of Self-Reported Aggression in Transgender Persons", *Journal of Sexual Medicine* 15 (2018), pp. 768–76.

[18]   S. N. Geniole, "Using a Psychopharmacogenetic Approach to Identify the Pathways Through Which—and the People for Whom—Testosterone Promotes Aggression", *Psychological Science* 30 (2019), pp. 481–94.

and brain development, in part due to its involvement with programmed cell death (apoptosis), an essential mechanism for the separation of fingers and toes during foetal development, for example.

The activity of this enzyme varies widely among the human and animal populations. Wolves and older breeds of dogs, like Siberian huskies and Samoyeds, show greater MAOA gene variability in comparison to modern breeds.[19] The gene is located on the X chromosome and since males only have one X, they have a reduced ability to moderate aggression compared with females. Following its identification and gene sequencing, many human and animal aggression studies have been conducted looking at the behavioural effects of different alleles and expression levels. Research suggests that a *low* activity genetic variation (MAOA-L) may increase the risk of aggressive and antisocial behaviour. Of course, defence lawyers were quick to use the emerging genetic evidence in excusing and mitigating criminal behaviour. McSwiggan and co-workers examined the criminal proceedings in which MAOA-L genotype was presented to the court, including five post-conviction appeals, two of which resulted in reduced sentences.[20] However, it is virtually impossible to determine what impact a particular allele would have on any human individual due to the complex interplay with other genes and the environment.

Cortisol

Cortisol is the main corticosteroid in humans and is synthesized in the adrenal glands that sit on the kidneys. Once released into the bloodstream it easily crosses the blood-brain barrier, and exerts multiple effects on anxiety, appetite, sleep and even cognition. Cortisol production has

---

[19] J. Sacco, A. Ruplin, P. Skonieczny et al., "Polymorphisms in the canine monoamine oxidase a (MAOA) gene: identification and variation among five broad dog breed groups", *Canine Genetics and Epidemiology* 4:1 (2017) at <https://doi.org/10.1186/s40575-016-0040-2>, accessed 30 January 2021.

[20] Sally McSwiggan, Bernice Elgera, Paul S. Appelbaum, "The forensic use of behavioral genetics in criminal proceedings: Case of the MAOA-L genotype", *International Journal of Law and Psychiatry* 50 (2017), pp. 17–23.

a diurnal fluctuation peaking soon after waking, followed by a steep morning rise and subsequent steeper fall throughout the day. Any deviation from this pattern is an indication of chronic stress or poor mental or physical health. Production is increased when experiencing stress, including exercise and surgery. In studies, it is often used as a biomarker for the stress response.

From a review of the literature, Adam and associates observed a significant association between the flattening of diurnal cortisol slopes and poor mental and/or physical health.[21] This was especially true for inflammatory and immune conditions, adding credence to the suggestion that stress can affect one's susceptibility to several forms of disease. Raised cortisol levels are common in the elderly and may contribute to Alzheimer's disease (AD) and dementia through atrophy in the hippocampus and a thinning of grey matter, thereby having deleterious effects on memory and cognition.[22] Emotional trauma in early life and the resulting impact of cortisol can cause some permanent changes in the brain, reducing cognitive and memory ability and increasing the risk of poor mental health.

Stress is often a precursor to depression, anxiety, post-traumatic stress disorder and schizophrenia. The role of cortisol and its disregulation is frequently investigated in psychiatry and many comparisons of salivary cortisol levels of patients and healthy people have been made. The data show an overall gender difference in the stress responses of men and women with major depressive disorder (MDD). Here men showed an increased stress response to psychosocial stress whereas women's responses are blunted.[23]

---

[21] E. K. Adam et al., "Diurnal cortisol slopes and mental and physical health outcomes: A systematic review and meta-analysis", *Psychoneuroendocrinolgy* 83 (2017), pp. 25–41

[22] S. Ouanes, and J. Popp, "High Cortisol and the Risk of Dementia and Alzheimer's Disease: A Review of the Literature", *Frontiers in Aging Neuroscience*, 1 March 2019.

[23] J. V. Zorn, et al., "Cortisol stress reactivity across psychiatric disorders: A systematic review and meta-analysis", *Psychoneuroendocrinolgy* 77 (2017), pp. 25–36.

Important research is underway to investigate cortisol-reducing interventions that could slow cognitive decline in AD and reduce depression and PTSD. There have been a few studies and trials of the efficacy of practising mindfulness by measuring saliva levels of cortisol, but results have been variable and inconclusive due to a lack of standardization in methodology.

The neuro-biochemistry of the human brain

Neurotransmitters are short-range cell-to-cell signalling molecules which are ubiquitous to all life forms, from microbes to plants and animals. The enzymes required for the biosynthesis and recycling of neurotransmitters and their cell receptors were present several hundred million years ago, and remain fairly well conserved in current life forms. Subsequent evolution led to the development of more complex signalling pathways. In microbes, they are used in cell-to-cell conjugation (for the exchange of DNA and chemicals). Normal plant metabolism and chemical defence employs histamine (e.g. in stinging nettles), glutamate (an amino acid), acetylcholine, gamma-aminobutyric acid (GABA), dopamine and serotonin that are chemically very similar to those synthesized in the human brain, where they enable signal transfer across the synaptic gaps connecting neurones. In addition to these, the human brain also uses norepinephrine. Their repurposing for neurotransmission allowed animals to become more mobile through the controlling of muscles and the development of brains. Neurotransmitters share overlapping functions. For example, both dopamine and acetylcholine promote cognitive processes, including learning, attention and memory. Later, we shall examine how neurotransmitters serve us and how they can have us at their mercy.

Some neurotransmitters operate as endorphins and are natural painkillers/opiates. The brain produces them in large quantities when we are falling in love, exercising or "high" in other ways. They cause ecstasy or euphoria and are important in relationship bonding and attachment. Dopamine, PEA (phenylethylamine), serotonin and norepinephrine (precursor to adrenalin) generate that rush making us feel the joy of life and infatuation. These endorphins are decreased during depression.

Dopamine is also a neurochemical modulator and exerts its effects in many regions of the brain, influencing the way we think, feel and behave. Its depletion in Parkinson's disease results in cognitive, emotional and motor disturbances. Dopamine is a major neurotransmitter of the reward system (also known as the pleasure or reward centre). The joy of success comes from this system and, importantly, learning is thereby rewarded. Drug, alcohol and other addictions arise through their stimulation of the dopamine reward system. Similarly, attraction and infatuation are driven by dopamine highs.

Histamine, a controller to be controlled

Histamine is infamous for its role in allergy, for which people take antihistamines with varying degrees of success. It is a small molecule with multiple functions throughout the body, where tissues express receptors for its engagement and subsequent effect. Histamine increases the permeability of blood vessels to facilitate entry of white blood cells and antibodies to control local infections. This is done by causing the smooth muscle of blood vessels to contract and shrink, thereby increasing pore size. It is the mediator of itching felt after an insect bite and during allergic reactions. Stinging nettles irritate our skin with their own histamine, and exacerbation follows with our own local histamine release. Bacteria and yeasts are also capable of producing histamine, but through a different biochemical pathway. Because of this, histamines are found in microbial contaminated food and in even in alcoholic beverages.

In humans and other mammals, histamine is produced by specialized white blood cells known as basophils and mast cells. Together with other specialized immune cells, these guard potential pathogen entry sites, notably the eyes, airways and skin of hands and feet and around the gut and blood vessels. Histamine also causes secretion of gastric acid, smooth muscle contraction for the bladder, uterus and, dangerously, the airways during an allergic reaction and asthma. In the brain, histamine acts as a neurotransmitter. Here it is involved with the sleep-wake cycle (hence antihistamines causing drowsiness), regulation of appetite, body temperature, hormone production and even cognition. Motion-sickness medication and some antidepressants are similar to antihistamines and therefore can also cause drowsiness and facilitate sleep.

Mood and brain biochemistry

Mood and mental health are influenced by diet, general health, life circumstances and genetics. Unfortunately, we often believe our negative perceptions about ourselves and our circumstances, based on untruths presented by a brain with a biochemical imbalance in its neurotransmittors. This is why medications that redress an imbalance in serotonin, for example (the so called "happy hormone") are so effective. Serotonin regulates and stabilizes mood, sleep, appetite, anxiety, impulse control and cognition. The precursors for synthesis of all our body biochemistry, including neurotransmitter synthesis are, of course, obtained in our diet. There is a growing body of evidence that strongly suggests our diets play a role in mood and behaviour disorders, including mood swings, aggression, bipolar disorder, depression, anxiety, seasonal affective disorder (SAD), eating disorders, obsessive–compulsive disorder (OCD), Attention Deficit Hyperactivity Disorder/Attention Deficit Disorder (ADHD/ADD), schizophrenia and addiction. These conditions appear to be on the rise in children. It is not surprising, then, that medical practitioners will encourage a healthy diet as part of a way forward in recovering from mental illness.

Artificially altering our moods

Most of us would like to feel generally contented, but realistically do not expect it all of the time. When bad things happen, if we become depressed or even just bored, we often look for that quick fix to lift our mood. Sometimes a cup of tea will not suffice, and we turn to chocolate (which contains PEA—see above) or other forms of sugar. Even simple blood glucose (two glucose molecules make sucrose, which is the sugar we put in tea) has the ability to lift the mood and alter behaviour in adults and children. This is because glucose is the only energy source that the brain can use. It is very rapidly absorbed and crosses the blood-brain barrier to give a sugar rush or even euphoria. The effects of low and high blood glucose are known only too well to diabetics.

If sugar is insufficient to raise the mood, alcohol, drugs or extramarital affairs will promote stronger intoxicating effects. All these stimulants produce rapid effects and operate by feeding the reward system, eliciting good feelings through dopamine and PEA highs. These neurotransmitters alter the perception of reality and keep us from thinking rationally. Thus, it is common to self-medicate in these ways. Unfortunately, the brain easily becomes addicted to these induced highs.

Alcohol quickly reaches the brain at a high dose, especially on an empty stomach. The quick fix to reduce stress and facilitate relaxation, albeit temporarily, can be irresistible. It can boost social and emotional experiences because it increases perceptions of likeability towards others and reduces inhibitions. Humans have been deliberately fermenting to produce alcohol since the Stone Age, but our interest in the beverage goes back ten million years when primates began to spend more time on forest floors. Here rotting fruit and fermenting nectar were encountered, which could reach up to 8 per cent alcohol. Janice and co-workers compared the gene sequences of alcohol dehydrogenase 7 (ADH7) of humans with gorillas, chimpanzees and bonobos. We all share a mutation, which other mammals do not have, which increases the efficiency of this enzyme in degrading alcohol fortyfold. This appears to be a mutation selected for by a common ancestor.

We often deliberately mess with our biochemistry in ways in which animals generally do not. However, there have been a few interesting exceptions, both scientific and anecdotal. Lara Giddings, the attorney general for the island state of Tasmania, reported to the BBC news on 25 June 2009 that wallabies were eating opium poppies and creating crop circles as they hopped around, high as kites. Australia supplies about half of the world's legally grown opium used to make morphine and other painkillers so, of course, efforts increased to prevent animals from getting into the poppy fields.

The consequences of alcohol for brain biochemistry

Liver enzymes (ADH7 in particular) rapidly metabolize alcohol into acetaldehyde, an unfortunately harmful metabolite. It is both carcinogenic and neurotoxic and therefore has health consequences following prolonged exposure. Studies using rodent models for chronic alcohol exposure suggest significant psychological decline, brain degeneration, cognition, learning and memory impairment, and elevations in anxiety, disinhibition, impulsivity and risk taking.[24] The neural stem cells (NSCs), which are responsible for neurogenesis (production of new neurones) in the adult brain show reduced survival.[25] Men and women respond differently to alcohol,[26] and it has been shown that female rats are more sensitive to alcohol-induced reduced NSC survival and differentiation.[27]

There is growing evidence to suggest that alcohol can have a similar deleterious effect on neurogenesis in adolescent humans and they do tend to consume more than adults, per occasion. Alcohol can affect human brain development, reduce attention span, learning and memory, and therefore could sadly, perhaps permanently, reduce a person's capacity for a successful future. Perhaps if personal genetic sequencing becomes a desirable service for a future generation, people will know in advance

---

[24] J. He, K. Nixon, A. K. Shetty, F. T. Crews, "Chronic alcohol exposure reduces hippocampal neurogenesis and dendritic growth of newborn neurons", *European Journal of Neuroscience* 21 (2005), pp. 2711–20.

[25] G. L. Ming, H. Song, "Adult neurogenesis in the mammalian brain: significant answers and significant questions", *Neuron* 70 (2011), pp. 687–702.

[26] A. Erol, V. M. Karpyak, "Sex and gender-related differences in alcohol use and its consequences: Contemporary knowledge and future research considerations", *Drug and Alcohol Dependence* 156 (2015), pp. 1–13; E. L. McGrath et al., "Spatial and Sex-Dependent Responses of Adult Endogenous Neural Stem Cells to Alcohol Consumption", *Stem cell reports* 9 (2017), pp. 1916–30.

[27] C. R. Schlagal and P. Wu, "Tipsy neural stem cells: chronic effects of alcohol on the brain", *Neural Regeneration Research* 14 (2019), pp. 67–68; W. C. McGrew and C. G. Tutin, "Chimpanzee Tool Use in Dental Grooming" *Nature* 241 (1973), pp. 477–8.

how their individual genetic backgrounds could affect their sensitivity to alcohol and any risks for addiction, alcohol-related recklessness and long-term health consequences.

Love and human brain biochemistry

Despite our faults as a species, we as individuals have enormous capacity for love, in comparison with other species. Love can take many forms, and these can have different biochemical correlates. During the infatuation stage of attachment, the rush of adrenaline-like norepinephrine results in a quickened heart and breathlessness at the sight of the desired one. At this stage, dopamine, responsible for the biochemistry of attraction, soars and alters the perception of reality. Phenylethylamine (PEA) soon saturates the "in love" brain, bestowing infatuation and euphoria. Dopamine and PEA promote sexual behaviour. Serotonin, the so-called happiness hormone, falls dramatically when the lover and beloved are apart, leaving a sense of emptiness and an obsessive preoccupation with the other person. Without realizing it, the lovers are in fact craving their next dopamine fix. Furthermore, they are subjected to an amphetamine-like neurotransmitter that increases risk-taking behaviour, like skipping lectures (or condoms). Lovers often find their emotions to be out of control and during an affair these feelings can include fear, stress, anxiety, guilt, frustration, and even rage. Here the stress hormone, cortisol, rises, subsequently reducing serotonin, thus driving the obsessive need for each other. Later, oxytocin emerges as the promoter of deeper, long-term attachment, bonding and trust. It is often known as the cuddle hormone.

Oxytocin is the food of love and bonding

Oxytocin is made within the hypothalamus and acts as both neurotransmitter and, for its long-distance effects on various regions of the body, a hormone. Is it essential in mammals for the bonding of mates and parents with their offspring? Studies have shown that grooming among the talapoin monkeys and affection between humans and their dogs can double the measurable blood oxytocin levels in all.

Vasopressin is another risk-taking hormone, which promotes physical and emotional mobilization. Possibly to help in the coordination of their fluctuating synthesis requirements, genes that regulate oxytocin and vasopressin are located on the same chromosome. They are closely related peptides and likewise, their neuronal receptors are similar. This facilitates behavioural fine-tuning and the balancing of relaxed and trusting care (by oxytocin) with the necessary vigilance for the defence of mates, offspring and territory (via vasopressin).

In humans, oxytocin is also responsible for making us feel more connected with others and facilitating feelings of awe and wonder when viewing a sunset and other examples of natural beauty. It can also generate the feeling of connection with a higher source, like God. As with most things biochemical, the effects of oxytocin are influenced by other genetic factors. The CD38 molecule regulates the release of oxytocin from neurones within the hypothalamus. In 2016, studies were conducted on the effect of intranasally administered oxytocin on spiritual and emotional responses to meditation in midlife men.[28] If given before meditation the subjects reported enhanced awe, wonder, gratitude, hope, inspiration, love and serenity, with effects lasting for several days. The strength of enhancement appeared to be moderated according to the variant genetic alleles for CD38.

It is likely that oxytocin is flowing through those people, mainly young, attending Christian events where inspiring talks are delivered and upbeat songs of praise are sung. They feel bonded together with love and a sense of connection to God. It is no surprise that there will be neurotransmitters that enhance our sense of spirituality and that these are the same as those for bonding between us and are shared with other mammals. There is a wonderful consistency in nature. It should be understood that the experience of our spirituality will be very personal

---

[28]   Patty Van Cappellen, Baldwin M. Way, Suzannah F. Isgett, Barbara L. Fredrickson, "Effects of oxytocin administration on spirituality and emotional responses to meditation", *Social Cognitive and Affective Neuroscience* 11 (2016), pp. 1579–87.

and influenced by molecules such as CD38 and oxytocin, and that the intensity of feelings, and the emotional expression of these, are not a measure of goodness or spirituality, and will be affected by other genetic/personality and environmental factors, including prior experiences and culture.

Taking steps to the control of our biology

Our ability to manipulate the fundamental processes of human life began in small ways thousands of years ago, for example with the tending of the sick and injured. Even before this time, natural selective pressures had slackened off from human evolution. Now, vaccination, medication and good nutrition in the affluent parts of the world have further eased natural selection.

Genetic engineering, however controversial, continues to take steps towards the elimination of genetic disease and the controversial improvement of foods. Early examples include inserting human genes into bacteria to instruct them to synthesize human proteins like insulin and growth hormone. Later, cow embryos were given human genes in order for them to produce human-like milk for baby feeds, and genes are borrowed from one plant species and inserted into another to produce pest- and drought-resistant crops. Transgenic mice are now widely used to express genes of the human immune system, making them better models for human disease, including COVID-19. Now we are seeing similar techniques applied to humans.

Since cloning the first human genome in 2003, the identification and understanding of genetics has developed exponentially. Molecular biologists and other specialist scientists are intensively engaged in gene therapy, gene editing, vaccine synthesis and cancer genetics. A new gene-editing technology, known as CRISPR (clustered regulatory inter-spaced short palindromic repeats), is cheap, easy, fast and accurate. It has given us the potential to alter the course of our genetic destiny. This is because the alterations are made in the embryo that will grow to adulthood and pass on those changes to his or her offspring. Theoretically, dozens of changes could be made to a single embryo. This notion is generally repulsive to people, but each generation becomes more and more used to technology, expectations from medicine become higher and we want quicker fixes to problems. Fortunately, genetic science is for the prevention and treatment of genetic disease and not for the creation of genetically enhanced babies. However, shockingly, two years ago in China the world saw the birth of the first genetically edited twin girls. Scientist He Jiankui offered a couple free infertility treatment in return for permission to genetically edit the embryos to confer resistance to some strains of HIV (human immunodeficiency virus). He was mimicking a natural mutation found in 10 per cent of Europeans. The implantation of the embryos had not been ethically approved and documentation had been forged. The scientific world, and the Chinese government, were outraged. In response to this the World Health Organization (WHO) established an international committee to devise guidelines on human gene editing. He Jiankui and his co-workers have been imprisoned. We may never know the outcomes for the health of these girls as they mature.

Can we preserve our dead bodies for a human-made resurrection?

Unsurprisingly, the answer to this question remains an emphatic *no*. Yet, a few of the world's rich have had their bodies or heads frozen after death in the hope of future resurrection if techniques have advanced sufficiently to allow a successful outcome. In the case of single-cell microbes, like protozoa, yeasts and bacteria, life can be put on hold for decades in cold nitrogen storage at about −80°C. Yeast and bacteria have cell walls to add to their protection during freezing. Animal cells, like sperm and 100 cell-sized embryos, require cryoprotection, otherwise the formation of ice crystals both within the cells and their medium would slice through them like swords. Tumour cell lines that originated from people or animals can be defrosted and grown again in culture long after the death of the donor. This is a legacy that some people have left to medical research which can go on indefinitely.

When considering freezing anything larger than a cell cluster, there are huge problems regarding the toxicity of the cryopreservative to overcome. This is because the penetration and subsequent removal of the cryopreservative agent from the cells packed together in an organ is to date impossible. In the long term, freezing cells is not really stopping the biochemistry of life, but rather slowing it right down to almost nothing. Molecules can nevertheless vibrate, even at such low temperatures, and will eventually vibrate their way to degradation. This obeys the second law of thermodynamics, stating that everything in the universe eventually reverts to its most thermodynamically stable state or chaos.

For now, we can prolong life by strict adherence to health regimes for diet, physical and mental exercise and by taking necessary medication. In this way, we are manipulating our environment to improve longevity, but genetic factors probably dominate. As we age our immune systems become less able to fight infections and cancers. Ageing studies on different strains (breeds) of mice, while living under optimal conditions, sees about 60 per cent of them developing tumours by the age of two years, if they live that long (personal observation).

Conclusion

This chapter has set out some of the science that lies behind human feelings, thoughts and emotions. Much remains to be discovered, but clearly any account of what it means to be human—and what it is that makes human beings both similar to, and distinct from, other animals—must take account of new facts. As knowledge and understanding of ourselves and our earth's co-inhabitants expands, let us hope that we will further respect the place and life that millions of years of evolution has bestowed upon us all, and not exploit the planet for our own ends.

Questions for discussion

1. If belief in God can now be described as "incompatible with science", how should a scientist of faith respond to this?
2. Given the expansion of technology in neuroscience and imaging, and the resulting explosion of information on brain structure,

function, genetics and neurotransmission, (a) where is there room for the soul in our life responses and (b) where is God in our religious experiences? (c) Could it be possible that our free will is overshadowed by fluctuating and varying neurotransmitter and hormone levels, such as occur during pregnancy, falling in love and depression?

3. Clearly our bodies are programmed by our genes, and the environment can influence their expression, for example artistic or musical talents. Could this be so for the gifts of the Spirit, for example kindness and love, or must they be independent from these factors?

Further reading

Philip Clayton (ed.), *The Oxford Handbook of Religion and Science* (Oxford: Oxford University Press, 2009).

David L. Nelson and Michael M. Cox (eds), *Lehninger Principles of Biochemistry*, seventh edition (New York, NY: W. H. Freeman and Company, 2017).

Flourishing dominion? Human and animal creatures in relationship

Margaret B. Adam

Initial questions about what it is to be a human might reasonably elicit responses declaring what a human is not. Some of these responses are obvious. Humans are clearly not upholstered chairs or candlesticks. Humans are infrequently confused with seas, mountains and plants. There is more potential for confusion between humans and animals, but humans are visually distinguishable from bedbugs and whales, chickens and cows.[1] Pigs' internal body parts and their genetic make-up share some similarities to those of humans, but a human is definitely not a pig. If, from a distance, bonobos, bears and Bigfoot look somewhat like humans, closer proximity or a telephoto lens help clarify that these are only human-*like*. If bonobos or pet dogs or parrots seem to display behaviours somewhat similar to human displays of emotion, language or reasoning, the behaviours are not the same as human behaviours.

---

[1]   Theological and philosophical discourse has made much of images of the animal or beast within humans, the superiority of human nature over animal nature, and the freedom of the human from its oppressive animal temptations. Here I use "creature" to indicate shared identity, and I specify the distinct identities of humans and animals, to reflect the most common human experiences of those differences. See also Celia Deane-Drummond, "Performing the Beginning *in* the End: A Theological Anthropology for the Anthropocene", in Celia Deane-Drummond, Sigurd Bergmann and Markus Vogt (eds), *Religion in the Anthropocene* (Eugene, OR: Wipf and Stock, 2017), pp. 173–87, here at p. 183.

Humans remain not bonobos, not dogs, and not parrots. Humans take comfort in their distinction from animals, and they so persistently identify themselves in contrast to animals, that the question, "What is a human?" prompts the confident answer: "A human is NOT an animal."[2]

However, the human/animal divide fails as an adequate marker of human identity, because it does not actually provide a single, firm, visible, and defensible border. The allegedly solid line between humans and animals is, in fact, blurry, variously located and permeable. Yes, of course, humans do differ from other animals. Science records traits, capacities, and biological specifications characteristic of most humans and not of most animals. Christians claim a uniqueness from creation, through baptism into the body of Christ, that humans do not share with animals. At the same time, human/animal divisions are not greater than the primary division between God and God's creation. A more apt definition of humans might be not-God, an identity that humans share with all of creation. Within the category of creatures, there are both differences and similarities between humans and each of the wide range of animal species. Humans have far more in common with pigs than pigs have in common with salmon or chickens. The gestation periods of cattle and humans are very similar; sheep have excellent memories and can identify many different sheep faces, as well as various sheep facial expressions of emotion.[3] The earliest stages of life of many creatures share similarities across species. Some humans treat other humans as if they were animals; some treat animals as if they were humans. As creatures, humans lack the divine perspective with which to locate precisely where a singular defining border between humans and animals lies. Too much focus on defining the human/animal border obscures the essential creatureliness of humans, downplays the shared purpose of humans and animals, and distracts humans from their identity in Christ.

A definition of humans that relies too heavily on species difference provides a thin account of who humans are and who animals are, let

---

[2]   David Clough, "Not a Not-Animal: The Vocation to Be a Human Animal Creature", *Studies in Christian Ethics* 26:1 (2013), pp. 4–17.

[3]   Keith M. Kendrick, "Brain Asymmetries for Face Recognition and Emotion Control in Sheep", *Cortex* 42:1 (2006), pp. 96–8.

alone the rest of creation. A definition of humans that rests too heavily on similarities among all creatures (or all of creation) squeezes out particularity, and it minimizes both God's infinite abundance and the uniqueness of each creature. Despite these risks, it makes little sense to consider the nature of the human apart from animals. The human inclination to defend the identity of humans from the identity of animals reflects not only human anxieties about superiority and hierarchies, but also the fact of shared creatureliness. Human uniqueness cannot be discovered through a quest for the real difference between humans and animals. More fruitful Christian considerations of human distinctiveness focus on relationships: humans, like all creatures, are composites of relationships. Humans are created to be in relationships with God, with other humans, with animals, with soil and plants, with the environment and its health, with ideas and truths, with past and future. Humans are born into these relationships; they live and die within them; these relationships intersect and influence each other. Christians become human through Jesus Christ's life, death and resurrection, which transforms all relationships, in hope now and in completion to come.

This chapter proposes a Christian account of humans as creatures who, like all creatures, are identified by their relationships with God, with each other, and with other creatures. God creates humans and animals into shared relationships of dependence, particularity and flourishing. In addition, God gives humans the distinctive responsibility of dominion in the image of God, a mediating relationship of divine care of animals.[4] Humans are often quicker to claim unique species superiority than to

---

[4] The focus of this chapter is the relationships between living humans and animals and God. One might also note that the two Genesis creation stories also mention human relationships with plants. In the first, God gives humans and all animals green foods and fruit to eat (1:29–31). In the second, God gives *adam* almost all of the fruit of the garden to eat (2:16). Also, in the second, God charges *adam* with tilling and keeping the garden of Eden (2:15). Scriptural interpretation throughout the Christian tradition sustains the position that God is creator of all that is, and that all that God creates reflects God. These claims support and promote human responsibility to care for all of creation and to participate in the urgent protection of the

claim unique species responsibility, and this is particularly the case in contemporary human relationships with the animals they breed and raise solely for human consumption. Human relationships fail to indicate the fulness of human distinctiveness when their relationships with animals are oriented more toward humans than toward God, more toward inhibiting than encouraging creaturely flourishing. Christians can better demonstrate the unique gift of human relationships by recognizing when their actions betray a dominion of objectification and commodification, and by accepting the responsibility of dominion in the image of God in their care for the creatures they consume.

God creates humans and animals to be creatures together sharing dependence, particularity and flourishing

Relationships of shared creaturely dependence

To be human is to share with animals a complete dependence on God, for their creation out of nothing, for their sustenance and survival, for their death and for possibilities of life beyond death. This relationship is the primary identity of all creatures: humans and animals are created by and dependent on God. God creates everything that is. Creatures depend on God for their existence, whether or not they realize it. They do not make themselves; they do not create anything out of nothing. Human and animal creatures are co-inhabitants of this planet (and beyond), and they share the goods of creation. If Christians accept their scriptural and theological biographical identity as creatures of God, then their relationships with other creatures should demonstrate their shared dependent cohabitation of the home God has created for them. Creatures and all of creation are limited and finite, because they are not divine, and cohabitation requires a distribution of finite resources.

Christians learn about their human, creaturely identity in part through their communal interpretations of scripture, where the story arc

---

environment—priorities which interact, rather than conflict, with care for animals—but such details fall outside the remit of this chapter.

of creation to salvation features human dependence on God, alongside animal dependence on God. The stories in Genesis 1 and 2 describe God's creation and ordering of everything that is. The stories of God's judgement and reordering of creation underscore the inability of humans to function without God's persevering presence and the effects of human frailty on all creatures. Animals *and* humans experience the effects when humans reject their dependence on God. The biblical flood, plagues, famine and wars all affected animals as well as humans, just as historical disasters cause animals and humans to suffer and die. God's directing and redirecting of humans who resist dependence also affect animals as well as humans. Biblical accounts of the Sabbath and Jubilee call for working animals to rest, as well as working humans. Prophetic anticipations of life aligned with God's order describe no beasts of burden, and no animals kill or are killed. Humans who place their hopes in God's gracious care of creation reflect that care when they provide justice and compassion to both humans and animals.

In Psalm 104, the psalmist lists the foundations for life that God supplies for creatures: earth, air, flowing waters, grass for cattle, plants for people, trees for birds, the sea for everything in the sea, sun and moon, day and night, life itself. Biological accounts of interdependence describe the extent to which creaturely life depends on other creaturely life, whether internal microbes, prey for predators, carcasses for scavengers, birds who eat ticks on mammals, cleaner fish who eat sea lice on salmon, discarded fur and hair for bird nests, and faeces to feed the soil to produce plants to feed animals and humans. All of creation is dependent. Humans and animals depend on many of the same life-supporting resources of creation. Animals depend on the human distribution of those resources. No creature is independent of God and creation.

Relationships of shared creaturely particularities

To be human is to share with animals the creaturely feature of particularity. Each creature is a distinctive individual, one of a species, of a family, in a location and at a time. This is the only way creatures exist. God recognizes, hears and cares for each human and animal creature. Humans in relationship with other humans and animals demonstrate both creaturely dependence and creaturely uniqueness, thereby reflecting God's infinite and intimate love for creation.

Humans, as a species, have capacities for reason, knowledge, culture, creativity, spirituality and social power. Not all humans have all of these capacities; biology, health, wealth and social systems determine the distribution and degree of human capacities. Some animals share some capacities with humans; most animals possess capacities that humans do not. Humans are still learning about distinctions among species, and between each species of animal and humans, but it is no longer legitimate to claim that only humans have feelings, cognitive functions, or emotional attachments. It is especially disingenuous to claim that farmed animals lack those characteristics, when industrial-scale farming attains financial success by ignoring or inhibiting farmed animals' unique physical, cognitive and emotional capacities. Most mammals and birds desire the positive parental presence and care appropriate to their species. Farmed animals do indeed suffer when they experience the mutilation, deprivation and crowding common to intensive farming systems.[5] Freedom to exercise species-specific capacities and behaviours improves their wellbeing. Human attention to the species-specific particularity of animals challenges the assumption that there is a single chasm of difference between humans and the set of all animals. Further, an emphasis on species-specificity is itself an insufficient account of creaturely particularity, because it fails to allow for the uniqueness of individuals within any one species. Pigs are more and less sociable; lambs are more and less lively; chickens may prefer dustbathing to resting in the shade of a bush. The larger the number of farmed animals, the less

---

[5] Intensive farming systems concentrate animals into a smaller geographic area, with limited movement and minimal (if any) access to the out-of-doors (or open sea). Animals are given feed designed to hasten their growth and develop their flesh for early slaughter and to generate animal products suitable to consumer preferences. Extensive farming systems provide more outdoor space and freedom to move, with minimal restraint and with indoor housing available for shelter as needed. Animals have more opportunity to forage for food they desire, gather in social groups, and birth and raise their young in species-appropriate manners.

possible it is to recognize the individuality of each animal. Too much weight on species specificity also distracts from the distinguishing lines that run across all creatures: old, young, sick, healthy; free or restrained; hungry or full; abandoned or in community; consumer or consumed. There are no generic creatures. There is no every-human, no every-animal, no every-sheep, to represent all humans, animals or sheep.

Humans who too quickly lump all non-human creatures together in a single non-human set risk overplaying human distinctiveness and underplaying animal uniqueness. Paul Waldau critiques this practice and names the presumption of human superiority that drives it:

> In effect, mere membership in the human species overdetermines the qualities of any individual human, while membership in the vague, undifferentiated group "other animals" underdetermines the features of many of the diverse biological individuals in that group, such that species membership of other animals often becomes irrelevant. This asymmetry is accepted because the status of human qua member of the human species taxon has been a favored status, whereas the status of any other biological individual qua nonhuman or member of its species taxon has been a disfavored status.[6]

This essay, with its articulation of the two categories, humans (one species) and animals (all the other species of creatures), may seem to follow precisely the status-favouring division that Waldau calls out. Waldau uses the terms human and non-human animals, in an effort to undermine the presumption that humans stand so far apart from and above other animals that the term "animal" does not even apply to them.[7] His strategy that highlights the great diversity within the category of animals should challenge Christians to exercise more humility when claiming a better-than-animal human identity. This essay appreciates Waldau's approach and yet perpetuates the human/animal distinction,

---

[6]   Paul Waldau, *The Specter of Speciesism: Buddhist and Christian Views of Animals* (Oxford: Oxford University Press, 2001), p. 110.

[7]   Waldau, Chapter 5, "What is an Animal?", ibid., pp. 89–110.

in order to emphasize the Christian identity of humans as creatures, with other creatures, in relationships of shared creatureliness. This focus risks placing humans above animals, in order to keep humans within the set of all creatures, but the main argument applies whether the labels are human/animal or human/non-human animals: the primary Christian identification of human is a creature of God in particular relationships with God, other humans and other creatures. At the same time, this essay will posit a human particularity that does set it apart from, although not above, those creatures frequently referred to as animals.

Christians claim their particular identity as the people of God, adopted into the body of Jesus Christ. Jesus lived as humans do, slept, moved, ate and drank as humans do. Jesus spoke in words, stories and language/s that people could receive. Jesus was more than human, as well: he was the fully human and fully divine presence of God amid and for humanity. As human and as incarnate God, Jesus was also a creature among creatures. Like all creatures, he was a particular body, and not a general, amorphous, life form. Like creatures, he was fleshy and finite, contingent and vulnerable, dependent on God and on others. Like creatures, he fitted within a species as a unique individual, of a particular family, in a particular location, at a particular time. He was not every-human, every-man, every-body.

The incarnation of God as a specific human illustrates God's saving grace for humans; Jesus is human, with humans, that they may participate in the fulness of humanness through Jesus Christ who is fully human and fully God. The very particular nature of the incarnation opens up life in Christ to all particular humans, in each and every of their particulars. No humans are the same as the fully divine and fully human Jesus Christ. The ultimate fulfilment of human identity, in the presence of God, is not more available to those with more apparent similarities to Jesus. Salvation does not require humans to be from Jesus' geographical region or century, to have the same body parts as Jesus, the same hair and skin, the same ancestry or heritage, the same physical and cognitive faculties. To be human is to be particular, and Jesus' particularity incorporates all human particularity into Christ's efficacious presence.

As far as we know, animal creatures do not share Christian narratives of God and creation. The Word of God seems to be a manifestation of God specifically directed toward human language, communities, limitations and bodies. It would not be fitting for badgers to have a badger Bible or for birds to sing melodies with human language lyrics. God's overflowing grace and wisdom provide for relationships with animals that we do not understand. To claim God as creator of all creatures is to acknowledge the particularity of both creatures and God's relationships with them. To be Christian is to claim and be claimed as a human creature whose primary family is Jesus Christ's body. The suggestion that this is the only kind of relation God has with creatures presumes to limit God and glorify humans, but the claim to a particular relationship with God in Jesus Christ names a relationship that humans can know, and it declines to conflate all creaturely relationships with God into one specifically suited to humans.

Jesus Christ, the human, shares creaturely specificity with the other animate creatures and shares in the finite existence of all animate and inanimate creation. In this way, Christ's relationship with humans in their humanness extends to the rest of the cosmos in all of its createdness. Again, we do not know what Christ's saving grace for dairy cows looks like from the perspective of a dairy cow, but we can develop human relationships with dairy cows (in person, or as consumers, retailers or corporate heads) that witness to the shared and distinctive creaturely identity we share with them, and to the peace of Christ that embraces all creaturely distinctions.

With sufficient community support, humans bond with, feed, teach and nurture their young. They form social groups and enter into complex intimate relationships; develop physical, cognitive and emotional skills; imagine, dream and draw on accumulated knowledge. They face few predators apart from themselves. They listen and read, make choices and plans. They spend portions of their lives completely dependent on human carers and aspire to (apparent) independence and long, healthy lives. No one human possesses the capacity to do and be all that humans as a species potentially do and are. Particularity rules out composite human creatures, and human frailty rules out perfection. At their best, humans do not set the value of other humans by degrees of fulfilled potential. Christians share with other humans the temptation to undervalue those humans who show the least likelihood of attaining or regaining independence, and most likelihood of needing more than they can contribute to the financially oriented economy of life.

A particular community may celebrate a human who achieves the features that the community values most highly, but that human cannot compete for superiority with one celebrated for features prized most highly by a different community. Further, a human distinguished by valued human attributes cannot claim superiority over animals whose creaturely distinctiveness consists of different attributes altogether. Fish swim faster than humans and lay more eggs than chickens. Sheep grow more wool than pigs and chew their cud, which is impossible for humans. Cows can detect odours many miles away, and humans can speak one or more human languages. Humans are superior to these animals only if human characteristics are the standard for all creatures. Augustine of Hippo follows the competition perspective when he shares the traditional assumption that humans are better than beasts because humans are better at (human) reasoning, and superior reason is what places humans in the closest relationship to God.[8] Yet Augustine also names the absurdity of a human claiming superiority over the

> many beasts which surpass us in the acuteness of their senses, in the ease and rapidity of their movement, in their strength, and in the greatly prolonged vigour of their bodies. What man [sic] can equal the power of vision of the eagle and the vulture? Who can equal the dog in his [sic] sense of smell? Who can equal in speed the hare, the stag and all the birds? Who can equal the strength of the lion or elephant? Who can equal in length of life the serpent, which is said to shed old age with its skin and return again to youth?[9]

Shared particularity, not competition, marks the relationships among humans, animals, creatures and God. Humans in relationship with

---

8   Augustine, *The City of God Against the Pagans*, ed. R. W. Dyson (Cambridge: Cambridge University Press, 1998), 8:15.

9   Augustine, *City of God*, 8:15.

other creatures must appreciate the others' particularity and shape the relationships' uniquenesses accordingly.

Relationships of shared flourishing in praise

To be human is to share with all of creation the primary purpose of giving praise to God.[10] Human and animal creatures express their shared dependence on God with their shared particularity by giving glory to God each in their creaturely-specific ways. Creation praises God by being the creation that God has created and is sustaining toward fulfilment. To praise God is to flourish as God's creation. "Creation's praise is not an extra, an addition to what it is, but is the shining of its being, the overflowing significance it has in pointing to its Creator simply by being itself."[11] Human praise often takes the form of intentional speech and song, willed actions and communal worship. The rest of creation praises in its own ways. Humans, the earth and earthworms all give glory to God by reflecting God's greatness, each in their turn, with or without speech and will.

The seas give glory to God by reflecting God in their breadth and depth, their provision of habitats for sea creatures, their contributions to weather and climate, and their mysterious beauty and power. When the seas are able to praise God in their sea-specific ways, they are flourishing. When the seas flourish, they are giving glory to God. The greatest good for creation, creation's uninhibited flourishing, is one and the same with giving glory to God. Praising God does not inhibit flourishing, as though there is some part of sea-ness reserved for sea-flourishing, apart from giving praise and glory. Praise and flourishing are inseparable; the purpose of creation is fulfilled in and as praising God. This glory-giving

---

[10] This chapter addresses praising and giving glory to God as aspects of one act, which effects creaturely flourishing. It is possible to add giving thanks to God to this discussion, but I am persuaded that it is an adequately distinct topic to leave out of this chapter. See Jerome H. Neyrey. "Lost in Translation: Did it Matter if Christians 'Thanked God' or 'Gave God Glory'?", *The Catholic Biblical Quarterly* 71:1 (2009), pp. 1–23.

[11] Daniel W. Hardy and David F. Ford, *Praising and Knowing God* (Philadelphia, PA: Westminster Press, 1985), p. 47.

relationship of creation and God is the shared purpose of all creation. The fulness of this purpose of creaturely life is constant praise, possible in part now and completed in the eschatological reconciliation of the cosmos in Christ:

> The heart of the NT proclamation is that through the Son, the Father is leading the whole created universe—cosmos and history—to the ultimate fulfillment of the kingdom (Ephesians 1:9–10). In its celebration of Word and sacrament, the church is transformed to see that the whole creation is a gift whose purpose is to praise its Creator.[12]

Human creatures' primary identity and purpose is to be praise-giving creatures of God in their human-specific ways. Humans flourish with their bodies, energies and strengths; their insights, imaginations and discernment; and in their gathering as community. Christians shape their flourishing as adopted members of the body of Christ, in which they embrace and enact their gifts of growing, nurturing and sustaining life, all to the glory of God. Christian flourishing in this life demonstrates hope in the fulness of flourishing, through Christ's death and resurrection, toward unabated flourishing with God. Christians participate in the fulness of flourishing through songs of praise and in the celebration of the Eucharist.

Physical and emotional health, adequate food and shelter, community and friends, freedom from violence, restraint and oppression, all contribute to the creaturely capacity to flourish. Humans who lack these conditions need relationships of nurturing, nourishment, protection and release, so that they can more fully live into the flourishing in which one's gifts, resources, body, mind and soul express God's greatness and illustrate the presence of Christ. Humans whose health, wealth, community and freedom exceed that which is necessary for flourishing may need relationships of shared asceticism and accountability in order to flourish in praise, and not simply in comfort. This flourishing is not

---

[12] Mike Pasquarello III, *Christian Preaching: A Trinitarian Theology of Proclamation*, (Eugene, OR: Wipf and Stock, 2011), pp. 183–4.

a matter of individual effort to fulfil potential, to unlock inner power or conquer an enemy. Rather, it is a matter of reflecting and returning to God the glory of God, in creaturely specificity.

This glory-giving relationship with God also manifests itself in human relationships with the creation with which humans share their primary purpose of praise. To flourish as human is to praise with, rather than diminish, creation's praise, which is already oriented toward giving glory to God. Chrysostom describes the praise of the heavens, not in sound, but in magnificence:

> "The heavens declare the glory of God." How then, tell me, do they declare it? Voice have they none; mouth they do not possess; tongue is not theirs! How then do they declare? By means of the spectacle itself! For when you see the beauty, the breadth, the height, the position, the form, the stability thereof during so long a period; hearing as it were a voice, and being instructed by the spectacle itself, thou admirest Him who created a body so fair and strange! The heavens may be silent, but the sight of them emits a voice that is louder than a trumpet's sound.[13]

The heavens flourish by being the heavens, free to praise God by reflecting the glory of God in their being. The less majestic, but equally enthusiastic, paving stones are also equipped with silent and loud voices. Jesus declares, on the way into Jerusalem, that the stones will shout out their own praise if his disciples are silenced from giving glory to God (Luke 19:40). Praise marks creation as of God, and it demonstrates the relationship between God and creation as giver and receiver of gift, giver and participant in that gift, giver, and reflection of the giver's glory.

The psalmist urges creation to praise God: earth, moon, stars; heavens, and the waters above the heavens; sea monsters and the depths of the sea; weather of all sorts; mountains and hills; and trees; "wild animals and all cattle, creeping things and flying birds!" (Psalm 148). They all praise God

---

[13]   John Chrysostom, "Commentary on the Statutes", Homily IX.4, *Nicene and Post-Nicene Fathers* vol. IX, ed. Philip Schaff (Grand Rapids, MI: Eerdmans, 1989), p. 401.

with their createdness, they "praise merely by being what they were made to be".[14] Animals flourish when they are free to express themselves with the traits and abilities given to them by God. Animals, like the heavens and humans, give glory to God in their own creaturely, species-specific and individual ways. Birds and whales sing, moles and rabbits burrow, ovines and bovines chew their cud, pigs wag their tails, all to the glory of God. As Elizabeth Johnson notes, echoing Chrysostom above, human self-awareness is not the prerequisite for creaturely praise:

> True, they do not articulate praise with the knowingness of human reflective consciousness. But they do so in accord with their created natures, ontologically, by which I mean in a way rooted in being, in reality. While they do not praise in the vehicle of human language, words are not of the essence.[15]

God does not need intention, extra effort or acts of supererogation; nor does God lack anything and need praise to fulfil that lack. Ian McFarland underscores the source of the glory that creation gives to God:

> When we say (paraphrasing the language of the Westminster Shorter Catechism) that the end of creation is to glorify God, the point is not to suggest that creation augments God's glory in any way, since whatever glory creation might give to God comes from God in the first place.[16]

Creation's highest praise is its own flourishing, of and for God's glory.

Human relationships of flourishing support, encourage and facilitate the flourishing of others, but humans frequently fail in their creaturely relationships by misconstruing flourishing as more human-focused than

---

[14] Peter Joshua Atkins, "Praise by Animals in the Hebrew Bible", *Journal for the Study of the Old Testament* 44:3 (2020), pp. 500–51, here at p. 501.

[15] Elizabeth Johnson, "Animals' Praise of God", *Interpretation: A Journal of Bible and Theology* 73:3 (2019), pp. 259–71, here at p. 269.

[16] Ian McFarland, *From Nothing: A Theology of Creation* (Louisville, KY: Westminster John Knox Press, 2014), p. 152.

God-focused, and more competitive than shared. In this way, humans inhibit others' flourishing for the (apparent) benefit of their own. Self-oriented, distorted, human flourishing is not the flourishing in which the best life of the creature reflects the glory of God. It is, however, an approach to flourishing that characterizes the rapidly spreading industrial farming systems in the UK. Christians can assess that account of flourishing, and their own relationships with industrially farmed animals, by considering what responsibility they might have for farmed animal flourishing.[17]

The responsibility of dominion in the image of God

To be human is to share dependence, particularity, and the primary purpose of flourishing with animals. These relationships fit within a Christian narrative of receiving and responding to God's active presence in creation, with the gifts of the Spirit and in the hope of Christ. Alongside these shared relationships, Christians claim a distinctively human relationship of responsibility for animals, a responsibility to reflect God's relationship with creation onto creaturely relationships in this world, now. Those with and without familiarity with the Bible refer to one passage of scripture when the question of human consumption of animals arises: "The creation story in Genesis 1 says that humans have dominion over animals." This response does not solve any of the pressing questions about animal consumption, systems of animal farming, or human relationships with animals more generally, but it is the most common point of entry.

In this first of two creation stories, God has created all the foundations of life and all the animals and pronounced them all good, and then establishes a relationship of human dominion over all the animals:

---

[17]   David L. Clough, David Grumett, Siobhan Mullan, Margaret B. Adam, *The Christian Ethics of Farmed Animal Welfare: A Policy Framework for Churches and Christian Organizations*, AHRC-funded Christian Ethics of Farmed Animal Welfare, 2020. <https://www1.chester.ac.uk/christian-ethics-farmed-animal-welfare/cefaw-policy-framework>, accessed 30 January 2021.

Then God said, "Let us make humankind in our image, according to our likeness; and let them have dominion over the fish of the sea, and over the birds of the air, and over the cattle, and over all the wild animals of the earth, and over every creeping thing that creeps upon the earth."

So God created humankind in his image, in the image of God he created them; male and female he created them.

God blessed them, and God said to them, "Be fruitful and multiply, and fill the earth and subdue it; and have dominion over the fish of the sea and over the birds of the air and over every living thing that moves upon the earth."

Genesis 1:26–8

The translation of the Hebrew, *radah* as dominion, or rule (Genesis 1:28), provokes sufficiently strong reactions that advocates of animal welfare, social justice and egalitarian social structures either propose a different translation or reject the idea altogether. Their concern is that dominion has been too often understood as domination, to the detriment of creatures; suggested alternatives to dominion include stewardship and care for creation, and each of these come with their own challenging associations. Those who are wary of insufficiently considered social change and innovative interpretations tend to reinscribe dominion as the essential translation of the passage. Thus, dominion is a flashpoint for disagreements about human/animal relationships, especially when discussing animals farmed for human consumption. Rather than handing dominion over to those who have determined its limited connotations, this essay proceeds to consider dominion within the phrase: "dominion in the image of God".

In Genesis 1, dominion over animals seems to depend on first being made in the image of God,[18] without much explanation about what

---

18   Paul Sands, "The *Imago Dei* as Vocation", *Evangelical Quarterly* 82:1 (2010), pp. 28–41, here at p. 38. Sands notes that "there is general agreement that dominion does not define the *imago Dei*, but the ideas are intertwined and inseparable. The syntax of 1:26 suggests that humans were created in the image *so that* they might exert dominion".

dominion or the image might be. The story so far shows God exercising dominion by providing creation with all it needs, including all the food humans and animals need, without predators or prey. As the stories of God with God's people continue through the books of the Bible, the picture of dominion fleshes out into God's realm, or reign, Christ's coming kingdom, the peaceable kingdom, the reconciliation of the cosmos, resurrection life after death, the fulness of flourishing in the presence of the Lord. Worship, ecclesial connections, mission, ministry preaching, discipleship, art, saints, visions, experiences of the Spirit, eschatological hope and theological study all offer occasional glimpses of God's dominion which should inform and form dominion in the image of God.

God's dominion is and does who God is, which is love.[19] God effects and manifests that love in creation, in constancy and presence with the people of God, in law and prophecy, in the incarnation, crucifixion, resurrection and ascension, in the Gospel, in the saints and martyrs, and in persevering peace. In God's dominion, all of creation flourishes. Humans cannot produce or sustain God's dominion love, for themselves or for animals, but they can receive the responsibility of reflecting it, in their relationships with animals. To flourish is to reflect God's creative glory back toward God, in the praise suitable to creaturely specificity. To exercise dominion in the image of God is to reflect God's dominion of flourishing onto the animals of creation, by encouraging, enabling and supporting their particular lives of praise. Dominion in the image of God shapes human relationships with farmed animals toward relationships of flourishing, of praise and glory.

The character of this responsibility can be described in the context of human virtues: know your animals so you can treat them well (Proverbs 27:23). It can be cast in terms of the Law: let the cattle eat some of the grain they are treading (Deuteronomy 25:4); give working animals Sabbath and Jubilee rest (Exodus 20:8–11; 23:10–12; Deuteronomy 5:12–15; Leviticus 25:6–7). Prophetic images of God's dominion remove the need for any creature to kill any other creature (Isaiah 11:1–9). And it is illustrated in

---

[19]   Christopher Morse, *Not Every Spirit: A Dogmatic of Christian Disbelief*, second edition (New York, NY: Continuum, 2009), pp. 125–7.

the lives of the saints who communicated and lived closely with animals (including Saints Anthony Abbot, Anthony of Padua, Cuthbert, Francis of Assisi, Melangel, Modestos and Mungo).

Humans persistently confuse dominion with domination in their relationships with each other, with animals and with all of creation. The narration of human dominion in the image of God as the responsibility of humans to share God's dominion in love in their care for animals names domination, oppression and abuse as sinful distortions of dominion. Domination as dominion also demonstrates the unreliability of human/animal boundaries. Human dominators claim the whole identity of humanness for their own small set of humans and place the line between humans and animals between them and all other creatures. They may rank non-human creatures in a hierarchy of "closer to" and "farther away from" their claim on human identity, but the distinction holds. Traditionally, the set inside this circle is predominantly white and male and powerful; outside concentric circles move from other white men, to white women, BAME men, BAME women, and to more and less useful animals.[20] Often, animals are given higher positions than some humans: for example, favoured companion animals might be ranked more highly than human service staff, and the financial value of a prize-winning, inseminating bull might push BAME women even lower on the less-than-human scale. Similarly, white powerful women can enact a comparable hierarchy that places oppressed BAME women lower than abused animals. Women are marketed as objects for sexual consumption as if they were animal products for food, while animals are marketed for consumption as if they were women as sexual commodities.[21] Throughout, the central characters place themselves in a position to use or benefit from those they have placed outside their self-identified set of humans. Dominion, not domination, must also characterize the treatment of farm, abattoir and processing-plant workers, whose flourishing is also diminished by

---

[20] Mmapula Diana Kebaneilwe, "The Good Creation", *Old Testament Essays* 28:3 (2015), pp. 694–703.

[21] Carol J. Adams, *The Sexual Politics of Meat: A Feminist-Vegetarian Critical Theory* (New York, NY: Continuum Publishing Company, 1990) and *The Pornography of Meat* (New York, NY: Lantern Books, 2003).

poor pay, dangerous working conditions, and a low ranking on the social hierarchy of valued humans to consumable animals. To flourish as human creatures living into Christ's dominion, Christians must undermine and disempower human domination and its malign effects on humans and animal creatures.

Dominion responsibility in the image of God over animals pertains to the treatment of all of the animals that humans breed, genetically alter, transport and train for their own use: for sport, companionship, laboratory research, fur and entertainment, as well as consumption.[22] McFarland underscores the breadth of this responsibility:

> Since all creatures have God as their sole source and condition of existence, all of them . . . are equally near to (or far from) God. It follows that a crucial measure of our commitment to love God as Creator of all things is our willingness to honour God's commitment to the flourishing of all creatures.[23]

In today's context of domination, the dominion of Christ seems too distant to imagine, and the flourishing of farmed animals seems a relatively low priority for daily life. Yet Christians, as human creatures, do eat on a daily basis, even as they work for the flourishing of humans and human social structures, wild animals and the environment. Those Christians who are able to choose what they eat should consider the kind of dominion they support when they consume farmed animal products. Today, more and more of the farmed animals in the UK are raised in recently developed farming systems which do not allow them to flourish. The mass production of laying hens, broiler chickens, fish, pigs, sheep, dairy cows and beef cattle identifies these animals as commodities, instead of creatures who might give praise to God in their dependent particularities before they are slaughtered for human use. The human responsibility of dominion in the image of God should facilitate, not diminish, farmed animals' flourishing. Human dominion care of farmed

---

[22] David L. Clough, *On Animals: Volume 2: Theological Ethics* (London: T&T Clark: 2019).

[23] McFarland, *From Nothing*, p. xi.

animals should value animals as creatures whose primary purpose is praising God, rather than serving humans. Stanley Hauerwas and John Berkman argue:

> Animals will not manifest God's glory insofar as their lives are measured in terms of human interests, but only insofar as their lives serve God's good pleasure. Similarly, humans manifest God's glory when we learn to see animals as God sees animals, recognizing that animals exist not to serve us, but rather for God's good pleasure.[24]

Humans can best exercise dominion in the image of God when they recognize and attend to the particular needs and desires of farmed animals, in order to enable the animals' flourishing, which *is* God's good pleasure. God is not limited, and God's commitment to creatures is not limited to some creatures and not others. Humans are indeed limited, but human commitment to animal flourishing should, at the very least, include animals farmed for human benefit.

Dominion in the image of God calls for close attention, humility and an orientation toward praising God always. In this way, humans can learn about the particular needs, capacities and delights of farmed animals as creatures whose flourishing can improve as their opportunities to praise God are increased. John Berkman describes the way the Lord shows Job just how much he has to learn about God's relationship with animals (Job 39).[25] Job's previous impressions of animals were based on their potential benefit to him, when, in fact, Job himself is not the point of animals:

> Job's task is to learn to see in [*sic*] God's diverse creatures not primarily as creatures that might hurt him, scare him, help him, or serve as food for him, but rather first and foremost as

---

[24] Stanley Hauerwas and John Berkman, "The Chief End of All Flesh", *Theology Today* 49:2 (1992), pp. 196–208, here at pp. 204–5.

[25] John Berkman, "The Story of Max", in Trevor Bechtel, Matthew Eaton, and Timothy Harvie (eds), *Encountering Earth: Thinking Theologically with a More-Than-Human World* (Eugene, OR: Wipf and Stock, 2017), pp. 42–3.

creatures who have their own ends in God, and in whom God exults. Job's task is also our task, to overcome our presumption that all nonhuman animals exist as instruments for human use and enjoyment.[26]

The task of Christians today, in the face of intensive farming systems, is to learn about how the creatures farmed for human consumption can and cannot flourish in those systems, and to promote and support systems that allow for increased flourishing.

To be human is to be in relationship with God in ways that reveal God and God's relationship with creation. To be human in the body of Christ is to participate in that relationship as a creature with other creatures. To be fully human, to fully flourish as human, is to be fully planted in the presence of God, singing never-ending praise. Christ alone, not humans, effects the fulfilment of humanness, of all creatures and of all creation. To be Christian is to anticipate in community Christ's already, and yet to be, completed dominion of resurrection life. Christians bear witness to that hope when their flourishing is praise and when their relationships of praise increase other creatures' opportunities for flourishing, especially those creatures whose praising is inhibited by human distortions of glory.

Questions for discussion

1. In what ways do the similarities and differences we know about between humans and animals matter? How do these help us consider what it means to be human?

---

[26] Berkman, "The Story of Max". Berkman further argues for a distinction between "the intrinsic goodness of all nonhuman creatures" and the purpose of nonhuman animals "primarily to glorify God", whereas I maintain that the two are one. The flourishing that is particular to each creature, human and animal, *is* that creature's praise to God; a pig flourishes by praising God in the most pig-appropriate ways and thereby revealing God's glory.

2. How do you praise God best? How do those you know and know about—friends, family, congregations, communities, animals—praise God best?

3. How should Christian communities address the flourishing of other human and animal creatures of God?

Further reading

David L. Clough, *On Animals: Volume 1 Systematic Theology* and *Volume 2 Theological Ethics* (London: T&T Clark/Bloomsbury, 2019).

Celia Deane-Drummond and David Clough (eds), *Creaturely Theology: On God, Humans and Other Animals* (London: SCM Press, 2009).

Pope Francis, *Encyclical Letter Laudato Si' of The Holy Father Francis on Care for Our Common Home*, at <http://www.vatican.va/content/francesco/en/encyclicals/documents/papa-francesco_20150524_enciclica-laudato-si.html>, accessed 30 January 2021.

Laura Hopgood-Oster, *Holy Dogs and Asses: Animals in the Christian Tradition* (Champaigne, IL: University of Illinois Press, 2008).

CHAPTER 11

Never unnecessary: Being human in the age of artificial intelligence

Eric Stoddart

The presence of the future

Artificial intelligence (AI) is a part of everyday life when you use a smartphone. AI curates your social media feed and offers you selections on music-streaming services. AI watches over your bank account to protect you from fraud and by facial-recognition technologies it identifies threatening individuals in crowded streets. AI detects disease and navigates you to your destination. This is the present for millions of people. Yet, will humans always have the upper hand over AI? If, to co-opt Irving Berlin's lyrics in *Annie Get Your Gun*, "anything we can do, AI can do better", then where does this leave us humans who have relatively little physical strength, limited information-processing capabilities and bodies vulnerable to decay and death? Will our descendants wonder why, through a series of relatively inconsequential small decisions, their predecessors abdicated control over AI and set the scene for humans being superfluous? Isaac Asimov's fictional, but influential, three laws of robotics are unlikely to protect us despite the optimism which they represent:

> 1. A robot may not injure a human being, or, through inaction, allow a human being to come to harm. 2. A robot must obey the orders given it by human beings except where such orders would conflict with the First Law. 3. A robot must protect its

own existence as long as such protection does not conflict with the First or Second Law. Handbook of Robotics, 56th Edition, 2058 A.D.[1]

In this chapter I argue that participation in the *transformatio mundi* (the present and eschatological transformation, not destruction, of the world) is a human activity which, although amenable to being supplemented by the use of AI, remains a human activity. In this light, humans ought never be rendered obsolete or unnecessary in the face of sophisticated AI. The consequences of job automation present a singular warning as to the medium-term implications for being human as AI unfolds. I find some assessments of how we might retain meaningfulness in work as tasks are automated to be overly optimistic. It is in bringing together theologies of work and of AI that the *transformatio mundi* emerges as that which cannot be delegated to AI. I avoid a Luddite eschewal of technologies and argue that being human both now and in the future is an interstitial practice to be undertaken in the spaces between the organic and the cybernetic. I conclude with indications of where theological articulations of work and AI will require further development if the worst of transhumanist ideology (the view that humanity should be augmented by technology to ultimately transcend our organic limitations) is to be averted.

"Alexa, have I been made redundant?"

AI impacts people's livelihoods now and, through projections of rates of automation in the workplace, significantly also in the medium-term future. Constructions by PriceWaterhouseCoopers from data gathered by the Organization for Economic Co-operation and Development (OECD) describe three waves of job-, and separately, task-automation rates over the next fifteen years.[2] Wave 1 (to the early 2020s) involves

---

[1] Isaac Asimov, *I, Robot* (London: HarperCollins, 1996 [1950]), p. 8.

[2] John Hawksworth, Richard Berriman, and Saloni Goel, *Will Robots Really Steal Our Jobs? An International Analysis of the Potential Long Term Impact of Automation* (PwC [PricewaterhouseCoopers LLP], 2018), available at

computational tasks being automated resulting in financial sectors (and those others that are primarily data-driven) being most affected. In a second, augmentation, wave (to the late 2020s) clerical support and decision-making will interact in real time with technology, and many tasks in semi-controlled environments such as warehouse movements will be performed by robots. To the mid 2030s an autonomous wave is projected that involves the automation of physical labour where tasks require manual dexterity and responsive systems in dynamic real-world situations such as transport and construction. There may be notable national differences where 20–25 per cent of existing jobs are at high risk of automation by the early 2030s in East Asian and Nordic economies, while in Slovakia this could be well over 40 per cent.[3] In the United Kingdom, it is expected that by the third wave a little short of 35 per cent of potential jobs will be at risk of automation. Looking instead at industries across the world, around 45 per cent of manufacturing jobs and more than 50 per cent of potential jobs in transportation and storage are at high risk of automation, particularly so in the third wave when autonomous vehicles become more prevalent.[4] It will be low- (and slightly less so, medium-) education level workers who will bear most of the brunt of the changes. Some sectors will likely see gains in jobs where technology boosts demand for goods and services such as in health and education (the latter perhaps being from older people seeking retraining).[5] What happens in the first wave for some workers will not happen until the second and third waves for others:

> highly educated women performing clerical tasks and highly educated men in analytical jobs could, for example, be relatively vulnerable in the short term. But, eventually, less educated men may face the highest risks as autonomous machines are deployed that are capable of independently performing manual tasks such

    <https://www.pwc.co.uk/economic-services/assets/international-impact-of-automation-feb-2018.pdf>, accessed 23 July 2020.

[3]   Hawksworth et al., *Will Robots*, p. 2.

[4]   Hawksworth et al., *Will Robots*, p. 3.

[5]   Hawksworth et al., *Will Robots*, p. 22.

as driving, as well as many factory and warehouse jobs that currently employ a higher proportion of men than women.[6]

The OECD recognizes that equitable and inclusive development of AI must be a priority lest "existing divides within and between developed and developing countries" are exacerbated.[7] People who are self-employed may be at particular risk because retraining may not be so readily available as in the corporate sector, and AI tools could well be priced beyond the capacity of individuals—although the most expert self-employed may benefit by holding specialist skills.[8] Reskilling does not solve the immense challenges for employment in the following decades. People do not all have the same intellectual capabilities; no amount of reskilling can turn every lorry driver into a biologist. Humans are not interchangeable across job sectors; sales work and social work demand different forms of emotional intelligence, not simply knowledge of different "products". This is not to deny that some people are able to reskill, nor is it to devalue particular jobs. Rather, the non-interchangeability of humans across domains of employment recognizes not necessarily the uniqueness but at least significant diversity in capabilities. The future for a high proportion of workers across the world is not simply uncertain but predicted to be highly challenging, if not bleak. These projections do not take account of existing structural unemployment which means that for many people there really are no opportunities for work.

---

[6] Hawksworth et al., *Will Robots*, p. 27.

[7] OECD, *Artificial Intelligence in Society* (Paris: OECD Publishing, 2019), p. 83, available at <https://doi.org/10.1787/eedfee77-en>, accessed 23 July 2020.

[8] Terri L. Griffith, Chester Spell and Katerina Bezrukova, *The Impact of Artificial Intelligence on Self-Employment* (Centre for Research on Self-Employment, University of Buffalo School of Management, 2019), p. 4, available at <http://crse.co.uk/sites/default/files/The%20impact%20of%20artificial%20 intelligence%20on%20self-employment.pdf>, accessed 23 July 2020.

"Yes Siri, yes Siri, three bags full, Siri"

Job automation occurs against a backdrop of a broader vision for AI. A transhumanist ideology looks beyond the limited capabilities and fragility of being human to augmented and then replaced humanity. The European Union's high-level expert group on AI proposes a working, although not comprehensive, definition that serves our purposes:

> Artificial intelligence (AI) systems are software (and possibly also hardware) systems designed by humans that, given a complex goal, act in the physical or digital dimension by perceiving their environment through data acquisition, interpreting the collected structured or unstructured data, reasoning on the knowledge, or processing the information, derived from this data and deciding the best action(s) to take to achieve the given goal. AI systems can either use symbolic rules or learn a numeric model, and they can also adapt their behaviour by analysing how the environment is affected by their previous actions.[9]

There is *narrow* AI (such as a language translation system) that operates within a single domain whereas *broad* AI is designed to cross domains and, using a variety of types of data streams, successfully encounters arbitrary environments (the latest autonomous "driver-less" vehicles are examples). A third category, *super* AI, envisages autonomous, reasoning systems that have capabilities far beyond those of humans. This is what science fiction writers have carved into popular imagination but what some computer scientists find theoretically possible in a (more or less) distant future.

A transhumanist, such as Max More, views humans' current evolutionary development as not a terminus but a staging post beyond which lies progress in applying technology to improve and reshape not

---

[9]   High-level Expert Group on Artificial Intelligence, *A Definition of AI: Main Capabilities and Disciplines* (Brussels: European Commission, 2019), p. 6, available at <https://ec.europa.eu/newsroom/dae/document.cfm?doc_id=56341>, accessed 23 October 2020.

just the conditions for human life but the nature of life itself.[10] More envisages a significant displacement in ethical priorities: "Transhumanists regard human nature not as an end in itself, not as perfect, and not as having any claim on our allegiance."[11] Futurists such as Ray Kurzweil anticipate non-biological systems that far surpass not only the thinking capacity of humans but that outstrip our emotional intelligence too.[12] The process of transcending biological roots by merging with technology will pass through a point in history referred to as the singularity, "a future period during which the pace of technological change will be so rapid, its impact so deep, that human life will be irreversibly transformed".[13] The prospects for humans in the transhumanist project lie in a combination of upgrading and then being superseded.

Yuval Noah Harari warns that humans will be deprived of the control they once held for they "are in danger of losing their economic value, because intelligence is decoupling from consciousness".[14] By way of explanation, cars, he suggests, replaced horses not because they were better at everything a horse can do—but because cars "were superior in the handful of tasks that the system really needed. Taxi drivers are highly likely to go the way of horses".[15] Such, Harari ponders, will likely be the fate of lawyers when AI can search and apply legal precedents as well as draw on brain scans to determine when someone is telling the truth or lying.[16] Similarly, teachers and doctors should expect to be fully replaceable as AI develops—not tomorrow, as he notes, but current technical challenges

---

[10] See also Fuller, Chapter 8.

[11] Max More, "The Philosophy of Transhumanism", in Max More and Natasha Vita-More (eds), *The Transhumanist Reader* (Oxford: Wiley-Blackwell, 2013), pp. 3–18, here at p. 4.

[12] Ray Kurzweil, *The Singularity Is Near: When Humans Transcend Biology* (London: Duckworth, 2005), p. 377.

[13] Kurzweil, *Singularity*, p. 7.

[14] Yuval Noah Harari, *Homo Deus: A Brief History of Tomorrow* (London: Vintage, 2017), p. 361.

[15] Harari, *Homo Deus*, p. 363.

[16] Harari, *Homo Deus*, p. 365.

"need only be solved once" to enable mass deployment.[17] Imagining later twenty-first-century economics, Harari asks about the future for "the useless class"; those humans who are no longer needed when AI can perform their tasks much better. The prospects for "superfluous people" are far from rosy.[18] Not everyone will be marginalized as a few, those who own the AI systems, will be an elite benefiting from the concentration of wealth and power. However, given that some legal jurisdictions already recognize corporations as "legal persons", AI systems might themselves be their own owners.[19] Not every human will be superfluous for a few may remain necessary to AI systems in a janitorial function but the future for most is "a massive new unworking class: people devoid of any economic, political or even artistic value, who contribute nothing to the prosperity, power and glory of society. This 'useless class' will not be merely unemployed—it will be unemployable."[20] Such effects would not only be felt in economics but in politics, because humans with votes are fickle, prone to folly, and likely to be known by AI systems better than they know themselves: "Google will be able to represent even my own political opinions better than I can."[21]

The future of which Harari warns is arguably rather too consistent for comfort with human decision-making in the past: "because these projects aim at surpassing rather than safeguarding the norm, they may well result in the creation of a new superhuman caste that will abandon its liberal roots and treat normal humans no better than nineteenth-century Europeans treated Africans".[22] Neocolonialism, in which AI is the colonizing power, may indeed reduce humans to mere spectators; useless and inferior beings to be dominated, amused, or in the darkest of visions, disposed of as waste.

---

[17] Harari, *Homo Deus*, p. 368.

[18] Harari, *Homo Deus*, p. 370.

[19] Harari, *Homo Deus*, p. 376.

[20] Harari, *Homo Deus*, p. 379.

[21] Harari, *Homo Deus*, p. 394.

[22] Harari, *Homo Deus*, p. 408.

The drudgery of freedom?

The prognoses of major job losses through automation may be unnecessarily bleak given that in previous stages of mechanization farm workers moved into newly burgeoning cities to take up employment in factories. However, as Martin Ford observes, the former linear growth of mechanization is not what we see with twenty-first-century automation which follows a more exponential increase: "we can anticipate that the coming years and decades will see far more progress than we might expect based on an analysis of history".[23] Furthermore, the major impacts will not only be on people with low skills but those offering information-based skills to the employment marketplace. The dependence of almost all areas of employment upon AI (in one form or another) makes the creation of a vast array of jobs to absorb displaced workers highly unlikely.[24]

The negative effects of unemployment are felt by individuals and communities. Research has shown that mass unemployment events hitting a community have negative impacts on people's health behaviour, such as drinking more, smoking, being overweight and drug misuse. In the first year, the risk of death from alcohol-related disease may increase by a factor of 2.6; of death from heart attack or stroke by 2.3; and of suicide by a factor of 3.[25] Households and families face difficulty repaying mortgages and may accumulate significant levels of debt that further increases financial hardship including constrained access to food. Parenting may suffer, with consequences for children's mental health

---

[23]   Martin Ford, "The Rise of Roots: Impact on Unemployment and Inequality", in Eva Paus (ed.), *Confronting Dystopia: The New Technological Revolution and the Future of Work* (Ithaca, NY: Cornell University Press, 2018), pp. 27–45, here at p. 28.

[24]   Ford, "Rise of Robots", p. 29.

[25]   Alisha R. Davies et al., *Mass Unemployment Events (MUEs)—Prevention and Response from a Public Health Perspective* (Cardiff: Public Health Wales, 2017), p. 1, available at <http://www.wales.nhs.uk/sitesplus/documents/888/Watermarked%20PHW%20Mass%20Unemployment%20Report%20E%2815%29.pdf>, accessed 27 October 2020.

and reduced educational attainment.[26] There may be no route out from being caught in a "low-skills trap" within a "culture of worklessness".[27] Community networks may dissipate as contact with friends and former colleagues lessens and social isolation becomes a normal everyday experience.[28]

If AI takes away employment for many in the medium term (into the 2030s)—let alone the more futuristic scenarios painted by Harari where humans become mere spectators to life—there will be significant sociological as well as economic impacts. Tom Boland offers one litany of unemployment. People can no longer self-define on the basis of their occupation. They lose a structured experience of time as well as the absence of status. In the absence of structure, "the precious gift of time becomes a burden"[29] and "being stuck within liminality creates a world that is boring, grey, repetitive and meaningless".[30] At a broader level, meaning and identity are lost, or at least seriously diminished in "self-devaluation", "societal devaluation", "state devaluation".[31] Agency is particularly important although this may be more available when unemployment hits in a rural rather than urban setting.[32] Overall, the impact of long-term unemployment is gloomy as illustrated by a US study by Pew Research. For durations of unemployment exceeding six

26   Davies et al., *Mass Unemployment Events*, p. 23.

27   Davies et al., *Mass Unemployment Events*, p. 24.

28   Davies et al., *Mass Unemployment Events*, p. 25.

29   Tom Boland, "Talk: Nothing to Be Done", in Tom Boland and Ray Griffin (eds), *The Sociology of Unemployment* (Manchester: Manchester University Press, 2015), pp. 11–29, here at p. 17.

30   Boland, "Talk", p. 18.

31   Jennifer Yeager and Jonathan Culleton, "Dialogue: Focus Groups with Young and Mature Unemployed", in Tom Boland and Ray Griffin (eds), *The Sociology of Unemployment* (Manchester: Manchester University Press, 2015), pp. 30–49.

32   Gordon B. Cooke et al., "Rural: Beyond Deprivation Theory: Examining Rural Experience", in Tom Boland and Ray Griffin (eds), *The Sociology of Unemployment* (Manchester: Manchester University Press, 2015), pp. 90–106, here at p. 104.

months, 46 per cent of people experienced strain in family relations; 43 per cent lost contact with close friends; and 38 per cent lost some self-respect.[33] It is projected that the COVID-19 pandemic will result in an 8.6 per cent loss in global working hours in the fourth quarter of 2020—this is equivalent to 245 million jobs.[34] In 2020, the World Bank expects the global economy to shrink by 5.2 per cent with Latin America and the Caribbean per capita GDP receding proportionally the most by 8.1 per cent.[35] Prior to the pandemic and with automation in the first wave and so not having its largest potential impact, people were living with unemployment rates in Kosovo of 48 per cent (2019), in Zambia of 43 per cent (2018), and in South Africa of 38 per cent (2019).[36]

John Danaher asks, from a philosophical perspective, whether life in a world without work will be worth living.[37] He is concerned about people losing the meaningfulness that work provides—not only directly in terms of work but in their non-work lives also. Nevertheless, Danaher finds reasons for optimism. The problem of distributing essential and

---

[33] Pew Research Center, *Lost Income, Lost Friends—and Loss of Self-Respect: The Impact of Long-Term Unemployment* (Washington DC, 2010), p. 2, available at <https://www.pewresearch.org/wp-content/uploads/sites/3/2010/11/760-recession.pdf>, accessed 19 October 2020.

[34] International Labour Organization, *ILO Monitor: Covid-19 and the World of Work. Sixth Edition* (2020), pp. 8–9, available at <https://www.ilo.org/wcmsp5/groups/public/---dgreports/---dcomm/documents/briefingnote/wcms_755910.pdf>, accessed 6 October 2020.

[35] World Bank, *Global Economic Prospects* (Washington, DC: World Bank Group, 2020), p. 17.

[36] International Labour Organization, "Which Country Has the Highest Rate of Labour Underutilization?", <https://ilostat.ilo.org/topics/unemployment-and-labour-underutilization/, accessed 30 January 2021. This is the U3 figure (most commonly used to report unemployment), being the percentage of the labour force who are without jobs and have looked for work in the last four weeks.

[37] John Danaher, "Will Life Be Worth Living in a World without Work? Technological Unemployment and the Meaning of Life", *Science and Engineering Ethics* 23 (2017), pp. 41–64.

non-essential goods and services to those many who are unemployed can be solved, perhaps by a universal basic income (although Danaher takes no view on this particular solution).[38] He does explicitly assume that the distributional problem *can* be solved but I would argue it is not readily apparent that the political intentions of the holders of capital mean that it *will* be solved satisfactorily.

Danaher engages with the problem in people's personal sense of values: "There is a danger that in robbing us of the dignity of work, increasing levels of automation could reduce our overall levels of flourishing." Danaher considers objections that argue that work is inherently bad, because it is often degrading and humiliating (although this is true for some it is not the case for all work) and bad because it robs us of authorial control over our lives (we have to work whether we like it or not). In terms of opportunity-cost arguments, work is distributed according to the labour market (including its geography) which can mean that some of us do not have access to work that is fulfilling in the way we, as individuals, need it to be. A non-work society could be more equal and in freeing people for leisure more opportunity for cultural and political developments could be opened up. Yet, as Danaher notes, income (usually from work) is necessary not only for food and healthcare but to pay for leisure activities.[39] However, non-monetary goods need not, he contends, be as tied to work as we generally assume: "People can, and do, achieve excellence, social contribution, community and status in leisure activities, voluntary charitable activities and hobbies. They tend not to because they are forced to spend their time in economically productive forms of work."[40] Danaher turns back to technological unemployment to argue that there is a danger that technologies might well be better at attaining "the True and the Good" and thus make our lives subjectively better but at the cost of severing a vital link: "the objectives will no longer

---

[38]   Danaher, "Will Life Be Worth Living", p. 47.

[39]   Danaher, "Will Life Be Worth Living", p. 51.

[40]   Danaher, "Will Life Be Worth Living", p. 52.

be ours".[41] This could leave humans with only the realm of the Beautiful as the domain in which to contribute and find meaning.[42]

Danaher's proposal is to tackle what he sees as our externalizing of technology such that it is only ever doing things to us. He suggests a more integrationist approach in which we merge ourselves with technology; becoming cyborgs (technologized humans)—for in that way, "We could have the best of both worlds: the benefits of the enhanced capacities of technology along with meaningful participation in the outcomes the technology facilitates".[43] This brings him to what we have already seen as a transhumanist position. Danaher argues that it may be in virtual realities (made possible by advanced technologies) that humans may find meaningful activities; meaning-making is not a preserve of the real world.[44]

Too much weight lies on Danaher's assumption that integration and equitable distribution of necessary goods and services will be available to everyone and not just a few, with the rest left as spectators. We now turn to the question of whether the goods of AI in respect to work are quite so theologically appropriate.

"Work, rest and play": the theological importance of work

Transformatio mundi

In his encyclical *Laborem exercens*, Pope John Paul II identifies the purpose of work as "making life more human" (§3) and "a fundamental dimension of [human] existence on earth" (§4).[45] The context of its publication in 1981 is the conflicting ideologies of capitalism and

---

[41]   Danaher, "Will Life Be Worth Living", p. 58.

[42]   Danaher, "Will Life Be Worth Living", p. 59.

[43]   Danaher, "Will Life Be Worth Living", p. 60.

[44]   Danaher, "Will Life Be Worth Living", p. 61.

[45]   John Paul II, *Laborem exercens* (1981) at <http://www.vatican.va/content/john-paul-ii/en/encyclicals/documents/hf_jp-ii_enc_14091981_laborem-exercens.html>, accessed 30 January 2021.

communism, neither of which, in John Paul's view, offer a theologically robust appreciation of work and workers. Humanity has been given a divine mandate of subduing and dominating the earth; a mandate of action that is part, although not the whole, of being human in the image of God (§4). The dignity of work is closely related to the personal dignity of humans as workers: "It is not only good in the sense that it is useful or something to enjoy; it is also good as being something worthy, that is to say, something that corresponds to [human] dignity, that expresses this dignity and increases it" (§9). The lack of opportunities for work undermines, therefore, not only people's economic potential but denies them dignity. John Paul highlights the responsibilities of those at national and international level who set or influence employment policy to address unemployment which "in all cases is an evil" (§18).

Work itself may be dehumanizing when, for example, "the mechanization of work 'supplants' [humanity], taking away all personal satisfaction and the incentive to creativity and responsibility, when it deprives many workers of their previous employment, or when, through exalting the machine, it reduces [humanity] to the status of its slave" (§5). For John Paul II, there is a moral benefit from industriousness which arises in conjunction with work and education (§10). The effort expended may be physically, emotionally or intellectually demanding, and such "toil" is not to be despised but embraced in being a disciple of Christ:

> The Christian finds in human work a small part of the Cross of Christ and accepts it in the same spirit of redemption in which Christ accepted his Cross for us. In work, thanks to the light that penetrates us from the Resurrection of Christ, we always find a glimmer of new life, of the new good, as if it were an announcement of "the new heavens and the new earth" in which [humans] and the world participate precisely through the toil that goes with work (§27).

Work is therefore not merely a vehicle for individual moral improvement, nor solely a means of earning in order to live. The cumulative effort of humans working (although this does not presume waged employment) is with a view to making the world a more humane place for all. Christians are able to appreciate their particular efforts in a light cast, as it were, from the future.

Miroslav Volf places work even more explicitly in relation to eschatology. Contemplation is primarily of God (not of work) and of God who has a particular future in mind for the world and therefore "Christian work must . . . be done under the inspiration of the Spirit and in the light of the coming new creation."[46] For Volf, this is grounded on a particular understanding of creation and new creation: "A truly *new* creation can never result from the action of intrahistorical forces pushing history toward ever-superior states."[47] This is not an eschatology of God's destruction of the world but of its transformation—transformatory action that is integral to being human: "without a theologically grounded belief in the intrinsic value and goodness of creation, positive cultural involvement hangs theologically in the air".[48] But, argues Volf, if the new creation is about the *transformatio mundi*, "then the results of the cumulative work of human beings have intrinsic value and gain ultimate significance, for they are related to the eschatological new creation, not only indirectly through the faith and service they enable or sanctification they further, but also directly: the noble products of human ingenuity".[49]

It is not just that work can be rendered meaningful but "the Spirit's salvific work", extending "to the whole of reality",[50] includes the humanizing of work.[51] This pneumatological understanding of work gives value to efforts this side of the eschaton because these are subject to the eschatological transformation to which they point and from which, for Christians at least, they are motivated. Work is valuable therefore not only for Christians: "If the world will be transformed, then the work of non-Christians has in principle the same ultimate significance as the work of Christians: insofar as the results of non-Christians' work pass

---

46 Miroslav Volf, *Work in the Spirit: Toward a Theology of Work* (Eugene, OR: Wipf & Stock, 2001 [1991]), p. 79.

47 Volf, *Work in the Spirit*, p. 84.

48 Volf, *Work in the Spirit*, p. 91.

49 Volf, *Work in the Spirit*, p. 91.

50 Volf, *Work in the Spirit*, p. 103.

51 Volf, *Work in the Spirit*, p. 116.

through the purifying judgment of God, they, too, will contribute to the future new creation."[52] (Here Ben Witherington, also writing to a broadly Protestant evangelical North American audience, takes issue with Volf's extension of *charism* of God's Spirit beyond the members of Christ's body, the Church.[53])

Volf has remarkably little to say about unemployment, reserving his observation to the claim that being without paid employment means "being free for other significant kinds of work".[54] There is no sign, however, of his appreciation of the poverty and dehumanizing effects of not only personal but structural unemployment. Volf does make an important distinction between those unable, and those unwilling, to work. Although work is not only a means to life, work is "an aspect of the purpose of life itself".[55] Volf makes a distinction between being human and living as "fully human"; refusing to work means "a person cannot live a fully human existence".[56] Although even the most degrading and dangerous forms of employment might still be redeemed, a refusal to undertake such work would appear to deny a person the possibilities of living as fully human. Volf is implying that *any* work is better than *no* work; a position that would be welcomed by an unscrupulous corporation, for it places all power in its hands and not in the hands of the working class. The *transformatio mundi* here seems kicked into the long grass of eschatological judgement.

Co-creating

Humanizing and transforming the world in the light of God's future for creation, at the current stage of AI development, does require human activity although we deploy technologies to assist. Pondering whether or not we may relinquish such activities when technological systems are sufficiently advanced forces us to consider the importance of creativity

---

52   Volf, *Work in the Spirit*, p. 118.

53   Ben Witherington III, *Work: A Kingdom Perspective on Labor* (Grand Rapids, MI: Eerdmans, 2011), p. 37.

54   Volf, *Work in the Spirit*, p. 156.

55   Volf, *Work in the Spirit*, p. 197.

56   Volf, *Work in the Spirit*, p. 197.

(a dimension of the meaningfulness of work) as an indispensable human characteristic. Dorothy L. Sayers, in a 1942 lecture, contends that work is, foremost, "the medium" in which workers offer themselves to God.[57] A person lives to work, not working to live, and work ought to be chosen and made available so that a person can make "the full expression of [their] faculties".[58] Reward does not come through remuneration for work but in being in a position to fulfil one's nature. Sayers stands against wages being higher than what is sufficient to live on and against restrictions that limit working hours because to do so is to impinge on the liberty of a person's own decisions about who is to be fulfilled in work.[59] In the midst of a war against fascism, which elevates commitment to serving the state above individual liberty, Sayers argues that engaging in divinely ordered work is the way to serve the community.[60] In what is, in effect, a critique that relativizes all appeals to *national* endeavour, Sayers concludes that, "If work is to find its right place in the world, it is the duty of the Church to see to it that the work serves God, and that the worker serves the work".[61]

Sayers confronts fascism; in the late twentieth century the threat of ecological damage by unbridled capitalism is the challenge for which Matthew Fox proposes a cosmology within which human work (not just paid employment) should be seen "as part of the ongoing work of the universe and all the species in it."[62] Inner work (of contemplation, interior, personal, soul-work) and outer work (of intellectual, physical, embodied activity) are, for Fox, joined. The inner feeds the outer; the outer is to be authentic to the inner. All humans are "creators" but Fox qualifies this capability: "To say that we are co-creators with the Spirit is to say that

---

[57] Dorothy L. Sayers, "Why Work?", *Letters to a Diminished Church: Passionate Arguments for the Relevance of Christian Doctrine* (Nashvillle, TN: Thomas Nelson, 2004), pp. 118–39, here at p. 128.

[58] Sayers, "Why Work?", p. 128.

[59] Sayers, "Why Work?", pp. 128 and 130.

[60] Sayers, "Why Work?", pp. 135–6.

[61] Sayers, "Why Work?", p. 139.

[62] Matthew Fox, *The Reinvention of Work: A New Vision of Livelihood for Our Time* (San Francisco, CA: HarperSanFrancisco, 1994), p. 297.

a wild and mysterious thing happens when we go about our work . . . Spirit may erupt at any moment and from any genuine act of creativity."[63]

Claiming a status as "co-creators" deifies humanity unless co-creation is understood as participation in divine labour. As John Hughes argues, ours is an "analogical participation", for although it is not possible to transcend the very differences between "the eternal unity of rest and action" and our daily round of work and rest, we are yet called to "be perfect as [our] father in heaven is perfect" (Matthew 5:48).[64] The telos of being human lies not in work; rather, "work must serve the higher end of worship and contemplation of the divine, the eternal Sabbath of the Beatific Vision".[65] Sabbath, on this side of the eschaton, has instrumental value in guaranteeing rest for bodies (and land) that are too easily exploited. The Sabbath is not, essentially, a period of inactivity from paid and unpaid work. Jesus healing on a Sabbath (Matthew 12:12) was him being about the work of his father (John 5:17). Neither is Sabbath synonymous with modern understanding of leisure. Hughes is helpful here in his juxtaposition of the *utility* by which human work is evaluated in non-theological discourse with the non-utility of God's working: "He does not create out of any need or lack in himself, nor instrumentally for any other purpose. God works for no other reward than his love for the thing made."[66] Sabbath is thus, analogically to God's non-utile activity, humans casting off the chains of utility. This is why someone who is unemployed has not entered a lengthy Sabbath of indeterminate duration. Unemployment does not symbolize the eternal rest in the beatific vision of God; unemployment symbolizes instead exclusion from participation in work and its possible benefits of wages and personal fulfilment.

Working encompasses much more than paid employment, but we should not underestimate the importance of being allowed to earn a living. Being *able* to work is far from the same as being *permitted* to work. Paid employment and performing tasks unpaid are both means by which

---

63 Fox, *Reinvention*, pp. 115, 123.

64 John Hughes, *The End of Work: Theological Critiques of Capitalism* (Oxford: Blackwell, 2007), p. 227.

65 Hughes, *End*, p. 225.

66 Hughes, *End*, p. 226.

humans can participate in the *transformatio mundi* that anticipates and practises the kingdom of God as it breaks into this world against the horizon of a renewed world promised to come. Unemployment is thus not "a price to be paid" for the greater profitability of automation. Lack of employment is dehumanizing in undermining human dignity. In the longer term, as neither leisure nor unemployment is Sabbath, so too being reduced to being spectators is not Sabbath. This is not to exclude AI from possibly being deployed in the yet-to-be-judged work of *transformatio mundi*, but it is to reject plans for a transhumanist future in which AI *replaces* humanity as those who are at work.

AI: harbinger or impediment to work as creativity and the transformatio mundi?

Although not uncritically, Antje Jackelén leaves open the possibility that improvements in the human condition brought about by the application of AI may have a positive relation to the messianic dimensions of the kingdom of God in, for example, healing those who are sick and feeding the hungry.[67] In her view, personhood need not be reserved only to those with a particular biological origin; the door is open for non-biological persons.[68] God is non-corporeal, so Jackelén also contends that imaging God need not be corporeal: thus "there is no principal theological reason to denounce the development of *techno sapiens* altogether".[69] There is a danger of creativity being narrowed to just technological creativity, admits Jackelén, although she imagines a future in which humans transform themselves into cyborgs rather than Harari's warning for the future of unnecessary humans. Jackelén is challenging an anthropocentric point of departure in questions of anthropology (theological and otherwise). Whilst there are indeed possibilities of "fruitful discourse" with transhumanist perspectives, she rather downplays possibilities of conflict between humans, cyborgs and AI.[70]

---

[67] Antje Jackelén, "The Image of God as Techno Sapiens", *Zygon* 37:2 (2002), pp. 289–302, here at p. 293.

[68] Jackelén, "Image of God", pp. 295–6.

[69] Jackelén, "Image of God", p. 298.

[70] Jackelén, "Image of God", p. 300.

In Eric Trozzo's view, humans ought not to surrender their future to a computational mode that is inadequate because it rejects divine in-breaking: "Pure calculation holds no space for hope in the future, for unforeseeable possibility to rupture the current trajectory of probability."[71] He finds a parallel with Jürgen Moltmann's important distinction between *futurum* (what comes next is nothing but continuity with the reality of before) and *adventus* (that which is coming *from* the future; hope in the kingdom of God).[72] Humanity cannot be self-constructed (and by implication in our view nor can it be self-deconstructed in deference to AI) on such *futurum* terms, for this is to deny that "our humanity is constituted by our relationship with divine creativity".[73]

Technology is confronted by theology, in the view of Brian Brock, over the former's illusory offer of control over the contingencies within which humans live.[74] As idols enslave with a false promise of salvation, so too does technology when humans make themselves subservient to what they have created.[75] Herein lies Brock's fundamental theological critique of all technology: "its replacement of . . . faith for reliance on a mechanism promising salvation without the risking of self in relationship".[76] Instead of seeking their end in "the freedom of the Spirit"—not merely freedom per se—any abrogating of moral responsibility to God in favour of deferring to a human system is to deny our proper relationship to God.[77] Brock is not rejecting technology lock, stock and barrel but challenging humans' surrender to the temptation of using it as another way of exerting power, not only over the material environment but also over other people. There remains, for Brock, space for technological systems to "play a part in

[71]   Eric Trozzo, *The Cyberdimension: A Political Theology of Cyberspace and Cybersecurity* (Eugene, OR: Cascade Books, 2019), p. 131.

[72]   Trozzo, *Cyberdimension*, p. 133.

[73]   Trozzo, *Cyberdimension*, p. 134.

[74]   Brian Brock, *Christian Ethics in a Technological Age* (Grand Rapids, MI: Eerdmans, 2010), p. 230.

[75]   Brock, *Christian Ethics*, p. 231.

[76]   Brock, *Christian Ethics*, p. 231.

[77]   Brock, *Christian Ethics*, pp. 259–60.

our finding ourselves in the love of the other".[78] It is placing trust in technologies as the solution to the human condition that Brock finds profoundly theologically problematic. The claims of artificial *intelligence* are contentious enough but are much less significant than what is, in effect, a hope of artificial *salvation*. The improvement of humanity is not the redemption of humanity.

Brent Waters helps us appreciate the mistaken perspective of that from which transhumanists contend we need deliverance. Waters argues that transhumanists "can discern no aesthetic qualities in the necessary. There is nothing beautiful at all about mortality".[79] Waters identifies an obsession with overcoming mortality (although I wonder if it might be more subtle) in terms of us desiring to hold on to what has been gained during life— not just material possessions, but knowledge and wisdom.[80] In common with the theological commentators we have already considered, he posits Christian eschatology as a bulwark resisting transhumanism: "The rule of Christ is not oriented toward a recovering of creation's origin but toward its destiny."[81] In so doing, Waters is also reorienting those theologies that neglect the teleology of the transformation (not the destruction) of the world. Waters is, in effect, arguing for a trajectory that reaffirms the human in the face of transhumanist cul-de-sacs. Although contingency and necessity are integral to being born and developing as human, Waters traces life as it is lived in relation to God as a life of "judgment, confession, repentance, forgiveness, and amendment of life".[82] It is life qualified by God which is not to be overcome (as by transhumanism) but enjoyed: life and technology "formed and guided by the hope of natality instead of the fear of mortality".[83]

---

[78] Brock, *Christian Ethics*, p. 213.

[79] Brent Waters, *From Human to Posthuman : Christian Theology and Technology in a Postmodern World* (Aldershot: Ashgate, 2006), p. 74.

[80] Brent Waters, *Christian Moral Theology in the Emerging Technoculture: From Posthuman Back to Human* (Abingdon: Routledge, 2014), pp. 105–6.

[81] Waters, *Christian Moral Theology*, p. 113.

[82] Waters, *Christian Moral Theology*, p. 107.

[83] Waters, *Christian Moral Theology*, p. 158.

AI threatens a theological understanding of work by devaluing the subjective dimension and by giving priority to efficiency. In more extreme developments, efficiency would be paramount, admitting no other considerations. Working in a way that is excellent cannot be synonymous with working efficiently. Pausing to assist a colleague has a moral value of compassion and consideration for another who is struggling. This might well be inefficient, but it might contribute to the dignity of both colleagues. Creative processes that include trial and error to achieve something beautiful may not be efficient. Scope for artistry in the workplace might be sacrificed and this might be a further way in which work is made less meaningful.

Work that remains available to those who integrate technology with their humanity could be further and further removed from any connection to human impetus. Just as being a cyborg is a matter of degree rather than a dichotomous category, work will cease to be work. A human designing a button for a semi-automated system and a human pressing that button is work. A group of humans designing a self-managing, autonomous system is also likely still to be classified as work. It is fair to describe as work the effort by humans to design machines that learn, so that AI can then take over operating systems. However, when a learning machine itself develops new learning machines to operate new systems, then human intervention is so far upstream that is seems meaningless to describe the activity as work. There comes a point where actions are so loosely attributable to human activity that humans become analogous to a deist's "watchmaker God" who sets the cosmos in motion and then steps back. AI might well be performing functions and operating but, from a theological perspective, not be working.

The need for redemption rather than mere improvement undercuts the optimism of transhumanists, such as Danaher, who assume that the distribution of goods and services to non-working populations will be fair and sufficient. Should highly automated systems reflect the ways in which capital is so readily concentrated in the hands of a tiny minority, it becomes acutely necessary to ask *for* whom people are working. Coupled with a move to janitorial tasks supporting the dominance of AI, the opportunities are curtailed for more than a small proportion of humans. The marginalization and even oppression of those who are poor, made poor and kept poor, is a theological issue of the uttermost importance. God's preferential option for those who are poor judges systems that privilege the rich. Those cast down from their thrones in Mary's song might less likely be kings and CEOs but AI systems. Cyborgs, billionaire funders of AI and systems designers will remain susceptible to sins of, amongst others, self-interest, prejudice, pride and greed. This is not to say that all developments of AI will denigrate human beings, but to be alert to the possibility that AI may make some humans more efficient at sinning. Furthermore, computer coding is a political act in the decisions taken over what to measure, how to measure it, and the ethical basis built into automated systems. An AI system need not be attributed with the agency to be "a sinner" to still engage in practices that are expressions of the sinful world.

At the heart of the issue is how the *transformatio mundi* is practised in the light of the eschatological new creation. As we have seen in Volf, the Spirit's salvific work is extended to all reality and this includes humanizing work. Without excluding the possibility that other creatures might, in their own way, be responsive to the Spirit of God, the element of *transformatio* is deeply linked to intentional activity. Human intention can surely be expressed through the technologies we develop and, like all human action, be passed through the purifying judgement of God. This becomes problematic when AI is the "actor", because once automation by artificial intelligence is so many steps removed from human initiation it is highly doubtful that the relationship with the Spirit of God remains intact. To argue otherwise would be to elevate a machine to a being of complex consciousness with the capacity to be compassionate and loving. We would need to attribute moral accountability to AI, rather than only to its designers.

More pressing for our discussion is whether by removing the need (and opportunity) for humans to work lifts from us the possibility of participating in the *transformatio mundi*. In the medium term, it would be deeply regrettable were considerable numbers of people denied access to an important domain in which they could be contributing to the *transformatio*. Work is not the only domain in which the *transformatio* can be practised, so all would not be lost as people could be involved in voluntary and unpaid activities under the inspiration of God's Spirit.

However, the transhumanist vision of humans being mere spectators of life would mean denying access to all but a few to a crucial avenue for the *transformatio*. If the future is more integrationist with technology then the theological problem is slightly lessened, but not avoided. It is not clear at what point on the continuum a cyborg loses the link with the organic (i.e. human). Cyborgs closer to the organic end of the continuum might well continue to be sufficiently human to be inspired by the Spirit of God. Establishing when that theological equivalent of the event horizon is crossed into a cyberstate requires consideration of experiences to which we currently have no access. To transcend the human would, at least at this point in theological development, mean crossing the boundary of the Spirit of God's inspiration; something which has hitherto been framed as requiring relationship with humans.

Onward Christian cyborgs

Being human is going to be more and more an interstitial practice of living in the space between human and artificial intelligence. As it becomes less necessary for humans to undertake dangerous tasks there may be a loss of income when there are not safe tasks available as replacement employment. However, there could be a difference in outcomes for those who are highly skilled in dangerous work and those who are in dangerous but low-skilled jobs. Cleaning after a nuclear contamination and some methods of mining may well be replaced by AI, but human workers will experience differential advantage based on existing valuations of their tasks. Similarly, the world might be less life-threatening as more aspects are directed by AI, but elite groups will likely benefit whilst the masses will find their environment more debilitating if poverty increases. The promised freedom from drudgery which transhumanists anticipate highlights the prospects for those whose work is not satisfying. AI and transhumanism seem to unfold as a capitalist project. Socialist imperatives of equity and shared responsibilities for everyone in communities do not appear prominent as future emphases.

When AI frees humans for leisure, the interstitial space will, in effect, be one of forced leisure; arguably an oxymoron. Taking a holiday can be enforced, but leisure is less a set of activities than it is a state of mind. The kind of leisure that emerges may not turn out to be recreational at all. If leisure is, at least in some ways, in a dialectical tension with other activities, what is the opposite pole going to be? We are familiar with vacations from work but when there is no work the practice of leisure dissipates. There is every possibility that humans will simply be bored and fall into acedia. To take the example of sourdough baking, which seemed to be symbolic of much middle-class activity during the first national lockdown in spring of 2020, there can be only so much bread baked in a world where humans are superseded by AI. Perhaps people of religious faith will fill their "leisure" time, freed from work and manual distractions, with contemplation and worship of God. However, interstitial worship could suffer from a loss of groundedness as toil and wrestling with our material and natural environment is lifted from us. Worshipping as if we were angels is to be limited to adoration that is disconnected from contingency and pain.

The time released to us by AI taking over so many tasks and jobs could let *homo ludens* (the human who plays) blossom, perhaps at first. However, just as all work and no play makes Jack and Jill dull people, *all* play and no work not only disengages humans from the transformation of the world but, like those of our Victorian predecessors who wallowed in excess leisure time, it also indefinitely postpones self-development.[84]

The offer of increased efficiency through not merely deploying but delegating to AI resonates with a utilitarian, cost–benefit analysis of not only specific technologies but of the human life integrally bound up in technologized environments. Being human is actually an inefficient condition—more so, it seems, if AI is able to do so many activities more efficiently. However, the virtue and skills of forgiveness towards other, fallible, people may be lost. It is absurd to forgive a device for either a system failure or a negative consequence for us. Being human has to keep on meaning that we offer forgiveness and praise to those who impact our lives. Refusing efficiency and continually reinjecting

---

[84]   Rebekah Lamb, "'The Lowest Place': Christina Rossetti and the Problem of Boredom", *The Journal of Pre-Raphaelite Studies* 26 (2017), pp. 23–49, here at p. 39.

human decision-makers into processes is already an important resistance to algorithmic decision-making.[85] In such a space, humans are able to serve each other. The alternative of relationships wholly mediated by AI points towards a future of cocooning from costly interactions of humility. The emptying of dignity that transhumanism posits under the guise of evolution of the species is not the kenotic self-emptying for others and for God that Christian spirituality extols. John the Baptist emulated this principle in his confession that "He must increase, but I must decrease" (John 3:30). AI, at least in the transhumanist vision, despite its assertions of improving humanity, seems to be calling for an idolatrous kenosis of human self-emptying in obedience to a technological master.

In the medium term, AI might extend individual freedom by taking on toil and effort, releasing time for the self, but society relies on bonds of responsibility to (and sometimes even for) one another that are expressed in commercial, political, cultural as well as familial relationships. Those cannot be substituted by AI—and perhaps this will be to the advantage of AI. Democracy is unlikely to be compatible with a transhumanist vision, lest the freedom of individuals expressed in political decisions interfere with the efficiency of the AI systems. In interstitial life there is a need *now*, not merely in the long-term future, for democratic accountability of AI systems. Unless we want to lose the social fabric and skill of decision-making more generally, it is vital that we retain control of such systems even while more and more information is processed. Humans do not always make optimal decisions and may on occasion make bad decisions—but decision-making in relationship to one another is a key practice. This, too, is an interstitial practice of being human, for it could well be that we are given freedom from paid employment and the ability to follow paths of non-paid forms of working. The analogy here is to those women who fought for financial independence from men through access to the same labour opportunities. Without work in the future people will lose economic independence from the state and be totally dependent upon such state welfare as is provided. In such a dependent state there is no space for politics when AI holds our pursestrings.

---

85   Virginia Eubanks, *Automating Inequality: How High-Tech Tools Profile, Police, and Punish the Poor* (New York, NY: St Martin's Press, 2017).

Humans—never trash, never unnecessary

What would a Christian of 2130 looking back to 2030 hope to see Christians arguing and practising in order to avoid the worst excesses of transhumanism? The current focus in theologies of AI is largely on discussions around the mind and how, if at all, AI can become conscious at some point in the future. Pressing developments in the ways automation is affecting employment opportunities suggest that a theology of AI needs to be more solidly grounded in social justice, and particularly with reference to God's preferential option for those who are poor. Being human is, for so many—perhaps even the majority—of those alive today, not so much a philosophical matter as a matter of practice. Optimistic claims of AI ushering in new opportunities may be true, but not for everyone. The emphasis on social justice becomes more pressing given the conditions of poverty under which so many people live today. However, if AI can alleviate now, or in the short term, some of the degrading circumstances in which people are being human then we must affirm its value.

Despite theologians of work responding to their context (such as Sayers to fascist totalitarianism, John Paul II to Reaganomics and Soviet communism, and Hughes to secular neoliberalism) the almost total absence of considerations of unemployment (and underemployment) in recent theologies of work is a major concern. Furthermore, there needs to be much more theological reflection on the cyborg as a worker and upon the continuum of work ranging from direct human activity through to automated systems designed by AI. How do we establish when work is no longer an activity linked to humans? This is connected to articulating a pneumatology that engages with technology. Should a theology of the Spirit of God include the potential for AI to be Spirit-imbued? The comparison might not then be with human intelligence but with forms of simple life and its organic sensory existence. Were this to be the case then our understanding of work would need to be expanded to encompass what is performed not only by humans but also by AI. The "work" of AI need not be the same sort of work as that of humans but may be of a different but no less theologically important form within our doctrine of (technologized) creation.

The harm to humans proscribed by Asimov's first law of robotics needs to be expanded beyond the notion of direct injury to individuals. Harms to which humans must not be exposed either through action or inaction by robots need to include unemployment and the ideological damage of rendering humans as potentially superfluous or useless. Theologically, Christians would want to include a preferential option for those who are poor into policies for AI development and encode such an option into the decision-making algorithms.

Questions for discussion

1. How is your work-life, and that of your family or friends, affected by AI?
2. What aspects of life might it be appropriate for Christians to hand over to AI now or in the next decade?
3. What would a Christian of 2130, looking back a hundred years or so, hope to see you arguing and practising at being human today in order to avoid the worst excesses of transhumanism?

Further reading

Margaret A. Boden, *Artificial Intelligence: A Very Short Introduction* (Oxford: Oxford University Press, 2018).
John Paul II, *Laborem Exercens* (1981) at <http://www.vatican.va/content/john-paul-ii/en/encyclicals/documents/hf_jp-ii_enc_14091981_laborem-exercens.html>, accessed 30 January 2021.
Eric Trozzo, *The Cyberdimension: A Political Theology of Cyberspace and Cybersecurity* (Eugene, OR: Cascade Books, 2019).
Miroslav Volf, *Work in the Spirit: Toward a Theology of Work* (Eugene, OR: Wipf & Stock, 2001 [1991]).

CHAPTER 12

Made in the image of God: Theology and transgender

Alison Jasper

Poetics and the image of God

I would say that any discussion of the likeness or image of God belongs within the realm of poetics, perhaps as Édouard Glissant's *Poetics of Relation* proposes it.[1] For Glissant, a literary critic of colour from Martinique, poetics is less a literary genre than a way of thinking and reading/writing, and even a way of being in the world, that particularly values those creative processes that begin with what may be broken or obscured in some way. The sources of this poetics are the "shattered histories" and "shards of vocabulary" that another Caribbean writer, Derek Walcott, refers to in relation to Antillean art.[2] These are definitions influenced by a powerful concern with Caribbean histories and cultures whose discontinuities owe much to Western colonial expansion and exploitation.[3] The context of scriptural composition is not the same, but the principle is certainly similar. And totalizing interpretations

---

[1] Édouard Glissant, *Poetics of Relation*, tr. Betsy Wing (Ann Arbor, MI: Michigan University Press, [1990] 1997).

[2] Derek Walcott, "The Antilles: Fragments of Epic Memory, Nobel Lecture", in Derek Walcott (ed.), *What the Twilight Says: Essays 3–35* (New York, NY: Farrar, Strauss and Giroux, 1992), p. 69.

[3] Mayra Rivera, *Poetics of the Flesh* (Durham, NC & London: Duke University Press, 2015), p. 3.

of the Bible—no more than totalizing interpretations of "empire" or "progress"—however comfortingly solid they might seem, can never be actually comprehensive or entirely innocent readings. They carry within them the seeds of their own eventual dissolution as the generations pass on and circumstances and knowledges change—sometimes, radically. What follows therefore needs to be seen as part of a process of reading and writing "poetically"; an approach that recognizes disruption, displacement and even, sometimes, irrecoverable loss. We cannot know everything about scripture. We must work continually to create these texts anew, recognizing our own limitations even as we remain vulnerable to, that is, capable of being affected by, their evocations of divine love.

What this might have to do with transgender begins with the ways in which the Christian scriptures (as themselves readers of earlier narratives or texts), and subsequent readers, have brought the symbolism of gender into their understanding of the creational order. The notion of the image of God is something that has wider scriptural resonance than the first three chapters of Genesis.[4] However, in the context of a short chapter,

---

[4]   There are, for example, many New Testament references to Christ as "the image of God" (e.g. 2 Corinthians 4:4; Colossians 1:15; Hebrews 1:3; Ephesians 4:24, and in John 1:14,18 Christ makes known the invisible God). In these contexts, it is through turning to Christ (2 Corinthians 3:15–18) rather than through our creation, that we are transformed into that same image equivalent to the new self (Colossians 3:10) that is the image of God. Thus the original creature of clay—or Adam, with whom we are all identified (1 Corinthians 15:22)—is distinguished from the image of heaven which is our hope in Christ (1 Corinthians 15:49). There are a very few New Testament references to wo/man made in the image of God that appear to conform more closely with the pattern of Genesis 1:26,27 (or Genesis 5:1), e.g. James 3:8–10. In 1 Corinthians 11:7, the apostle Paul abandons his more characteristically theological approach to the question. Reverting to the Genesis 1–3 narrative he uses this to defend the kind of normative gendered hierarchy that would no doubt have been recognized by a substantial proportion of church members: "For a man ought not to cover his head, since he is the image and glory of God, but woman is the glory of man."

we can only begin to open up this discussion. Genesis 1–3 seems an appropriate place to begin.

In the beginning: Genesis: 1–3[5]

Genesis 1:26,27

> Then God said, "Let us make humankind (Hebrew: *adam*) in our image, according to our likeness . . .
>> So God created humankind (Hebrew: *adam*) in his image,
>>> In the image of God he created them; male and female he created them.

Genesis 2:21–24

> So the LORD God caused a deep sleep to fall upon the man, and he slept; then he took one of his ribs and closed up its place with flesh. And the rib that the LORD God had taken from the man he made into a woman and brought her to the man. Then the man said,
>> This at last is bone of my bones
>> And flesh of my flesh; this one shall be called Woman,
>> For out of Man this one was taken.
>> Therefore a man leaves his father and his mother and clings to his wife and they become one flesh. And the man and his wife were both naked, and were not ashamed.

This story of human creation in the image and likeness of God is also, as Glissant and Walcott suggest about the literature of the Caribbean, composed from shards and discontinuous histories, though of a different kind. In the book of Genesis, linguistic differences and variable styles reveal traces of older literary texts and are scattered with references to mythologies and ritual practices; all forms of the poetics of ancient Middle

---

[5] See also Taylor, Chapter 1, Adam, Chapter 10.

Eastern knowledge and culture, and especially of the Jews. The book of Genesis, by common scholarly consent, has been constructed from strands woven together by one or more later editors or redactors.[6] Thus, the first account of the creation of a "creature of clay" (NRSV Hebrew: *adam*) in Genesis 1:26–7, attributed to the so-called "Priestly" source, is more recent than the second account of creation that appears in Genesis 2–3.[7] In the view of von Rad, the first account is in clear contrast to the second account—even though their purposes, he suggests, coincide. This first account is not, like the second, "masterly narrative" composed by the so-called "Yahwist" author, something that encompasses "the whole of human life with all its heights and depths",[8] but constitutes a matter of doctrine.[9] The first account, as we now read it, introduces the notion of a divine image or likeness as pattern or model for humankind,[10] but perhaps more, the mirror of a certain divine purpose.[11] In the context of this first strand, God creates and sustains and endures in dominion and control—and enjoyment! Humankind, formed in that image, is represented by a couple (Genesis 1:28), whose purpose is thus to create and domesticate the environment—sex and birthing seem assumed—and to thrive in it. The issue of sin does not arise here; everything is good.

---

[6]   See Gerhard von Rad, *Genesis: A Commentary* (revised edition), tr. John H. Marks (London: SCM Press, [1961] 1972), pp. 24–9. Also, see Susan Nidditch, "Genesis", in Carol A. Newsom & Sharon H. Ringe (eds), *The Women's Bible Commentary* (London: SPCK and Louisville, KY: Westminster John Knox Press, 1992), pp. 10–25, p. 11.

[7]   Nidditch, "Genesis", pp.11–12.

[8]   von Rad, *Genesis*, p. 25.

[9]   Ibid., p. 61; p. 47.

[10]   "The terms 'image' and 'likeness' are probably not to be differentiated: the double phrase is simply for emphasis. It clearly defines human beings as resembling God in a way that is not the case with the animals (cf. 1:28 and Psalm 8:3–8). The nature of this resemblance is not apparent, however, and *hypotheses abound*." R. N. Whybray, "Genesis", in John Barton & John Muddiman (eds), *The Oxford Bible Commentary* (Oxford: Oxford University Press, 2001), p. 43, emphasis added.

[11]   von Rad, *Genesis*, p. 59.

Dominion and control are declared and stated but do not explicitly invite the kinds of misogynistic interpretations that have bedevilled the history of biblical interpretation in relation to the story of "Eve" in Genesis 2–3.[12] God is not a founding patriarch in this sense.

But of course, in consequence of the present arrangement of the texts, the Yahwist creation story in Genesis 2–3 is now governed by the notion of creation in the likeness or image of divinity that appears in Genesis 1. In Genesis 2, taken as a different narrative thread, the first clay creature (Hebrew: *adam*)—and this is before the couple or sex and gender come into play—is given the task of "tilling and keeping" (Genesis 2:15), but additionally, is invited to give other creatures names. Theopoetically speaking, this expands the notion of divine likeness or of the image of God in the human creature, to include a cooperative or "co-creative" role. It also hints at a certain divine curiosity; the divine has invested in this human independence or freedom (Genesis 2:19). And this, as it were, trope or theme of curiosity has an interesting effect when we come to look at what the woman (Hebrew: *ishshah*) does next. Created from the clay of the first earth creature, this second creature that comes out of the first, is different, and initially, separate. The creation of a second creature clearly represents a divine purpose of growing community and mutual support (Genesis 2:20). But, as a character, this second creature's first act is not to give or offer help in a way that would indicate the dominion of either God or human, but to be curious about the world in which they find themselves. First there is the snake and the tree and the snake's account of what the fruit can do. This is something the tradition has tended to associate with a distinction of gender—the second human as wife/female—and to interpret in terms of error and disobedience. But perhaps this second creature should also have credit for contriving a necessary interruption to the stasis of Genesis 2:2–3. By the time we reach the end of this story in Genesis 3, that dominion declared in Genesis 1 has been laid out in gendered and hierarchical terms. Nor is there any doubt, at the end of this second/earlier account, about the relationship between creator and creature. This is a fall, a break-up, the agonizing destruction of the

---

[12] See Jenny Daggers, *The British Christian Women's Movement: A Rehabilitation of Eve* (London: Ashgate, 2002).

primal bond. At the same time, unlike the first/later story, it also contains something new: the story of an ongoing relationship between God and God's people. A narrative of convincing depth and complexity starts here. Humans have become more than ciphers or symbols. As an etiological as much as a cosmogonical or theological account, at the end of Genesis 3, the conjugal couple has been set up to reflect "the foundation of social and cultural relationships for the writers of Genesis".[13] And yet, theopoetically speaking, by binding the two accounts together, this image and likeness of God as characteristic of the creational order becomes more about allowing a space for relationality, curiosity and newness—an opening up to the twists and turns of our connexions with the divine—than about laying down the (potentially totalizing, patriarchal) law of male responsibility and heterosexual privilege.

Relations between the sexes as a source of symbolism: anthropological insights

Putting the two accounts of creation in Genesis back together again, the hierarchical relations between two gendered creatures established by Genesis 3:16 is thus brought under the aegis of "the image and likeness" of God in Genesis 1:27. Something about this—for many within the tradition—*unsatisfactory* relationship comes also to reflect something about God. God in relationship, like the two creatures of clay in relationship, is saddled with dissatisfaction and being misunderstood. This is described, so evocatively, in terms of a hurtful and disappointing response to divine love (Genesis 3:22). In this way we can agree with von Rad, that this story reflects the complexity of human psychology, and perhaps also say that it expresses something of the perplexing unknowability for humankind of divine desires.

To return to the symbolism of gender, a hierarchical, primarily heterosexual relationship is an anthropological commonplace. In these terms, "almost everywhere the conditions of maleness and femaleness

---

[13] Nidditch, "Genesis", p. 13.

are used to make statements about various areas of social life".[14] And, anthropologist Marilyn Strathern suggests, it is also a tendency within human cultures to foster the development of gender stereotypes. More, it is a necessary condition of making relations between men and women such a resonant symbol within this kind of myth-making to have those stereotypes. It is the existence of stereotypes, describing and evaluating certain kinds of gendered behaviour,[15] that grounds gendered performances. Within the evaluation of gender lies the power of the symbol to regulate social relations (typically, from the contingently more powerful, male perspective). More theopoetically speaking, such representations also provide a basis for exploring the complexity of relations—divine, human, environmental, embodied. One example amongst many to which Strathern refers is taken from the work of an anthropologist, Gregory Bateson, who studied the Iatmul people of Papua New Guinea in the 1930s. In this example, Bateson describes forms of occasional transvestism practised by both women and men. His explanation of this behaviour was that it allowed for the expression of aspects of experience that, in terms of the gender stereotypes developed in this group, were foreign to the norms of their everyday experience:

> The men by their unreal spectacular life are perfectly habituated to the "ordeal" of public performance. But they are not accustomed to the free expression of vicarious personal emotion. Anger and scorn they can express with a good deal of over-compensation, and joy and sorrow, they can express when it is their own pride which is enhanced or abased; but to express joy in the achievements of another is outside the norms of their behaviour.[16]

---

[14]   Marilyn Strathern, *Before & After Gender: Sexual Mythologies of Everyday Life* (Chicago, IL: Hau Books, 2016), p. 6.

[15]   Strathern, *Before & After Gender*, p. 33.

[16]   Gregory Bateson, *Naven: A survey of the problems suggested by a composite picture of a New Guinea tribe drawn from three points of view* (Stanford, CA: Stanford University Press, [1936] 1958), p. 201.

Thus, a cultural norm had apparently been created in which the symbol relationship between men and women mediated through stereotypes (of dress, speech and demeanour) had somehow to be reversed when, for example, the achievements of sisters' sons were to be acknowledged and celebrated. For the men, to adopt women's clothing and bearing, it could only be in terms of buffoonery, maintaining by these indications of comic distaste, that this could never be the normative expression of an all-important masculinity that had nothing to do with such womanish silliness. The point is not to "pass" as female without comment, and femaleness is deliberately "dressed down" as disreputable. Not surprisingly, Bateson reports a significantly different response amongst women in their cross-dressing, in which the women took great pride when they adopted the stereotypical behaviours—and clothing—of men.[17] Male gender, embedded in stereotypical behaviours such as dress, is typically coded as superior to female, carrying within it, in these circumstances, no sense of real or assumed humiliation. But what is equally interesting here is Strathern's suggestion that this transgressive Iatmul practice, having itself become a social norm, allowed not simply for the expression of a man's pride in his sister's son's achievements but also for the recognition of the women's role in the make-up of the group. It was a way in which a prized masculinity could give some recognition to its more-than-superficial dependency on female roles.[18] In a similar way, whilst the theopoetics[19] of Genesis might not be sufficiently transgressive to satisfy an ideological

---

[17]   Strathern, *Before & After Gender*, p. 41.

[18]   See, ibid., pp. 129–74.

[19]   *Theopoetics* is a contemporary trend or movement in theology that "brings art into intimate connection with theory and theology into a generative relation with imagination" (Heather Walton, ed., *Theopoetics* (special edition), *Literature & Theology*, Vol. 33, no.3, [September 2019], p. 229). It has links with an older spiritual tradition of *theosis*—concerned with the transformative process whose aim is likeness to or union with God. In the past, this has been particularly associated with the Eastern Orthodox churches—and with incarnational theology (ibid., p. 229). Notable authors associated with theopoetics include Catherine Keller, John Caputo, Richard Kearney, Mayra Rivera and Heather Walton.

perspective (such as feminist or trans activism), it does make some allowance for the tensions and fractures of stereotypically gendered relations—shards of contested sociality—to find some expression. Thus different readings of Genesis emerge, from midrashic constructions of Lilith[20] to various modern feminist revisions[21] following Adrienne Rich's definition of the term as "entering an old text from a new critical direction".[22] My own Strathern-influenced reading of the first couple is only one more in a very long list. In this case I suggest they illustrate an understanding of interdependence that is, perhaps as much as anything, the likeness and image of God's purpose for creation.

The image and likeness of God: the creational order of loving interdependence

What has any of this to do with the issue of transgender in the contemporary context of the Christian Church? In what follows, specific reference is made mostly to the situation of the Scottish Episcopal Church and to Scottish legislation, but it is intended that this example should serve as one illustration within a much wider conversation.

As indicated so far, one reason why the previous discussion is significant is the fact that the accounts of creation in Genesis 1–3 set up the relations between the (two) sexes as a key symbol of the image or likeness of God. Therefore, of course, to subject this account of sociality to deconstructive analysis seems to strike at the heart of the divine for

---

[20] Marianna Ruah-Midbar Shapiro, "The Temptation of Legitimacy: Lilith's Adoption and Adaption in Contemporary Feminist Spirituality and Their Meanings", in *Modern Judaism—A Journal of Jewish Ideas and Experience* 39:2 (2019), pp. 125–43, <https://academic.oup.com/mj/article-abstract/39/2/125/5418984?redirectedFrom=fulltext>, accessed 30 January 2021.

[21] Caitlin Matthews, *Sophia: Goddess of Wisdom, Bride of God* (Wheaton, IL & Chennai: Quest Books, 2001). See also, Phyllis Trible, "Eve and Adam: Genesis 2–3 Reread", *Andover Newton Quarterly* 13 (1973), pp. 374–81.

[22] Adrienne Rich, "When we dead awaken", *College English* 34:1 (1972), pp. 18–30.

some readers. But as already suggested, it is not so much the divine as a specific interpretation of scripture that is at stake here. The theopoesis of former times has been essentialized and concretized. Certainly, the connubial interdependencies and vexations of the Genesis account allow for a particular narrative arc to rise up from this point. The image of the divine, set up in this way, connotes a mutually significant relationship. It continues to be of profound, if sometimes traumatic, consequence throughout the Old Testament and is then powerfully refracted within the New. But any attempt simply to equate this poetic discourse with the context-related, binary gender interdependencies of twenty-first-century cultures is inevitably challenged. Some of these challenges, such as the existence of stay-at-home or even pregnant Dads, might be dismissed as exceptional or simply sensational. But some new ways of being in the world have deeper and more awkward implications. One example is the newly acknowledged importance, in the crisis of COVID-19, of "front-line workers". We are suddenly aware of food shop assistants, shelf-stackers, care workers and bin-collectors, amongst others, as people whose roles cannot be dispensed with. We depend on them leaving their homes and going out into a potentially dangerous environment in order that all our fundamental bodily needs can be catered for. Yet their generally much lower wages, and the sense in which their needs for protection were at first played down, show just how little they were regarded or even noticed. These are workers whose primary focus links them, by long cultural association, with the subordinated feminine. Their belittlement represents a persistent cultural and Christian tendency to "displace flesh onto women—and, more startlingly, to deploy the term as almost equivalent to sin".[23] And, whilst many Christians seem to think we now live in a "secular" age, it is notable how, as a community, we still manage to oppose flesh with spirit in this way. You could perhaps characterize the COVID-19 challenge to the way in which readers read the Genesis myth of interdependency as peculiarly transgendered, opposing stereotypes with salient realities.

The reality of transgender in contemporary Scotland is determined, in a legal sense, by the 2004 Gender Recognition Act (GRA) (Scotland),

---

[23]   Rivera, *Poetics of the Flesh*, pp. 52–3.

which provides for the award of a certificate of gender recognition in cases, for example, where changing gender is seen as grounds for divorce. A certificate of gender recognition is thus of more consequence than it might seem at first glance, since it is on this basis that previously cisgender[24] relationships can be dissolved. Adjustments to provisions within the NHS alongside the Act illustrate a slow, and sometimes uneasy, process of change, based on a range of principles that are not always cohesive. An understanding of human equality that also recognizes the challenges of human diversity reflects the classically liberal outlook of the nineteenth century. This has been stretched and tested by forms of "identity politics" as well as powerful neo-liberal influences—stressing our assumed freedom of choice—in the twentieth and twenty-first centuries. With the emphasis shifting away in more recent times from the constitutional model of personhood (defined by efforts to establish equal rights and responsibilities by law) towards a greater accent on individual autonomy, identity is increasingly seen to be bound up in the extent to which we can choose to do our "own thing"[25] or "be [our]selves".[26] For some trans activists this is the reason they object to the Gender Recognition Act (Scotland) of 2004.[27] The Act requires that two professionals, one of whom must be "practising in the field of gender dysphoria" or a chartered psychologist working in the same area, attest to the presence of gender dysphoria as a prerequisite for a legal change in gender recognition. This is then perceived as an effort to subject passionately held convictions about identity and personal choice to inappropriate adjudication by medical professionals; to medicalize an issue that is not about medicine or

---

24 Cis or cisgender is a term referring to "[s]omeone whose gender identity is the same as the sex they were assigned at birth. Non-trans is also used by some people". Stonewall, *Glossary of Terms*, <https://www.stonewall.org.uk/help-advice/faqs-and-glossary/glossary-terms#c>, accessed 30 January 2021.

25 Strathern, *Before & After Gender*, p. 209.

26 Stonewall: <https://www.stonewall.org.uk/about-us/our-mission-and-priorities>, accessed 30 January 2021.

27 Scottish Government, 2004, *Gender Recognition Act* <https://www.legislation.gov.uk/ukpga/2004/7/crossheading/applications-for-gender-recognition-certificate>, accessed 30 January 2021.

biology at all. But, as Strathern recognized, there are consequences to this background shift away from establishing freedoms and responsibilities in law, with reference to objective criteria, towards expressions of personal freedom and identity that are obviously also evidential but which seem more subjective. Thus interest groups wanting others to cede rights that validate their autonomously and subjectively chosen identities increasingly find themselves in conflict.[28] For example, in recent times we have seen some interest groups appealing for the fuller expression of women's rights (against patriarchal oppression, say) coming into conflict with transgender interest groups representing the fuller expression of, most significantly, an autonomously chosen transfemale identity (against *cisgender* patriarchal oppression).[29] No doubt partly in response to these growing tensions, the GRA (Scotland) has recently been subjected to wide consultation (2019–20).[30] Significantly, the comparable Act in England was confirmed without change this year (2020), whilst the consultation in

---

[28] Strathern, *Before & After Gender*, p. 209.

[29] In the summer of 2020, there was considerable media interest in the author J. K. Rowling's online expressions of sympathy for women who oppose the idea that gender cannot be determined by biology, see <https://www.jkrowling. com/opinions/j-k-rowling-writes-about-her-reasons-for-speaking-out-on-sex-and-gender-issues/>, accessed 30 January 2021. The idea that gender is not defined by biology but that it is a matter of cultural construction and socialization has been held to be true within mainstream feminist scholarship and opinion, and, increasingly, more widely, since at least the publication of Judith Butler's work *Gender Trouble* in 1990. The matter of concern in this debate was that the autonomously chosen female identity of transwomen placed at risk the choice of women defining themselves in biological terms, to establish safe, biologically-defined "female" spaces on that basis. In other words, the debate pitched autonomous identity-choice against freedoms and protections enshrined in law and precedent. There is passion on both sides.

[30] Scottish Government, 2019, *Gender Recognition Reform (Scotland) Bill: A Consultation by the Scottish Government*, <https://consult.gov.scot/family-law/gender-recognition-reform-scotland-bill/>, accessed 21 October 2020.

Scotland has been put on indefinite hold.[31] It is clear then, that in Scotland (as elsewhere), we are struggling to do justice both to a continuing—if less prominent—constitutional model of human rights and responsibilities in law, and to more liberal and also subjective readings of spaces such as the body. But what the critical gender analysis that feeds into these debates also shows is how these uncertainties are reflected more broadly in our constructions of reality. For Christians, for example, they continue to impact on understandings of the divine as well as social and economic categories.[32] In such a situation, for queer theologian Marcella Althaus-Reid, "heterosexuality makes of every courageous human being a Queer, indecent person. Only very hypocritical people may claim to live according to the rules, *contra natura*".[33] In other words, normative stories, for Althaus-Reid, do not represent reality, but only how certain people at certain times believe human beings ought to be.

Summing up here, being made in the image of God as male and female (Genesis 1:27) is, I would argue, not just about producing a normative vision of human society.[34] And in particular, it cannot be equated with the idea that it is God's will that human beings should be aligned with culturally specific ways of understanding binary sex/gender. Queer theologians like Althaus-Reid and Linn Tonstad propose that we focus instead on the *theology* that is at the heart of the story of creation and redemption. This is God's option or choice to side with fleshly and suffering humanity in the midst of its complex and ever-changing interrelationships with God, world and each other. This should be the target, rather than formulating and imposing normative, would-be totalizing moral structures. Another way of putting this would be to say that limiting the image of God to one pattern of human social interaction betrays a troubling overconfidence. In God's derisive words to Job, perhaps, it would be like trying to "draw out Leviathan with a fish hook" (Job 41:1).

---

[31] <https://www.bbc.co.uk/news/uk-scotland-scotland-politics-48702946>, accessed 30 January 2021.

[32] Marcella Althaus-Reid, *Indecent Theology: Theological Perversions in Sex, Gender and Politics* (London & New York: Routledge. 2000), p. 2.

[33] Ibid., p. 120.

[34] Linn Tonstad, *Queer Theology* (Eugene, OR: Cascade Books, 2018), p. 68.

Reading the story in Genesis can thus be said to be about revealing the layers of the text that help us to uncover and expand our own thinking. Rather than handing down one solution to a single issue, the exercise is better understood as reflexive and poetic and, in this way, better able to speak to the reality of different lives. There could be a description of the nature of God that is, indeed, compared to the sanctity of conventional binary gender patterns; perhaps even patriarchal ones. But this is simply not the only possible interpretation—and the midrashic tradition is only one of many indications that different meanings can be adduced to this text about the image of God, this being "the Rabbinic method of coping with socio-political and theological change and of reintegrating this change into tradition".[35] And, understanding this narrative thread as itself located within a composite text, put together over centuries and now overlaid with further centuries of reading and interpreting by human beings from many different backgrounds, ought to make us expect complexity. Within a Christian context still marked by the impact of the Reformation, even the principle of *sola scriptura* has itself to be interpreted. We need to acknowledge that Martin Luther did not assume people would actually go off to read and understand the Bible in complete isolation from all other formative influences such as their family or church or his words of wisdom. Interestingly, in his case it is clear that his own formative influences included the "standard methods of humanist philology and textual study". These were part of the "toolkit" he used himself "to unseat the [previously] dominant, official understanding of the text".[36]

So here is an alternative "queer" theopoetic reading of the image of God in Genesis 1–3. It emerges out of my own ongoing critical reading of theological and biblical texts over many decades, contextualized by feminist biblical criticism and many years of teaching in publicly funded schools and universities, superimposed on a background in church worship and church community. God's image is to be found within the

---

[35]   Elisabeth Schüssler Fiorenza, *Wisdom Ways: Introducing Feminist Biblical Interpretation* (Maryknoll, NY: Orbis Books, 2001), p. 149.

[36]   John Riches, *The Bible: A Very Short Introduction* (Oxford: Oxford University Press, 2000), p. 74.

interdependence to which the Genesis story points—it functions like a signpost that indicates a direction but does not attempt to represent the destination. Contemporary debates about transgender within Scotland provoke a shift of critical attention towards the presumed cisgender or heterosexual conformity of the story. Critical attention points towards a purpose of fostering interdependence. As a Godlike purpose, it must be expected to feed our imaginations if not to move us out of our comfort zones. It resonates with biblical scholar R. N. Whybray's comments on the plurality of God in the creation accounts.[37] If there is plurality, inter-relatedness and interdependence in the act of creation, then we would expect to see that in what is created. And this is also reflected in the clear interdependence that is displayed in the whole of creation, something, moreover, that we have tended to ignore with increasingly dire consequences for ourselves. In this sense, what the reflection or, perhaps better, refraction of transgender does is take us away from the narrowness of one cultural reading of interdependence (heterocispatriarchalism[38]), where Strathern's meticulous scholarship suggests we may indeed see the burnishing of certain gender stereotypes. Instead, I suggest a much more stirring contemplation of our fundamental, Godlike, relatedness and interdependence in orgiastic Trinitarian mode.[39] Ever happy to

---

[37]   Whybray's commentary on Genesis 1:27 is, we might say, typical of Barton and Muddiman's commentary, marked by learned, diligent biblical scholarship, whose authors have been inducted into a particular academic tradition, owing its origins to the principles of higher criticism formed and developed within the European context of "modernity". Their interpretation notes the discrepancies between the "Let us make" and "in our image" of verse 26 and the "in his image" of verse 27, putting them down to a passing reference, in the case of verse 26, to "a court of heavenly beings who exist to do God's bidding" (Whybray, *Genesis*, p. 43).

[38]   A recent neologism that combines a feminist critique of patriarchal perspectives with a queer critique of normative heterosexuality and a trans critique of cisgender privilege.

[39]   See Tonstad, *Queer Theology*, p. 94; Marcella Althaus-Reid, *The Queer God* (London & New York, NY: Routledge, 2003), p. 3.

employ shock tactics to challenge "the phallus of the church",[40] Althaus-Reid contemplates the socially conservative sensitivities of dictators and dictatorships in the South American contexts of her youth, which ignored those who cried out to them for freedom and justice. Instead they mobilized the resources of the Church and its theology, metaphorically as well as actually, to lay down the law against non-conformity expressed in sexual, political and theological tropes. Althaus-Reid's project was thus dedicated to the rediscovery of God outside the heterosexual and cisgender ideology that dominated this Church,[41] and others. She puts it in terms of "theological queering" which is "the deliberate questioning of heterosexual experience and thinking which has shaped our understanding of theology, the role of the theologian and hermeneutics".[42] And, as she says, this process requires

> from us, not only honesty and courage, but also a critical engagement with queer theory, non-heterosexual and critical heterosexual theology. It also requires us to come clean about our experiences, which in some way or other always seem destined to fall outside the normative sexual ideology of theology.[43]

And yes, in terms of our day-to-day lives, it requires us "to read *contramano* (against the grain) when we contemplate issues of heterosexual institutions such as marriage or the subversiveness of popular spirituality in many non-Western cultures".[44] In Linn Tonstad's words:

> Heterosexuality as a system doesn't deal with truth. Theological heterosexuality deals with fictions, ideas of what human beings ought to be like that are divorced and distanced from the reality of human, bodied, sexual life. Yet those fictions get used against people. Poor women are called indecent or undeserving if their

---

40   Althaus-Reid, *Queer God*, p. 23.

41   Ibid., p. 2.

42   Ibid., p. 2.

43   Ibid. p. 2.

44   Ibid., pp. 2–3.

lives don't conform to heterosexual, middle class ideologies of sexual behaviour. They are often called underserving by politicians whose own lives bear no trace of the decency they seek to impose on others.[45]

This piece has suggested then that the stories of creation in Genesis, in a poetic sense, have woven the story together with the story of gendered relations, implying through an initial conjunction of texts that this complexity of human and divine relations is not driven forward simply by divine providence—that might have taken us to Genesis 2:3—but by the complexity of relationality as a characteristic of both human redactors and their evocation of divine beings. If we can rely on the anthropological scholarship of Strathern, the specific nature of this/these story/ies draws on widely established, etiologically framed threads that reflect deeply embedded stereotypes of difficult but key human relationships with parents and with our own sexuality. But theopoetically speaking, this does not tie us to specific representations as we struggle to create these texts anew, acknowledging our limitations, our inability to know everything. In these circumstances, what we could say about transgender is that it seems to disrupt—as perhaps the Genesis story/ies sought to disrupt—a problematic and fundamentally impossible scene of Edenic serenity with its totalizing (and ultimately self-limiting) implications.

We are still troubled: coming to some theopoetic conclusions

So, to come back to the beginning of this chapter, what answers are there to the question "What troubles some thoughtful Christians about transgender?" and how is this connected with the story in Genesis 1–3? The perception that transgender "distorts the creational order of male and female"[46] is crucial for some. Transgender—a desire for a

---

45   Tonstad, *Queer Theology*, p. 76.

46   Evangelical Alliance, *Transformed: A brief biblical and pastoral introduction to understanding transgender in a changing culture.* <https://www.eauk.org/

differently gendered identity or a response to the perceived pain of gender dysphoria—is, according to this view, one of the consequences of living in a fallen world. And that is a powerful way of acknowledging how the pain we experience seems sometimes inexplicable and unresolvable. But in view of what has already been said about the symbolism of binary gender—that it has been used throughout human experience and all over the world to express and preserve a range of very different social forms of human interdependence—one needs, arguably, to be careful not to short-circuit the workings of the metaphor. A male/female monogamous relationship may indeed serve to express something about human/divine relationships.[47] But it cannot be said to have exactly the same purpose. And Genesis 1–3 might equally well be understood as a matter of theopoetics; speaking of God or of the divine in relationship with the created world in terms or words that make sense within the contingencies of certain contexts passed on *via* a discursive tradition[48] that both acknowledges the authority of the text and its capacity to "forge meaningful connections"[49] within widely differing conditions and circumstances. In the narrative we read today, the fallenness of creation is convincingly summed up through the juxtaposition of Edenic serenity and order, and the turbulence—and creativity—of love, desire, care, curiosity and distrust. But identifying the *specific forms* of the story in Genesis with "the creational order" is surely to miss the point. On this basis it might as well be said that the creational order is distorted by our slaughtering animals and eating meat when it would appear that God provides plants, fruits and seeds to eat (Genesis 1:29–30), rather than other animals.[50] This is certainly not to

---

resources/what-we-offer/reports/transformed-understanding-transgender-in-a-changing-culture>, accessed 30 January 2021, p. 10.

47 Ibid., pp. 10–11.

48 See Talal Asad, *The Idea of an Anthropology of Islam Occasional Paper Series* (Washington DC: Centre for Contemporary Arab Studies, Georgetown University, 1986).

49 See John I'Anson, & Alison Jasper, *Schooling Indifference: Re-Imagining RE in Multi-Cultural and Gendered Spaces* (London & New York, NY: Routledge, 2017).

50 See also Adam, Chapter 10.

dismiss the urgency of considering whether our meat-eating propensities as a species are threatening the whole environment, but rather to say that this text does not provide us with answers to this specific dilemma. Moreover, concerned Christians are often themselves engaging in a process of hermeneutics with theopoetic implications, for example when they read, in the creation narratives of Genesis, the loving acceptance of individual people whatever their identity, colour, belief or personal history.[51] It would be hard to read this straight off the pages of Genesis 1–3 in a specific or literal sense. This hermeneutics is informed by reading the New Testament. And whilst this could hardly be said to be the wrong thing for Christians to do, it does have to be admitted that it changes what we see in the text and how we understand what we are reading.

An analogy between the divine creator and a monogamous cisgender, male/female couple, in which male domination of female is laid down, by the end of Genesis 3 is one representation of the text. Yet the narrative allows for a much wider range of interpretation. This is also a rich and psychologically complex notion of the divine image that combines dominion with recognition of how things do not go easily to plan but whose disruptions can also, sometimes, be creative—an unknotting or moving of things on as well as a breaking or tearing of connections. There is an impressive tension here that militates against a tendency to reduce the image or likeness of God to a simple form, always moving backwards towards what is perceived as originating purity. It proposes instead a story of how we desire the realization of divine purposes within the intricate interdependencies of every new and often heterogeneous reading of the text.

Gender symbolism in Christian theology has been identified for many decades by liberation theologians interested in Christianity's relationship with the poor and marginalized: their conclusions have tended to point to the way in which the Churches in many contexts and across many generations have presumed to sacralize forms of questionable hierarchy or dominion in the name of theological concepts such as divine sovereignty, the Fatherhood of God or indeed the image of God, for reasons that have more to do with the exercise of forms of power than with theopoetics or

---

[51]   Evangelical Alliance, *Transformed*, p. 5.

even dogmatic theology. In an anthropological context Strathern makes a similar claim; stories and mythologies in many parts of the world, based on stereotypical gender traits, normalize patterns of male dominion and entitlement. She also reads into these narratives and structures various ways in which they *recognize* interdependence between men and women. And, as a matter of fact, this kind of reading is not ruled out in Genesis 1–3. As suggested above, the heterosexual cisgender couple can be presented as a reflection or image of divine creative purpose alongside the recognition of problematic interdependencies both between human beings and between divinity and created worlds.

So, one reason why the issue of transgender may be troubling to some Christians today is because it challenges what has sometimes seemed like a straightforward connection between the scriptural texts and stereotypes or values that have become part of a framework for making sense of the world. In respect of gender. for example, we might be tempted to map onto Genesis 1–3 a pattern of monogamous cisgender relationships, without giving much thought to the fact that this is a text constructed more than two and a half millennia ago and in a widely different cultural context to our own. Patterns of relationships that have grown and developed specifically out of the contingencies of Western industrial and colonial societies over the last two or three hundred years can only ever be superficially equivalent to those that characterized the worlds of those writers and poets who first put the sacred writings of the Jews together. Either way, historically and culturally contingent practices and values cannot be made to bear too much theological weight. To say that the creative or even problematic nature of relations between men and women represents something of the divine purpose is not the same as saying that any specific example of that relationship could properly determine the creational order.

Of course, this is not the only reason why Christians are made uneasy by the increased visibility and volubility of transgender people and of their demands. Clearly, as citizens of the twenty-first-century world— and, more specifically, of Scotland—we are all aware of how transgender has been framed within contemporary discourses of identity politics and human rights and made possible, in some ways, by the increased sophistication of medical procedures and other therapies. Christians are required to take a position as citizens, even when discussions about how transgender impacts on the laws of the country do not defer to our theological presuppositions. Understandably, it can seem discouraging. Some people continue to want civil society to align its attitudes towards transgender with particular—liberal or conservative—readings of scripture. But, putting asides these kinds of alignments, Christians *could* return to the theopoetics of Genesis 1–3 to find something useful to say in the present contingencies. The image of God expresses a divine purpose for human lives but not in legislative terms. The narrative directs our thoughts towards human interdependencies and divine love, but it is necessarily underscored by the capacities and limits of our human imaginations. In terms of an imaginative capacity, the divine is read, theologically, as incarnational: to make the creative purpose of divine love evident requires the recognition of mutual (God, world, human) interdependence within those ephemeral circumstances. The theologian Mayra Rivera provides new resources for reflection on this, understanding the theological notion of flesh in terms of a corporeal imaginary she describes as "carnal".[52] In the carnal imaginary, the contingencies of human existence and interrelating, and the limitations this imposes on the knowledge we seek, lead to a notion of our own human incarnation in the image of a divine emptying into the world. For Rivera, this flesh is, in theopoetic terms, essential: "unless I can embrace my own flesh and its beginnings in the flesh of another, I cannot love other fleshly beings—nor can I understand the incarnation".[53] The image of God is thus an outpouring into a world of relationality and interdependence. In these terms, the creational order is not at all about insisting on

---

[52] For Rivera, a "carnal" is distinguished from a "somatic" imaginary of the bodily and material. Both find space within Christian scripture (Rivera devotes attention to both the Johannine and Pauline as well as to Patristic interpretation), but she argues against the emphasis she detects—equally within contemporary Western, Cartesian ways of thinking—on the somatic (*Poetics of the Flesh*, p. 153): "The somatic strand represents flesh as inessential . . . .we dream of fleshless bodies freed from the weight of earthly substance, the menace of death or the determinations of our social histories."

[53] Ibid., p. 154.

cisgender—however resonant the image has been over the centuries and however common a human practice it has been—but much more profoundly, it is about insisting on our investment in each other and in the world. This does not imply that contingent matters of ethics, law or social polity are not important, because they matter to and in our fleshly lives. The texts of scripture remain but they remain, in the flesh, as a basis for our ongoing work of theopoetics, drawing shattered histories and shards of vocabulary together afresh in every new age.

Questions for discussion

1. Mayra Rivera is particularly aware of a strand (she calls it the "somatic") within Christian theology that deems our corporeality, ultimately, unnecessary. Those who emphasize an understanding of human life that resides in some kind of eternal substance, like a soul, may see human bodily and material needs (including a sexual nature) as secondary or derivative. But another strand (she calls it the "carnal") perceives the earth(l)y as essential both to the human and the divine (Rivera, *Poetics of the Flesh*, pp. 153–4). Whilst not arguing against the idea that both strands have their place, she thinks we cannot really understand the Christian doctrine of the incarnation outside of this carnal framing. In what ways would you say that a carnal framing has to assume cisgender or heterosexuality? What alternative symbolic representations (moving away from the patriarchal) might help us to reimagine this incarnate divine in whose image we are made?

2. How, if at all, do the creation narratives in Genesis help us to understand the bodily, sexual and gendered nature of the God whose image Christians believe they bear?

3. Jo Clifford's controversial one-woman play, *The Gospel According to Jesus Christ, Queen of Heaven*, which portrays Jesus as a transgender person, premiered in Glasgow in 2009. It has travelled the world, generating applause and vitriol in equal measure. What factors could be at work in producing such extreme responses?

Further reading

Jo Clifford, *The Gospel According to Jesus, Queen of Heaven* (Edinburgh: Stewed Rhubarb Press, 2019).

Surya Monro, *Gender Politics: Citizenship, Activism and Sexual Diversity* (London & Ann Arbor, MI: Pluto Press, 2005).

Julia Serrano, *Whipping Girl: A Transsexual Woman on Sexism and the Scapegoating of Femininity* (Berkeley, CA: Seal Press, 2007).

Stonewall is an organization that seeks to champion LGBT+ people and their needs, and its support for people "being themselves" allows for the option of radical and invasive medical procedures. Its website is a good place to find out more about transgender: <https://www.stonewallscotland.org.uk>, last accessed 30 January 2021.

Tara K. Soughers, *Beyond a Binary God: A Theology of Trans* Allies: A Theology for Trans* Allies: 9 (Church's Teaching for a Changing World)* (New York, NY: Church Publishing, 2018).

Afterword

David Fergusson

Every generation has a definition of the [human] it deserves.
Abraham J. Heschel[1]

This is a remarkably rich collection of essays on a theme of fundamental importance to the ways in which we think of ourselves. Informed by careful scholarship and imaginative reflection, its findings are presented in a lively and accessible style. I anticipate that the volume will prove immensely useful to students and others as they reflect upon the central concept in theological anthropology.

The *imago Dei* has long struck me as both indispensable and yet problematic. Appearing in the opening chapter of the Bible, it is easily appropriated by accounts of human dignity and worth. If asked to elucidate their theological commitment to social justice and care, a church committee or agency will generally appeal to our humanity as created in the image of God. That seems right. Yet, if we ask what is intended by the concept, several difficulties quickly come into view.

There is the exegetical problem that the text itself remains cryptic. Outside the opening chapters of Genesis, the Hebrew Bible says virtually nothing about the key terms translated as "image" and "likeness". At best, we find some consonant remarks about human distinctiveness. In the New Testament, the divine image tends to be deployed as a Christological or soteriological category—James 3:9 might provide the anthropological and ethical exception. Protestant theologians have often attempted to harmonize the different references to the image of God. The story goes

---

[1] Abraham J. Heschel, *Who is Man?* (Stanford, CA: Stanford University Press, 1965), p. 23.

that the original image was lost with the Fall in Genesis 3 and only restored by Christ, the second Adam, who is the bearer of the true image. This scheme has some advantages, but it runs into difficulty. The text nowhere suggests that the original image of God was lost, nor that it ceases to be a universal characteristic of the human condition. Calvin duly reflects this tension, qualifying his claim in one place that the image is lost by noting elsewhere that some vestiges of our former glory remain.[2] These problems are a good example of the dangers in an oversystematized approach. We can learn here from David Kelsey's insistence upon the different plot lines in Christian theology, all of which must be interwoven in theological anthropology but without allowing any one to dominate at the expense of the others.[3]

Philosophical problems also beset traditional attempts to specify the *imago Dei*. Through much of the tradition, it is identified with the rational or spiritual element of our human nature. Doubtless, this reflects the influence of Greek philosophy, especially the Platonic dualism of body and soul. If, as humans, we are distinguished by the possession of a rational and immortal soul, then the *imago* can readily be identified by that defining spiritual component of our make-up. Despite widespread support, this strategy has also faced formidable criticism.[4] Hebrew anthropology does not allow a bifurcation of our nature into a body-soul duality—its key anthropological terms are more psychosomatic and holistic. Others have charged this interpretive tradition with an overintellectualizing of our condition. This has generated various negative consequences. Our embodiedness and sociality tend to be denigrated in such approaches. Those with learning difficulties can too readily be regarded as subhuman when this trajectory becomes firmly established. Bias towards a masculinist left-brain rationality has also been discerned here. And, finally, the elevation of intellectual functions may ironically

---

[2] Cf. Randall C. Zachman, *Reconsidering John Calvin* (Grand Rapids, MI: Eerdmans, 2010), pp. 6–34.

[3] David Kelsey, *Eccentric Existence: A Theological Anthropology*, two volumes (Louisville, KY: Westminster John Knox Press, 2009).

[4] Fergus Kerr has described its hold over the Western imagination in *Theology After Wittgenstein*, second edition (London: SPCK, 1997).

result in our soon being surpassed and even superseded by the advent of intelligent machines. No longer the exclusive domain of science fiction, this is rapidly becoming a threatening reality.

A further and increasingly pressing anxiety is that the tendency to set human beings apart from other forms of creaturehood will have poor ecological outcomes. If the essential and immaterial component of our existence is godlike and not shared by other creatures, then our bonds with animals are likely to be weakened, as well as the value we place upon our shared habitat. Anthropocentrism has arguably become the most recent theological heresy, though this can take different forms, some more benign than others. But the idea of a special status in the created order, even a central one, which is authorized by the image of God, can rapidly result in the loss of companionship, solidarity and belonging with the rest of creation. These problems are accentuated by the association in Genesis 1:27–28 with the function of "dominion". Although this can be more pastorally inflected in stewardship models of creation, the language of dominion has often generated notions of rule, control and disposability. Against this background, eco-theologians have been quick to point out the inherent difficulties of traditional constructions.

One option that has attracted some commentators is towards a more deflated account. Acknowledging that the concept of the *imago Dei* has been overdetermined in the past, we can adopt other approaches to theological anthropology. These might recognize that the concept functions as an initial placeholder in Genesis 1, awaiting further content as the stories of humanity, Israel, Jesus, and the Church unfold.[5] This has the advantage of abandoning attempts to unlock the concept by searching for an essentialist definition, as if the *imago* were a clue in a crossword puzzle. In general, this is where my own sympathies lie, though it is important not to neglect the simplicity and ethical significance of

---

[5]   A narrated approach is advocated by Mary McClintock Fulkerson in "Contesting the Gendered Subject: A feminist account of the *imago dei*", in Rebecca Chopp and Sheila Greeve Davaney (eds), *Horizons in Feminist Theology: Identity, Tradition and Norms* (Minneapolis: Fortress, 1997), pp. 99–115.

the concept itself.[6] However we describe it, if we are all made in the divine image, then there is an equality, a dignity and a value bestowed upon each human life that must evoke our respect. Other philosophies might approach this in different ways and with alternative conceptual schemes, but here at least is one that should mobilize the adherents of the Abrahamic faiths.[7] This is not to be downplayed, even while challenges remain in showing how other creatures have their own worth in the created order. Some approaches have helpfully attempted to invigorate the *imago Dei* with a richer set of meanings. Douglas John Hall, for example, has argued that imaging God requires a multidimensional set of relationships with God, other people and other creatures—these are the essential "counterparts of our being".[8]

The importance of this collection resides in its capacity to explore these problems from different angles. Instead of a simple essentialist approach, these essays afford a variety of perspectives that both expose many of the problems and pitfalls in accounts of the *imago Dei* while offering a refreshing array of constructive proposals. Along the way, light is shed not only upon the human condition but also upon our understanding of God and creation. Here we are reminded that the problems of theological anthropology are not there to be resolved once for all, but must be urgently tackled afresh in the different contexts in which we find ourselves.

---

[6]   I have attempted to develop a deflationary approach in "Humans Created According to the *Imago Dei*: An Alternative Proposal", *Zygon* 48:2 (2013), pp. 439–53.

[7]   Abraham J. Heschel argues that a distinctive contribution of Judaism was its understanding of the metaphysical dignity of the human from the concept of the divine image. See "The Concept of Man in Jewish Thought", in S. Radhakrisnan and P. T. Raju (eds), *The Concept of Man* (London: Allen and Unwin, 1960), pp. 108–57, here at p. 131.

[8]   Douglas John Hall, *Imaging God: Dominion as Stewardship* (Grand Rapids, MI: Eerdmans, 1987), pp. 123–8.

Index